Political Economy of Illegal Drugs

Whether we like it or not, illegal drugs are widely consumed and a huge source of revenue for criminals and an expenditure for governments throughout the world as they attempt to police their misuse. Examining the thorny issue of drugs within an economics framework is an exercise that is not only timely but also helpful.

This book attempts such an analysis with admirable rigour and originality. Analysing the behaviour of drug consumers and sellers, Pierre Kopp explores in detail the difficulties of implementing successful drug policies. He considers the role of organized crime, the laundering of drug money and the complexities of tracking organized criminals.

Policy-makers around the world searching for ways to contain the drug problem will welcome this book. It will also be of great interest to students and researchers of applied microeconomics, criminology and, in particular, the economics of crime.

Pierre Kopp is Professor of Economics at Pantheon-Sorbonne University, Paris I, France.

Studies in Crime and Economics
Edited by Peter Reuter
University of Maryland
and Ernesto U. Savona
University of Trento

Volume 1
Political Economy of Illegal Drugs
Pierre Kopp

Political Economy of Illegal Drugs

Pierre Kopp

Routledge
Taylor & Francis Group

LONDON AND NEW YORK

First published 2004 by Routledge
11 New Fetter Lane, London EC4P 4EE

Simultaneously published in the USA and Canada
by Routledge
29 West 35th Street, New York, NY 10001

Routledge is an imprint of the Taylor & Francis Group

© 2004 Pierre Kopp

Typeset in Times by Wearset Ltd, Boldon, Tyne and Wear
Printed and bound in Great Britain by Antony Rowe Ltd,
Chippenham, Wiltshire

British Library Cataloguing in Publication Data
A catalogue record for this book is available from the British Library

Library of Congress Cataloging in Publication Data
Kopp, Pierre.
  [Economie de la drogue. English]
  Political economy of illegal drugs / Pierre Kopp.
    p. cm. – (Routledge studies in crime and economics ; v. 1)
  Includes bibliographical references and index.
  1. Drug traffic. 2. Drug traffic–Economic aspects. 3. Drug abuse–
Government policy. 4. Drug abuse–Economic aspects. I. Title.
II. Series.
HV5801.K66 2002
338.4′736345–dc21

                                                    2003043148

ISBN 0–415–27138–X

Contents

Figures

Tables

Note on the text

Throughout the book, when discussing policy-makers, drug dealers and drug users, we have referred to them as 'he', although we are aware that there can be female policy-makers, drug dealers and drug users.

Introduction

Why write an economics study that discusses drug trafficking and consumption? Of course, intuitively, the word 'drug' evokes an image of enormous sums of money, but an economist's work should not be reduced to an accountant's inventory of cash flow. The economic approach consists in examining the consequences that drugs circulating on the market have on consumer and dealer behaviour. Effectively, drugs are psychotropics that influence the perception of the individuals who consume them, but they are also forms of merchandise, which are exchanged in the marketplace and have particular characteristics.

There is never a drug debate that does not very quickly begin to discuss the pros and cons of prohibition. For some, the intrinsic harm of drugs justifies their being banned; the existence of illegal markets is a result, regrettable of course, but one that a more repressive policy could do away with. For others, it is precisely repressive public intervention that is the root of all evil because it plunges the consumer into the midst of a web of transactions which are not only illegal, but are, above all, dangerous. The dogged opposition between these two theses explains the recurrent nature of drug policy debates. We should note, in passing, that it is in fact the societal debate which, by focusing on the violent nature of the functioning of these illegal markets, has invited economists to discuss the characteristics of market functions, and it is not the latter who have invited themselves to a debate where their presence has been requested by nobody.

The controversy on the root of the evil created by drugs dates back to an old and deep opposition between different economic approaches, notably liberal and interventionist. In order to determine when intervention is justified, it is possible to adopt a fairly simple rule that the most liberal authors would not contest. Consider as established that individuals are the best judges of their own well-being. Then, as long as an individual's actions affect only his well-being, and not that of other members of society, he must be free to act as he wishes. The rule is clear, but putting it into practice is less so.

First, is a drug-consuming individual still the best judge of his well-being? As Gary Becker has argued (Becker and Murphy, 1988), the inclination for drugs could certainly be considered as rational. We could then consider that the individual arbitrates between present satisfaction obtained from drugs and the future inconveniences of such consumption. From this perspective, the drug consumer would permanently optimize his behaviour, taking into account the signals sent by such market intermediaries as price, intensity of repression (when drugs are banned), or availability of health care programmes. On the other hand, we could consider that, far from being rational, the drug consumer is under-informed or irrational, concluding that at the time of taking drugs for the first time he is unable to measure the future consequences of this action and thereafter is no longer able to stop. The principle of consumer sovereignty would thus cease to be applicable, and we should implement an active paternalistic type of policy that would protect the consumer from himself. To decide whether the drug consumer is really the best judge of his well-being or whether he has lost the attributes of his sovereignty, due to the drugs, is thus a far from trivial question. The answer essentially depends upon our representation of the entry conditions to the career of drug consumer.

Second, does drug consumption affect only the drug consumer? If that were the case, there would be no need for public intervention, except that designed to protect the consumer from himself, as mentioned earlier. Here the question is different; if the behaviour of some people affects that of others, then without doubt there are good reasons for public powers to regulate access to drugs. The question is extremely thorny. Literature on drugs tends to rather quickly present the risks run by drug consumers as externalities. The question is not without importance as the presence of an externality is generally a good reason to insist upon state intervention.

Nobody doubts that most drugs have negative consequences for those who consume them.

It, however, in economic terms, does not concern externalities, as it is not a third party who is affected by drug taking but the consumer himself. The problems that the consumers inflict upon themselves, therefore, in no way constitute a good reason to diverge from the principle of letting people decide for themselves. However, drugs affect not only those who take them, but also third parties. Under the influence of drugs, individuals can commit crimes, and markets are often known for their violence. If it is established that the consumption of some affects the well-being of others, there is good reason to abandon the rule that advocates respecting individual choice to consume. The problem is that it is not easy to assign a specific reason for externalities characteristic of the drug market. For some, the case is clear; it is the psychoactive nature of the products consumed that modifies the consumer's behaviour and instigates violence or behaviour that is dangerous to others. For others, it is because drugs are not permitted that markets are violent. Does the danger of drugs to third parties stem from the drugs or the laws that prohibit them? Once again, our apparently simple rule, which is supposed to serve as a guide of whether or not to set up public intervention which deprives the citizen of the right to exercise his freedom of choice, turns out not to be particularly helpful.

Thus, we can observe that the rational discussion of benefits and disadvantages of intervention to regulate drug use does not have a simple conclusion. Its outcome depends too restrictively upon each one's opinion of the relative weight to be accorded to the individual rights of the citizen and the State's role in permitting a clear outcome. In this sense, any discussion relating to drug legislation cuts into those debates that have been agitating society for at least two centuries and do not appear destined for rapid solution. This is why the approach in this book focuses more on a discussion of drug policy as it is actually implemented as opposed to attempting a comparison of the theoretical merits of drug policy extremes such as total prohibition or total legalisation. The fact that it seems to be impossible to determine, in normative terms, what the drug laws should be does not remove the obligation to examine the consequences of existing laws and the possibilities of modifying them in order to improve social well-being. In any given institutional framework, generally that of drug prohibition, the public policy-maker must choose a public drug policy. Discussing the strategic basis for this and its consequences constitutes, in our eyes, a more exciting task than re-opening the debate that juxtaposes prohibition and legalization.

Anyway, can we really talk about 'drug policy'? In many countries so-called drug policy is in fact the uncoordinated aggregate of sometimes incoherent measures. Often, for example, the actions of the Minister of Health and Welfare and those of the Interior Minister turn out to be contradictory. Henceforth, we will place under the term 'public policy' a set of laws, regulatory dispositions or measures, the coherence of which we do not prejudge.

In other respects, a purely economic analysis of drug policy can often appear to be somewhat simplistic. Standard economic theory generally considers that the economist's work is done once he has identified the sources of inefficiency in a public policy. Of course, some go further and compare the benefits of different corrective therapies. Rare are those who question the feasibility of the solutions proposed. This delicate problem of policy implementation recommended by economists reveals the limits to the territory covered by this discipline. Ascertaining the conditions of implementing a proposed public policy demands verifying its compatibility with the existing institutional framework. Moreover, one must also question whether or not a political majority exists to uphold it, and anticipate its potential adverse effects. Of course, economic analysis reduced to its most simple expression, the analysis of rational choices, can handle all of these tasks. A less ambitious conception of the science of economics would limit itself to recommending a multi-disciplinary study of conditions of implementation, choosing between a plea for collaboration, of uncertain outcome, with other social sciences, and economic reductionism within a range even more disputable.

Finally, the best evaluation of any given public policy is not necessarily the bearer of change. Such a view, certainly somewhat cynical, but nourished by the practice of evaluation, leads to the attitude that it is not a good idea to count on the reasoned evaluation of drug policies having a great effect. Sociologists have long since abandoned the overly optimistic instrumentalist position, which envisions the well-meaning public policy-maker, warned by a perfectly neutral evaluator of the flaws in his policy, correcting them without any resistance. The virtuous loop between evaluation and change is infinitely more complex. This is why practitioners generally consider that the first merit of evaluation is to force the actors to sit down at the table and clarify their position. The virtue of evaluation is not to guide change in a normative sense but to set off an administrative dynamic that serves as a catalyst for transformation. The position of those sociologists who are most impassioned by political science is even more draconian. For them, evaluation is but one of many facets of political competition. One evaluates only to use the result of the evaluation in the struggle for power. The benefit of evaluation would then be to force the competing political teams to clarify their projects. Transparency thus imposed by competition would then favour the elimination of the most obviously incoherent proposals.

Furthermore, can we seriously discuss drug policy without distinguishing between the different products? On the one hand, we can recognize that what is justified in the case of cannabis is perhaps not so in the case of heroin. On the other, current practice is in fact characterized by fairly uniform public drug policies which cover all products, the subtle distinction between products often being relegated to the background. We will adopt this attitude, although it is somewhat frustrating, treating drugs in general and not distinguishing between the products, except to make certain qualifications. In any case, what are the best criteria for distinguishing between the products? A necessarily too rapid inventory underlines how much each discipline adopts a taxonomy of drugs adapted to the questions it raises. Neurobiologists point out common actions of the different substances on the neuro-receptors that constitute in their eyes, a rational basis for a multi-substance drug policy. They do point out, however, the differences in intrinsic dangers among the various products. Certainly, in the laboratory, cocaine appears to provoke more serious problems than cannabis, but cannabis is more often associated with tobacco, which that produces numerous cancers. What should we conclude in relation to the dangers posed by the two products? It seems to us, then, that a classification of products by level of danger is of little assistance in designing public policy. On the contrary, Freudian psychoanalysts defended the idea that the specific characteristics of the products were secondary, addiction being a pathology unrelated to the product, which represents only a symptom.

This thesis partly explains the initial opposition of this profession in some countries, such as France, to surrogate treatments. What is the use of treating the symptom? The most formalistic lawyers uphold the opposition between legal and illegal substances. Historians remind us that some countries tolerate cannabis more than alcohol, and at certain periods cocaine was legal in several developed countries. Economic analysis, as we apply it, distinguishes between the products when the impact on the social cost of a measure varies in relation to the product considered.

Finally, when we evaluate a public policy in general we should be mindful of the strategic objective it indicates. Most often the public policymaker is careful to keep from overtly announcing the objectives assigned to a drug policy. Is it a question of eradicating drugs, reducing consumption, banning their circulation, or limiting the negative consequences of consumption? We should note that public drug policy often consists of a combination of measures aimed at different objectives, brought under the umbrella of a general presentation intended to artificially unify this heterogeneity. Such heterogeneity in fact is not necessarily to be condemned. It is logical that different sectors of society have very different needs for public policies which the State cannot avoid. The evaluation of a public policy often consists, therefore, in testing the effectiveness of announced measures, then trying to evaluate their effects, and finally verifying if the effects observed follow the direction of the announced strategy. Economic evaluation of public policy diverges somewhat from this schema of evaluation. This, in fact, is what makes it both interesting, as well as irritating.

In fact, unlike other disciplines economic analysis claims the right to discuss the value of strategic objectives chosen by the public policy-maker. Even more importantly, mainstream economic analysis of public policy does not do away with the complexities involved in specifying the nature of the objective that the policy-maker should assign to the policy. Economic theory, such as is usually used by economists, considers that good policy must facilitate more efficient allocation of resources: that which allows the achievement of a given result with the least cost. Good public policy thus must correct the inefficient allocation of resources by the markets. Such a description generally suffices to discredit the economic approach among those who are afraid of seeing a public drug policy reduced to correcting markets in the direction of greater efficiency. It is interesting to note that this policy might be reformulated in an equivalent manner in the following format: the efficient policy for drugs is that which allows minimization of the social cost that the drugs impose on the collectivity. This formulation is generally better accepted. Without insisting here on this point, let us point out once more how much this normative obsession constitutes the specificity of economic evaluation of public policies. Where other evaluation methodologies are content with measuring the space between the objectives and the results, or are transformed into accompanying a learning process of change in public organizations, economic analysis claims the right to test the public policy in view of an objective which it judges unavoidable: collective well-being, meaning the efficient allocation of resources or the minimization of the social cost (no matter what the formulation), and not that advanced by the public policy-maker who is supposed to represent the democratic majority.

The aim of this book, then, is to introduce the reader to the economic evaluation of public policies. When, for example, the public policy-maker increases police presence in the street, this increases the probability of the arrest of dealers and consumers. The cost of drugs increases and the consumer can react by reducing his consumption, by changing products or by adopting another form of use. The effect of public action therefore depends upon the complex interaction between market and consumer behaviour. Other than seeing therein a means of satisfaction *pro domo* for the economists whose profession it is to study this type of interaction, the reader will easily understand how an adequate understanding of consumer and dealer behaviour represents a prerequisite for the examination of their activity on the market.

Written for economists who are looking for concrete illustration of the use that can be made of classic microeconomic tools, this work is also addressed to policy-makers. Some will find pleasure in delving into the detail of some presentations using formal mathematical language; others will discover that their train of thought may be maintained by skipping over the more technical parts. By providing a better understanding of drug policy and offering a framework for discussion wherein the merits of different proposals can be compared, this work should prove a useful instrument for evaluating public drug policy. Finally, when the success of a policy depends upon the interaction between individual behaviour, prices, and markets, there is no doubt in our mind of the importance of economic analysis.

Overview

The first chapter analyses the flow of drugs. The suppliers constitute the primary actors in drug markets. Producers, importers, wholesalers, and retailers form a chain of distribution. The behaviour of each of these actors affects not only drug price, but also allocation of the value created by the different protagonists. In other respects, the organizational methods of supply determine the conditions under which drugs are distributed, the degree of violence on the drug markets, and the influence of organized crime. Each of the supplier groups (importers, retailers, criminal organizations) adopts strategies that differ greatly from those of a classical legitimate firm. Uncertainty, limited rationality, opportunism, and betrayal create specific strategies, a thorough understanding of which is the key to an efficient public policy.

Also, the most frequently proposed hypotheses about the behaviour of drug suppliers are too often deficient. The major traffickers are invested with a power of monopoly that guarantees price control and makes them, unwittingly, play a regulatory role, as the monopoly rations the supply. The small resellers are often presented as being representatives of a class of new businessmen in full enrichment phase. In underlining the strong competition that reigns between the suppliers, and by drawing attention to the high flexibility of the organizations in the drug supply network, we interpret, in a unique manner, some of the difficulties facing repressive public policy when it attempts to eradicate drug supply.

At the end of the drug chain, laundering the money represents a crucial and necessary step. Only the biggest criminal organizations use the more sophisticated instruments offered by the international financial system to launder their profits. The other smaller traffickers content themselves with unrefined and less costly methods. The analytical schema of laundering strategies becomes coherent after revising, downward, the sums produced for laundering as estimated by those wishfully called the best experts in the area.

Chapter 2 is devoted to drug addiction. If addicted consumers react paradoxically to the price signals engendered by public policy, then it is the efficiency of the latter that should be questioned. For some, drug consumers are not responsible economic agents, but individuals whose economic behaviour has become abnormal as a result of their affinity for drugs. This thesis poses problems because it repudiates the value that the act of consumption represents for the individual. In short, drug consumption disappears behind addiction. Yet, demand for drugs cannot be reduced to a choice that is imposed upon a subject who lacks free will. We ought, therefore, to understand the motivation for an individual's initial choice in favour of drugs and then describe how an individual, even though he has become a regular consumer, nevertheless preserves a palette of choices that he uses to try to optimize his drug consumption in an environment full of temptations, where the main variables are income, price, dependence, and the pleasure that drugs procure.

The question of whether economic analysis can help to define the framework of good drug policy is at the heart of Chapter 3. In the sphere of drugs, where ideology and moral judgements are omnipresent, it is worth knowing what kind of policy an economic approach, based on research into policy effectiveness, would favour: that is, minimization of the social costs generated by drug consumption and trafficking, or the sum of the increased negative externalities and utility procured for those who consume drugs. Taking an interest, admittedly in rather abstract terms, in the form of an optimal drug policy allows us to indirectly bring to light the economic cost (sometimes exorbitant) of any policy that deviates from this norm. In concrete terms, society must be aware that by deviating from optimal drug policy it is wasting resources. Unfortunately, a quick review of the literature illustrates that although mainstream normative analysis performs well in evaluating the marginal effects of drug policy (new treatment or inroads into criminal policy) it is incapable of clearly indicating which of the two important regimes (prohibition or legalization) should be recommended. The stream of analysis called 'Law and Economics', as initiated by Coase (1937), consists of an interesting approach, distinct from traditional normative analysis.

In Chapter 4, the issue is no longer to decide whether we should prohibit or legalize drugs, but to determine which public policy should be retained within an institutional framework where prohibition is a fact. So, from a normative point of view, governments should therefore implement public policies aimed at maximizing social welfare, i.e. minimizing the social cost of drugs.

Notwithstanding this lengthy practice of treating externalities, normative economic analysis encounters real difficulties playing its role of aiding decision-making, the reason being that conventional economic analysis ties the reduction of social costs to intermediate objectives. Classical analysis of externality correction is inspired by the work of C. Pigou (1920) and the study of crime economics developed by G. Becker (1968), both of which aim at minimizing social costs. However, the former proposes accomplishing this by bringing society to an optimal level of consumption of illegal drugs, while the latter suggests attaining this result by reducing criminal activity to an optimal level. Nothing proves that the orientation of a public policy toward attaining an optimal level of one or the other of these variables (consumption and crime) guarantees maximization of collective well-being, or, in other words, minimization of the social cost of drugs. All of the difficulties where drugs are concerned stem from the fact that the level of social cost – that is, the severity of the harm inflicted on society by drugs – does not depend exclusively on either the level of consumption or on the level of activity of the illegal market. The means of suppression can in itself affect welfare in more important ways than in the trivial sense of tax distortion.

Departing from the view that drug policy cannot be reduced to the search for a hypothetical optimal consumption level any more than an efficient crime level, Chapter 5 tries to define the normative objective which should be established in public drug policy? The search for efficiency seems shocking when applied to the area of social policy. It is, however, intertwined with the objective of social drug cost minimization, and thus solidly establishes the basis for those policies entitled 'harm reduction'. Minimization of social drug cost is thus the main objective of drug policy. The objective of economic efficiency may be attained by an infinite variety of allocations of social resources. If we limit ourselves to the examination of arbitration between two groups of individuals – the non-consumers of drugs and the drug consumers – the heart of the problem when creating a drug policy lies in determining whether the principal beneficiaries of the policy should be the first or the second group. In practice, there exist many groups of actors concerned by drug policy. Thus, the public policy-maker must subtly negotiate the fact that any public action relating to social cost, even a neutral one, benefits certain groups and penalizes others. Second, the same public action may affect external factors generated by drugs and thus the social cost, in two directions. We should then calmly accept the fact that public policy is not only a vector of efficiency, but also a powerful factor in regulating the distribution of wealth.

Chapter 6 deals with the implementation of public drug policy. The conventional approach for reducing externalities is based on the hypothesis that repression increases the price paid by the consumer of drugs, and is thus a motivation to reduce consumption. Action aimed at demand constitutes the key to all anti-drug policies geared toward reducing consumption, but effectiveness critically depends on the degree of demand elasticity of drug consumers: that is, on the consumer reaction to price change. We will see that not only can the particularities of drug price-demand elasticity intervene and thwart the expected effectiveness of the repressive policy. The drug suppliers' organizational methods can also play a negative role in policies aimed at reducing consumption. Briefly, from the supply side and the demand side, there exist valid reasons to conclude that increase in repression does not necessarily engender a decrease in consumption.

Drug policy is the result of a combination of several instruments, particularly repression and treatment. How can we most efficiently combine these two instruments? Economic analysis supplies the rule, and the observation of implemented policies emphasizes how far away governments are from it. A multiple equilibrium approach explains why a sub-optimal public policy can prevail for a long time.

Chapter 7 continues the previous discussion in regard to the fight against organized crime and money laundering. It is fairly apparent that policies implemented run up against several obstacles, but, without it being a real consolation, we can say that the theories put forward really do advance our thinking. In matters of organized crime, on the other hand, we remain more skeptical about the range of the analyses undertaken. According to hypotheses we consider to be unrealistic, various authors have argued that the presence of organized crime is not necessarily more destructive to collective well-being than its absence (Buchanan 1974). Whether it is about controlling mafia activity or the participation of banks in laundering, modern economic theory uses agency models. In this context, we illustrate the difficulties of the Principal, the State, to calibrate a system of incitation that forces the agents (the banks or the mafia) to submit to its objective function. In the banking area, we observe a marked difference between the European model in which banks cooperate in the struggle against laundering following the adoption of rules (Cooter 1995) and the Anglo-Saxon model in which the legal responsibility of the bank (corporate liability) forces them to participate in the reform of the banking system. The Continental system produces results that are difficult to measure, and while in vogue in the US, it has important weaknesses: in some cases it is optimal to not survey the activities of bank personnel (Arlen 1994).

Part I
Behaviour and strategies

1 Drug supply and criminal organizations

The suppliers constitute the primary actors in drug markets. Producers, importers, wholesalers, and retailers form a distribution chain. The behaviour of each of these actors affects not only the drug price, but also the allocation of the value created by the different protagonists. In other respects, the organizational methods of supply determine the conditions under which drugs are distributed, the degree of violence on the drug markets, and the influence of organized crime. Each of the supplier groups (importers, retailers, criminal organizations) adopt strategies which differ greatly from those of a classic legitimate firm. Uncertainty, limited rationality, opportunism and betrayal create particular strategies, a thorough understanding of which is the key to an efficient public policy.

Combining theoretical analysis with empirical data is not an easy thing to do, particularly as the latter on drugs are rare and not very reliable. This is no doubt due to the desire of international organizations responsible for fighting drugs to furnish, from the beginning of the 1990s, some definite estimates of the different fluctuations, despite the fact that knowledge was still very much in an embryonic stage. This was responsible for the circulation of figures, which, upon being repeated, ended up becoming accepted as reliable information. However, the most summary examination cannot but discover many fallacies. Profits are often take to be incomes, as if traffickers had no production costs or risks to cover. Similarly, reference prices are confused with retail prices, which makes no sense when measuring an international drug trade flow in which exchanges are made at wholesale prices.

The most frequently offered hypotheses about the behaviour of drug suppliers are also too often simplistic. The major traffickers are invested with a power of monopoly that guarantees price control and makes them, despite themselves, play a regulatory role, as the monopoly rations the supply. The small resellers are often presented as being representatives of a class of new businessmen in full enrichment phase.

In underlining the intense competition that reigns between suppliers, we thus offer new factors to explain the drop in drug prices, particularly on the retail market of the United States in the past fifteen years. By drawing attention to the high flexibility of the organizational forms in the drug supply network, we interpret in an original manner some of the difficulties facing repressive public policy when it attempts to eradicate drug supply.

We notice how lively are the controversies about the behavioural interpretation of these actors, their strategies and the amounts effectively in play. The stakes are high, regarding the calibre of public policies, particularly repressive ones. No doubt, the hypotheses made about the behaviour of actors turn out to be determinant in the discussion of different methods of public intervention.

Illegal distribution: the flow of drugs

The most frequently used drugs are of natural origin (cannabis, cocaine, heroin); the others are of manufactured chemical origin (ecstasy, LSD, etc.). We have fairly accurate statistics for evaluating the surfaces engaged in both the cultivation of opium, from which heroin is made, and of coca leaves. On the other hand, the data concerning the culture of cannabis is of mediocre quality. This is because high turnover and a great dispersion of plantations into small production units characterize the agriculture of cannabis. The fact that some of the production is accomplished indoors further complicates data collection. As for statistics relating to synthetic drugs, they are rare and often disputable.

Drug production

At the point of production of drugs of natural origin, we find cultures for which it is interesting to specify the surface area. UNDCP (2001) notes that opium occupies the cultivated surface area of between 240,000 and 280,000 hectares, or approximately 26,000 km^2. This represents a global production capacity of 400 tons of heroin, which can be contained in 40 trucks (see Table 1.1 and Figure 1.1). For cocaine, 180,000 hectares are sufficient to ensure the 900 tons produced annually, a quantity that would require 90 trucks to transport.

Table 1.1 Historical production data for opium (metric tons)

Country	1988	1990	1992	1994	1996	1997	1998	1999	2000
Afghanistan	112	157	197	3,146	2,248	2,804	2,693	4,565	3,276
Burma	1,125	1,621	166	1,583	1,760	1,676	1,303	895	1,097
Other Asian	482	507	383	356	226	207	190	173	219
Colombia	–	–	90	205	67	90	100	88	88
Mexico	67	62	130	265	121	160	160	131	109
Total	2,794	3,760	4,143	5,620	4,355	4,823	4,346	5,764	4,691

Source: UN ONDCCP, 'Global illicit drug trends'. Reproduced from Reuter and Greenfield (2001).

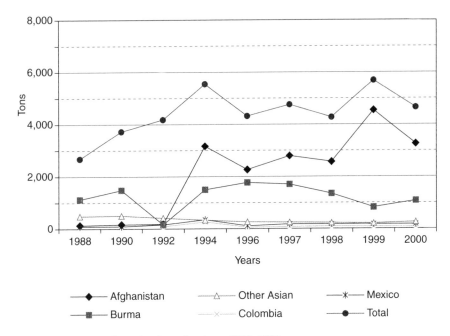

Figure 1.1 National production of opium, 1988–2000

Despite the difficulties related to estimating production and particularly those posed by the precise measurement of cultivated surface area, the number of harvests, and the rate of turnover, it appears that Afghanistan and Myanmar[1] dominate world heroin production, representing between them 85–90 per cent of annual production. As illustrated in Table 1.1, their relative position varied over the years, but remains very large. The annual production of opium during the 1990s was around 4,000 tons, from which approximately 400 tons of pure heroin were made.

Cocaine production from coca leaves is essentially concentrated in three Andean countries (Bolivia, Colombia and Peru) (see Table 1.2 and Figure 1.2). Colombia plays a special role in that it partly imports the leaves and the paste, and then refines them into cocaine. Although fairly simple from a

Table 1.2 Historical production data for coca leaf (metric tons)

Country	1992	1993	1994	1995	1996	1997	1998	1999
Bolivia	803	844	898	85	751	701	529	228
Colombia	296	317	358	2,293	3,029	3,470	4,376	5,214
Peru	2,239	1,555	1,653	1,836	1,747	1,302	956	692
Total	3,339	2,717	2,909	4,979	5,527	5,403	5,861	6,134

Source: UN ONDCCP, 'Global illicit drug trends', Reproduced from Reuter and Greenfield (2001).

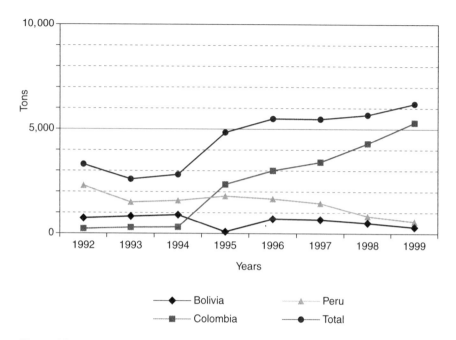

Figure 1.2 National production of coca leaf, 1992–1999

technical standpoint, this last stage in the production holds the risks of the laboratories being discovered and destroyed, which explains why numerous producers of leaves and paste prefer to leave the final refining process to a Colombian organization.

The distribution of cocaine production among these countries underlines Colombia's growing role in global production, which explains the civil war in that country and the traffickers' desire to bring coca leaf production sites closer to the refining laboratories. The volume of pure cocaine production has been around 900 tons a year over the past ten years.

The data relating to the production of cannabis and marijuana is more difficult to collect. UNDCP (2000) indicates that more than 120 countries reported the existence of cannabis plantations. It would seem, however, that Morocco, South Africa, Nigeria, Afghanistan, Pakistan, Mexico, Colombia, and Jamaica are the main producers. The lack of data concerning the United States is troubling since this country is certainly the largest consumer in the world and disposes of an abundant production.

Once produced, the drugs must be exported to the consumer countries. In the process, a non-negligible portion is seized by police and customs officials. Around 30 tons of heroin, 300 tons of cocaine, and 4,000 tons of cannabis and marijuana are confiscated each year. The drugs that are not seized are then cut and distributed in the various national markets.

A first somewhat striking observation shows that only 12 to 18 tons of heroin end up in the American market: at most only 5 per cent of the total quantity of heroin available. According to Reuter and Greenfield (2001), around 60 tons of heroin are consumed in the other developed Western countries and certain Eastern countries, for a total consumption of 80 tons in Eastern and Western Europe. Three-quarters of the heroin produced is therefore consumed in Third World countries, particularly in Pakistan, Afghanistan, Iran, Myanmar and Thailand. Despite weak prevalence rates, and compensated for by a large population, it is reasonable to assume that Asia shelters around 10 million regular consumers of heroin.

Analysis of drug seizures raises an interesting question. Reuter and MacCoun (2001) have suggested that the ratio between drug seizures and population size is an indicator of the volume of drug shipments destined for a country. The fact that between 1985 and 1994 Holland had a higher number of seizures than all the other EU countries for three drugs (cannabis, heroin, cocaine) demonstrates the role played by Rotterdam as the port of entry for drugs for the rest of Europe. The same is true for Spain, where a high ratio also reflects an analogous position.

Figure 1.3 examines the question of seizures from a slightly different angle. We note that the average quantities of heroin seized in the EU countries and the United States correlates very well with the number of problematic drug users, which is not the case with cocaine. We could therefore conclude that the heroin shipments are destined to replenish the national markets, while the shipments of cocaine enter at one point of the European territory and are then dispatched to the various local markets. This hypothesis is confirmed by the fact that the average seizure of heroin is smaller than that of cocaine.

Trade flow

Having once determined the zones towards which the drugs are dispatched, it is logical to multiply the approximate quantities by the prices, which are often difficult to ascertain. The publication by UNDCP (1997) of a study estimating global drug commerce to be approximately $400 billion a year considerably complicates the discussion. The figure put forward by UNDCP does not reflect trade flow, but is an estimate of the turnover or total retail expenditure. This estimate is obtained by multiplying the street price of the drug by the amount consumed. First, without even discussing the relevance of such an indicator, it is necessary to discuss the price samples that are used by the authors of the study. In the case of the heroin market, UNDCP (1997) holds that the global market for this drug represents around $107 billion. Reuter and Greenfield (2001) use the terms of this calculation, but this time without neglecting to consider the fact that the price of the heroin consumed in the Third World countries is lower than that in developed countries. They thus arrive at a global

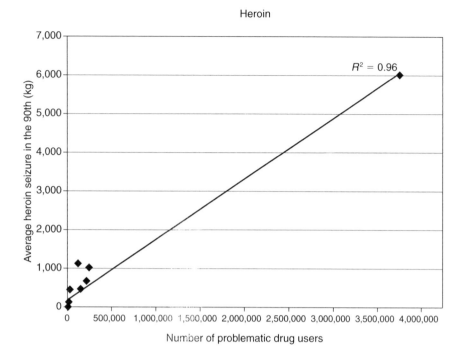

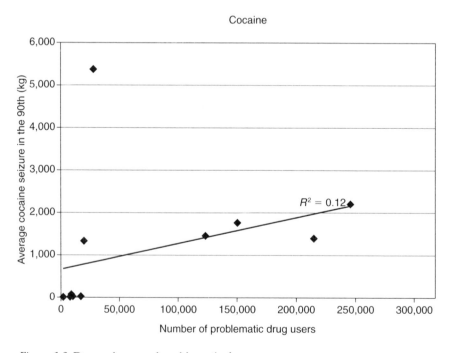

Figure 1.3 Drug seizure and problematic drug use

turnover figure for the heroin market of $12 billion for the United States and $5 billion for the rest of the world, or a total of $17 billion. Second, this figure is far removed from a trade flow figure. In absolute terms, most of the value added in the supply chain accrues when drugs are distributed within consumer countries. In true trade terms, a more reasonable estimate of the total of illicit drugs, heroin, marijuana, and synthetic drugs, is only about $20–25 billion per year (Reuter 1997),[2] (see Table 1.3).

The drug trade flow is an indicator of international drug commerce. Once the drugs are exported to the consumer countries, they are resold and the margins are taken off all along the distribution chain. It still remains to understand how to distribute the value added throughout the production chain (see Table 1.4).

We can see clearly from Table 1.4 how the added value is concentrated at the time of drug exportation from the source country to the consumer country. The mark-up at this stage is 2,100 per cent for cocaine and 2,700 per cent for heroin. Certainly, the mark-up rate is equally high at the point of retail drug sale, but the margin is then shared between a multitude of final resellers while the importation phase is concentrated in a few hands. Consequently, the portion of the value of the drug once dispatched (landed value) – for example, to the United States – represents only around 12 per cent of the retail price of cocaine and heroin.

International trafficking and mark-up

The traffickers' ability to pass on, and eventually increase cost by increasing the price depends largely on the degree of competition that pits one

Table 1.3 Illegal drug trade flow and total retail expenditure ($ billion)

	Reuter (1997)	*UNDCP*
Total retail expenditure	–	$400
	Heroin: $27	Heroin: $107
Trade flow	$20–25	–

Table 1.4 Prices and mark-up (heroin and cocaine)

Distribution chain	*Price $ per pure kg equivalent*	*Mark-up (%)*	*Distribution chain*	*Price per pure kg equivalent*	*Mark-up (%)*
–	–	–	Opium (Pakistan)	90	–
Leaf (Peru)	650	–	Heroin value of the raw material in a kg of heroin (Pakistan)	900	220
Export (Colombia)	1,050	60	Export Pakistan (kg)	2,870	220
Import (USA)	23,000	2,100	–	–	–

function against the other. According to the Colombian economists, Krauthausen and Sarmiento (1991), in producing countries drug traffickers make up a cartelized oligopoly, which means that the traffickers respect an informal agreement destined to avoid price wars and the collapse of the market. That said, at the limits of the oligopoly, we observe the activity of smaller traffickers, in competition with each other, who share less than 20 per cent of the market. Caulkins (1990) goes in the same direction and considers that competition is weak between big traffickers, deducing from this a model of price formation, of 'mark-up' type, which indicates that the increase in prices is 'multiplicative'. This hypothesis of monopolistic price activity applies to the case of cocaine, implying that an increase of 10 per cent of the price of a coca leaf creates an increase of the same percentage in the retail price of cocaine. We contest this oligopoly thesis, which claims traffickers are sufficiently cartelized to be capable of preventing the drop in drug prices. The competition in producing countries is lively, and the ability of traffickers to pass on the rise in cost is more limited than Caulkins supposes. In fact, his model fits poorly with the empirical data.

In contrast to the proponents of the cartel hypothesis, Kennedy *et al.* (1993) consider that strong competition reigns between big traffickers and propose a model of formation of an 'additive' type. As a result of competition, the models of Kennedy *et al.* consider that the traffickers can only pass on to the drug's final price that rise in cost which is effectively observed. This hypothesis of competitive pricing leads to a model of retail price formation for the drug that is very different from that of Caulkins.[3]

The first consequence of choosing a mark-up additive is to explain why a substantial rise in the price of coca leaves, due for example, to increased repression in the source countries only engenders a very small increase in the street prices of cocaine. Thus, the tripling in price of the leaves necessary to produce 1 kg of cocaine only engenders an increase in retail price of 2 per cent. The mark-up is the economic reward paid to smugglers, wholesalers and retailers of cocaine, for their work. It is presumed to be equal to the sum of the opportunity cost of their time, a premium to offset: their risk of legal sanction and their vulnerability to theft and coercion by other illegal actors; monopoly profits that may accrue to established distribution organizations (and the cost they incur to deter potential new arrivals); the cost of other goods and services (such as transportation equipment and storage) which they purchase; and payments they make to evade law enforcement. The assumption of a fixed mark-up between the export prices of cocaine in producing countries and the retail price to consumers implies that the economic rewards for trafficking will be primarily related to the quantity of cocaine sold rather than to its value (see Table 1.5).

Table 1.5 Additive vs multiplicative mark-up models of illegal drug importation

Level of the network	Authors	Competition	Model for price formation
	Krauthausen and Sarmiento (1991) Caulkins (1990)	Weak competition; Cartelized oligopoly; Presence of small dealers in competition with each other.	Multiplicative model (Caulkins): the increase in price is 'multiplicative'. This hypothesis of monopolistic price implies that an increase of 10 per cent in the price of the coca leaf engenders an increase of the same percentage of the retail sales price.
Producing countries	Kennedy, Reuter and Riley (1993)	Strong competition; Non-cartelized oligopoly.	Additive model: the traffickers can only pass on the increase effectively observed of their cost to the final price of the drug. Thus, the tripling of the price of the leaves needed to produce 1 kilo of cocaine engenders only a price increase at retail of 2 per cent.

Drug sales and income

The organization of a network for drug distribution is composed of four levels: production, international trafficking, wholesale distribution and final distribution. The network resembles a double tunnel, with lanes moving in both directions, upon which we find several thousands of agents engaged in production and distribution, while in the middle, the international traffic and wholesale traffic are concentrated in the hands of a few.

The ability of each link in the chain to generate the margin depends upon their ability to sell at a price higher than purchased. One part of the margin covers the costs, and the other part generates the benefit. All along the chain of production and distribution different intermediaries ensure a functional role and cover their cost by adding a margin to the purchase price of the drug. According to the degree of competition, they may increase the price and make profits by exploiting their control of the situation.

After having specified how the sale price of drugs is determined at the different levels of the distribution chain, we should question the revenues that each group of actors obtains from its participation in the traffic.

Source countries

To begin, how much do producing countries benefit from drugs? As far as most producing countries are concerned, we do not have much information. According to NCIS, however, coca occupies a fairly important position in the economies of Bolivia and Peru. Table 1.6 reports these estimates, for which the methods of calculation are not always clear.

The figures are complex to interpret. It is true that, for example in the case of cocaine, the actors in the chain who are based in Colombia only take up 1 per cent of the street sale price. Yet, this sum is very large when compared to the Colombian GDP, and it is concentrated in a few hands, causing visible effects on Colombian society.

Table 1.6 Position occupied by coca in the Peruvian and Bolivian economies

	Bolivia	Peru
Value of production of coca (millions of dollars)	313–2,300	869–3,000
Coca exports (millions of dollars)	132–850	688–2,100
Total revenue (millions of dollars)	246–442	743–1,200
Number of jobs (in hundred thousands)	207–463	145–700
Cultivated surface	35,000–55,400	115,530–166,500
Part of the economy of coca:		
Of the GDP	6–19%	2–11%
In exports	15–98%	14–78%
Of the exterior debt	7–25%	3–18%

Source: NCIS (1989).

It is also obvious that the essential part of the added value in the production chain of cocaine is localized in the United States without the aggregate revenue of millions of small resellers having a very significant macro-social impact. Finally, the essential data remain unknown: we know nothing or next to nothing about the functioning and the profits of criminal groups who act in the North and South of the continent and who play a major role in the importation and distribution of wholesale drugs in the United States. It is important to note that the functioning of the Colombian part was partially brought to light during the dismantling of the Medellin cartel, while the part operating on US territory remains the submerged part of the iceberg. Since criminal rings are essentially transnational, it is thus somewhat meaningless to speak of Colombian cartels or American criminal organizations.

Wholesale trafficking and profits

The biggest mystery continues to surround the part of the drug sales chain that operates in the consumer countries. If, at the level of international traffic, we are able to formulate plausible hypotheses, we know almost nothing about the functioning of the segments of the chain that enable the drugs to move from the wholesalers to the final resellers, where the picture becomes clear once again. In fact, literature (though scarce) exists which is devoted to the role of the small resellers. However, we know almost nothing about the actions of the dealers situated between wholesale and retail (sales of quantities of drugs running from 10 to 500 grams).

Although the mark-up additive model seems adapted to describing the exportation of drugs to consumer countries, it, however, poses problems when we attempt to apply it further upstream along the distribution chain, in the passing of drugs from wholesalers to retailers. Effectively, a simultaneous drop in the street price of cocaine and an increase in repression have been observed in the United States over the past twenty years. It would therefore seem that wholesalers and resellers were not able to pass the increased cost of risk to customers (see Figure 1.4).

In order to explain this situation, we have proposed a model of (wholesale) drug market structure in consumer countries (Kopp, 1996a). Following this model, at the wholesale level, the capacity of the drug resellers to add the rise in cost onto the prices is determined in an endogenous manner by the threat represented by the entry of small traffickers into the market, attracted by the price rise. The drug market therefore functions as an oligopoly composed of competitive bands of insiders, an arrangement resembling what is generally designated as organized crime,[4] which is subject to strong pressure by marginal traffickers (outsiders) desirous to cross the entry barriers in order to profit from the opportunities of such a market. The insiders protect themselves from repression by corruption, violence and trickery. In these conditions, for them, the risk of being arrested dimin-

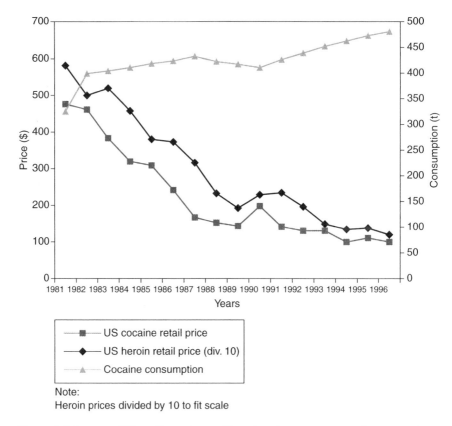

Figure 1.4 Average US retail cocaine and heroin prices per gram and consumption

ishes and the high prices generate a large profit. On the other hand, the outsiders are effectively exposed to the risk of arrest, which constitutes a real cost for them. The price is not sufficiently high for them to stay long in the market. This is precisely what explains why a crowd of candidates for juicy profits do not invade the drug market. Lacking specific know-how or the benefits of good connections, the outsiders cannot gain a foothold in the market. This unequal exposure to risk provides the explanation for the enduring oligopolistic nature of the drug market.

Retail sales

The last stage in the distribution chain, the retail level, places the dealer and the consumer face to face. To be consistent with our previous argument, we will stick to the subject of the constitution of the retailers' income. In order to better understand the functioning of districts where there is heavy traffic, Reuter *et al.* (1991) studied the population imprisoned between 1985 and 1987 for selling drugs in the city of Washington, D.C.

The results can be summarized as follows: from the viewpoint of the prison statistics, the dealers in the street are in the majority black (99 per cent), young (40 per cent aged between 18–24) and male (90 per cent). Also, the street dealers have a lower than average level of education and a history of involvement in various forms of delinquency, as indicated by their numerous arrests for other crimes. The figure on arrests carried over to the total population underlines the prevalent participation of people in the area in small drug trafficking. Some 10 per cent of the individuals born in 1957 were charged with a drug offence between 1985 and 1987. For those born between 1957 and 1963, the percentage fluctuates around 11 per cent. The probability of a young black male aged 19 years old residing in the district to have been condemned for a drug-related crime in 1986 is 33 per cent. These figures must be viewed in the context of the living conditions of blacks in the district: in 1986, 82 per cent of the people living in poverty were black. These figures are corroborated by Tillman's study (1987), which indicates that between 1974 and 1985, in the State of California, 66 per cent of blacks born in 1956 were arrested between the age of 18 and 29, as compared with 34 per cent of whites. Blumenstein and Graddy (1981–1982) and Mauer (1990) corroborate these results. Finally, Tillman (1987) indicates that between 1972 and 1979, 10.5 per cent of blacks were in prison, compared with 2.4 per cent of whites (sample of 12,000 persons aged between 14 and 21 in 1979).

For a complete picture of things, repression should thus be considered. In the district in question, of the 24,000 dealers, 14,000 of which are regular, 1.4 per cent face the risk of being killed, 7 per cent being severely injured, and 22 per cent being imprisoned. By carefully distinguishing the population of more or less professional users-resellers from those of the dealers, it appears clearly that the actors of the first group do not get rich in the drug business.[5]

Criminal organization

In examining the role of importers, wholesalers, and retailers, we quickly begin to realize that they could organize themselves and create criminal organizations. The image of criminal organization is generally associated with wholesale traffic rather than the resale of the drug at the retail level. Is this accurate? Finally, do we really know why criminal organizations only sometimes appear?

The monopoly thesis

Why, in the world of crime, does something other than individual criminals exist? Intuitively, it is tempting to theorize a relationship between the formation of criminal enterprises – that is, criminal organizations (not individual) – and economies of scale, to which the question of monopoly is linked (Andreano *et al.*, 1980). It seems 'natural' for an enterprise, regardless of the market in which it operates, to exploit available possibilities in order to gain a monopoly position in a more or less significant segment of the market. What firm would refuse to occupy a monopoly position? It may, however, be that this position is impossible to achieve (for legal reasons) or too costly to achieve and/or to defend relative to the advantages that it can bring. But a criminal enterprise has available a tool that 'legal' businesses do not, namely, violence. One can then consider the question of whether violence permits a sustainable monopoly position, and whether it can lead to a stable equilibrium (the operator of the monopoly succeeds in rendering his position 'uncontestable').

The theory of organized crime developed by Schelling (1967) and Buchanan (1973) proposes transposing, case-by-case, illegal market results with those derived from observations of classical markets by industrial microeconomics. Such a step brings these authors to prognosticate on the capacity of organized crime to impose its monopoly on criminal activities. Such success hinges on the facility with which criminal organizations succeed in eliminating competition from petty criminals when they step on their territory. In effect, entry into the world of criminal activity is limited by the action of various barriers (moral scruples, ignorance of the networks, etc.). These barriers reinforce the monopoly and facilitate the existence of abnormal profit. The market for illegal activity should be treated much like a classical market, the threat of repression and the risk of being arrested being simply considered a supplementary cost which moves the curve of supply towards the top.

We know that a monopoly position offers a certain number of advantages. The monopoly allows the criminal enterprise to attain a large size and to benefit from the economies of scale that accompany this. Moreover, the criminal enterprise that holds a monopoly can fix a monopoly price that brings additional profit. It can also play for a drop in prices to prevent the entry of potential competitors to the market. Organized in a monopoly, criminals improve their chances of successfully modifying laws. For example, activity aimed at changing a law concerning the operation of casinos can be more fruitfully conducted by a single organization than by a collection of individuals. By organizing themselves into a monopoly, criminals become 'rule makers'. They offer a 'mode of governance' to the criminal milieu.

In a monopoly situation the prices paid are high and the quantities exchanged low. This explains why Buchanan (1973) accorded an advantage to a criminal monopoly. He pointed out that a criminal organization in a monopoly maximizes its profit for a quantity of goods produced that is lower than that of the competition (and this at a higher price). As a result, according to Buchanan, the collectivity gained an advantage from a crime monopoly. Such a thesis found a receptive audience among American policy-makers and popular opinion, to whom organized crime could constitute an unwilling ally in the fight against the explosion of a proteiform criminality.

Contestation of the monopoly thesis

Recent work contests the idea that the monopoly prevails as a natural form of criminality. On market structure, Reuter (1983) and Kleiman (1989) highlight the difficulties of criminal organizations to effectively close the drug market to candidates at entry in order to impose their monopoly. Reuter criticizes the Mafia myth, which, according to him, holds that the Mafia continues to cash in on its prestige, even though it no longer possesses sufficient power to maintain its organization at the level of its reputation. According to this author, the Mafia is weakly centralized and has high coordination costs, which is characteristic of illegal operations. The insufficient information available and the low degree of definition of the property rights of each of its subgroups deprive the Mafia of a part of its profits that its size should permit it to collect.

As for the drug market, nothing indicates that big dealers constitute a real monopoly. The strong competition to which they are subjected leads us to conclude that the market is structured like a non-cartelized oligopoly, the members of which wage a price war. The ability to combine the necessary resources for the exercise of an illegal activity (network, connections, corruption, etc.) is crucial to accessing the market. The access to these resources has different modalities. Certainly, big dealers, who benefit from these resources, see their cost level go down. On the other hand, candidates for market entry, more sensitive to risk, have higher costs (Kopp 1996a). The big dealers therefore benefit from an absolute cost advantage. They carry out their illegal activities sheltered from entry barriers, however we should not consider that they are completely invulnerable. In fact, the entry candidates can see their arrival on the market facilitated by a repressive policy that creates a rise in drug prices. Such a price rise pulls the price of the drug above the profitability mark for small dealers and accelerates their entry. Furthermore, we should consider the different sensitivities to risk by the agents. The cost introduced by the risk does not convert at the same rate for all traffickers. Although exempt from networks that would protect them efficiently from risk, some small traffickers nevertheless penetrate the market and compete with big dealers. Real risk-lovers, they benefit from a cost function that is advantageous, as they do not attribute the same cost as the others to risks they run.

These few observations indicate how the thesis of the tendency towards monopolization of criminal activity and drug traffic is, and has been for several years, questioned. In the absence of a real crime monopoly, there is no reason to think any longer that traffickers would practise a self-limitation of drug supply. On the contrary, the instability of the entry barriers and their relative permeability warn that the supply of drugs will remain abundant.

Should the collectivity therefore regret the absence of such a monopoly of the traffic? Once the analysis includes the externalities created by criminal activities in terms of violence and social anomie, it seems, to the public policy-maker, useless and in bad taste, to think that there is a choice to be made between a situation where a small group of traffickers monopolize the market and one where competition prevails among the suppliers. Although it has met with great success, the thesis of criminal pursuit of monopoly power is strongly debatable.

Oligopoly with a fringe member

The most frequent form of criminal market organization appears to be that of the oligopoly, where several large organizations exist and divide the market in an unstable manner. The battles among the Chinese triads and the conflicts between the New York Mafia families illustrate such a situation. As a result, no organization succeeds in establishing a position of lasting monopoly over a market segment, and the oligopolistic structuring appears to be a sort of makeshift monopoly.

This, however is not a pure form of oligopoly. A number of criminals – bank robbers, drug dealers, certain drug wholesalers, and numerous arms dealers – do not belong to a criminal organization and constitute a fringe of independent criminals. This situation leads the crime oligopoly to be of a particular type, a non-cartel oligopoly with a fringe group. This configuration describes a situation in which several criminal organizations coexist without reaching a real agreement among themselves, surrounded by a periphery of independent criminals. The two worlds are far from being impermeable, and the independents sometimes enter organized criminality or form new organizations, while some members of organizations reclaim their independence.

To be sure, the independents maintain connections with the organized criminal world: they avail themselves of the services of various experts (false papers, weapons, etc.); sometimes they appeal to a criminal organization to procure its smuggling channels or to benefit from its protection. But they remain outside the organization. Assuming that it were possible for them to enter it, it could prove to be more advantageous for them to buy the services of a criminal organization rather than to belong to it. From the organization's point of view, it may be advantageous to limit its size. It is indeed likely that beyond a certain size, the admission of an additional member is counterproductive. The organization's operating costs, notably the risks of defection, infiltration or disloyalty, increase with size. Thus there exists a certain threshold beyond which recruitment of a new member generates additional cost greater than the gain which could be expected. In other words, there exist diseconomies of scale that lead large organizations to offer their services to other criminals rather than seeking to integrate them into the group. The expectations and interests of each group thus coincide to limit the growth of criminal organizations.

In short, even though it may appear that criminal organizations do not inevitably seek growth by bringing in outside criminals, but rather try to eliminate them in order to monopolize the markets and in that way suppress competition, there will always exist a certain number of candidates for entry who will penetrate the crime market, thus preventing a real monopoly.

Inside the criminal organization

Each criminal organization of the oligopoly functions autonomously. We have, however, too often a tendency to apply operating schemas observed in legitimate enterprises. Thus for a long time Medellin's cartel was presented as having a perfect hierarchy, a sort of IBM of the criminal world. It is basically in the particular methods of illegal transactions that we must look for the structural roots of criminal organizations involved in drug trafficking.

Illegal transactions

The institutional environment closely determines the measure in which the agents are going to cooperate or, on the contrary, compete. One can consider that the regime of drug prohibition constitutes a specific modality of institutional arrangement which plunges the agents into the world of illegal transactions and gives birth to particular forms of organization which can be enlightened by 'transaction cost' theory.

The primary characteristic of an illegal transaction is its effect of depriving the agents who engage in it of all possibility of recourse to the law. The contractors are not obligated to respect the engagements made other than by the threat that weighs upon them from their partners if they do not keep their part of the bargain. The illegal character of the transaction favours opportunistic behaviour. Private violence does not constitute a brake on the amount of opportunism when the contractors must remain in contact within the same market. Given the fluidity of drug trafficking compared with other criminal activities (gambling, prostitution), and the weakness of the fixed costs involved, it is often tempting to break the contract and swindle the other. The second characteristic of an illegal transaction is its tendency to bring about innovation. The agents who constitute the drug economy constantly experiment with new rules, thus transforming the prior market organization and creating new forms. The environment is not transparent: the illegality of the transactions and the absence of a stable network give rise to great complexity and uncertainty, producing somewhat irrational behaviour on the part of its agents. The drug economy sees its mode of functioning being transformed without ever becoming stable. The movement and the sclerosis are, in the eyes of the agents who put them into practice, the product of rational strategies, but in reality they are composed by chance, exchanges of doubtful information and behaviour that is more or less rational and opportunistic.

Criminal networks

The uncertainty and the limited rationality of the agents influence them to reason in the short term (Turvani, 1994). In this context, the agents who choose to carry out the illegal activity of drug dealing in an institutional environment marked by repression group themselves in organizations which differ from classical firms and react in sometimes surprising ways to changes in their environment. Thus criminal organizations can often be better described as 'criminal networks' rather than 'criminal firms'. These networks present interesting organizational characteristics.

On the one hand, as opposed to legal markets where the agents tend to gather missing information and organize themselves so as to minimize the costs of transactions, traffickers organized in networks block the circulation of information, and, for security reasons, break up the production chain. This is why the operation of the network does not follow one vertical line where the hierarchy of the firm reflects a functional division of productive activity. On the contrary, numerous agents in the network rise or slide back along the chain, short-circuiting the intermediaries and carrying out operations directly. This mobility is explained by the fact that the knowledge necessary for drug trafficking is not very specific (Kopp 1992b). This form of flexible specialization is made necessary by uncertainty, which prevents standardization of merchandise and procedures. Production is only possible at the price of reorganization and perpetual redefinition of the procedures guiding transactions. In contrast to legal firms, the specialization here is accompanied by great instability.

On the other hand, organizational efficiency in a network is measured not by the efficiency of each agent in accomplishing specific tasks, but in the ability of all to create new markets, more or less independently of their position in the network. In effect, each agent of the network attempts at all times to set himself up independently, in addition to his activity within the network.

All networks are not identical. Traditionally, the South American cocaine networks always bet on global market expansion and are not necessarily disturbed by the excessive dynamism of some of their members. This is not necessarily verified in the case of Asian heroin networks, but on this point, our information is still very incomplete.

Criminals like simplicity

Contrary to what one might think, a priori, criminal organizations are fragile. The reason for this is that they must face a considerable amount of transaction costs. Transaction costs represent inescapable costs of operating an exchange system – in other words, in the framework of a market economy, what it costs to turn to the market to carry out the allocation of resources and to transfer property rights. These include all the costs that are not direct production costs. Production costs relate to the expenditures to produce the good or the service (purchase of goods, transportation, storage, etc.). Transaction costs, for their part, correspond to the array of expenditures necessary to the existence and functioning of the market. Production costs most often involve an actual payment, while transaction costs, which occur all the same as an additional charge, are generally not paid out. For example, the violence that drug dealers bring to bear among themselves in order to control a territory constitutes a cost of organizing of the market. Without it they cannot gain access to this market. There are, however, exceptions to this rule. For example, expenditures made to their lawyers by traffickers are a part of transaction costs and are paid out.

In concrete terms, for the market to function properly, it is not enough that suppliers and consumers of a product exist. Also necessary is an appropriate institutional environment that permits the parties to the exchange to enter into contracts, to see that they are respected, and, in the case of non-fulfilment, to take action against the defaulting contracting partner. Such an environment does not function without costs; a small part of these costs is socialized through public expenditures, notably the cost of maintaining the judicial apparatus,[6] but the major part is taken on directly by the players in the market.

To minimize the costs of their participation in the market, criminal organizations must continually simplify organizational structures whose very simplicity is transformed into a handicap. They are obliged to give in to constant compromise in order to avoid seeing the uncertainty and absence of formal rules, characteristics of their environment, transformed into as many sources of inefficiency. The success of their strategy is not guaranteed, and, confronted by a correctly targeted public policy of enforcement and even the least bit of aggression, criminal organizations must display boundless ingenuity in order to maintain their operations. In fact, criminal organizations are far from being technically out of reach of enforcement agencies. The real difficulty public action faces consists of adopting plans of action that are suited to what criminal organizations really are, and not the image that one has of them.

Criminals seek rules

Criminal organizations do not lie outside the general rules of human organizations. The exchanges they undertake are accompanied by transaction costs that, as we have seen, correspond to the costs of organizing exchanges and the market. The rules with which organizations of the criminal world equip themselves, therefore, are aimed at minimizing these transaction costs and rendering the exchange more profitable. We will see that the constraints that these bring weigh heavily on their chances of emerging as winners in a selection process that pits them against the enforcement agencies.

The surrounding secrecy and impossibility of observing the actions of each of the members of the production network make assessing the contribution of each to the final product more complex. As a result, it is difficult to determine the property rights of the different players; moreover, it is tricky to see if they are respected because it is impossible to turn to the legal authorities. The costs of criminal transactions are therefore unavoidably high, since the conflicts involved in the distribution of criminal proceeds are numerous. The proper functioning of the market is slowed by quarrels, conflicts, and the settling of scores, all of which impose higher costs on criminal organizations.

To try to reduce these costs, criminal organizations may be tempted to proceed to vertical integration. In other words, by bringing within the organization the greatest possible number of levels of the criminal network, it is possible to limit the extent of conflicts. As long as the head of the organization retains authority to set rules of retribution for everyone, this kind of vertically integrated structure is effective. When the head of the organization loses his authority, notably because law enforcement compromises the proper functioning of the channels of communication within the organization, this form of organization is no longer viable. When control over the assessment of goods and services and the contributions of each member are not assured through the hierarchy, the organization implodes. Vertical integration ceases to be effective and the organization splits up into a multitude of autonomous cells (compare, for example, cocaine cartels). There exists a true relationship between the reduction of transaction costs by vertical integration and their increase by lengthening the chain of command.

More generally, criminal organizations often deem it wise to restrict their recruitment to a small group coming from the same family or the same village. This allows them to minimize the risks of betrayal, but at the same time it limits their possibilities of enlarging their market. When they want to widen their zone of influence, criminal organizations are compelled to broaden the network of individuals with whom they work. They must then enter into sophisticated contracts with numerous partners. These contracts are even more difficult to enforce because the State cannot intervene. Criminal organizations can turn to a variety of strategies to counter this difficulty. Depending on the context, and in particular, on the type of enforcement policy they face, they will have to regulate the level of violence practised within the organization. When public authorities are relatively indifferent to murders perpetrated in the criminal world, organizations tend to increase internal violence to ensure that commitments made are kept. If such a strategy triggers harsh police action, they will reduce internal violence, or, at least, its visibility.

The impossibility of appealing to the State to referee conflicts among criminals contributes to increasing the costs of criminal transactions. That is why criminal organizations may be tempted to put alternative systems into place (of the council of wise men sort). Most often, these systems quickly fall apart. Organizations must then either resort once again to violence to settle their conflicts or deliberately limit the complexity of the contracts they enter into among themselves or with independent criminals. This is because the simpler the contract, the easier it is to see to it that it is honoured. The common expression of 'dividing up territories' reflects this situation well. The sharing of territory is an especially primitive type of contract between two organizations. It is only effective because all the more complex forms of cooperation that include payments according to participation by several groups are a source of disputes that, in the absence of an impartial arbiter, will inevitably degenerate into violent conflicts. We see again a process of compromises between the wish to limit transaction costs by implementing sophisticated modes of cooperation between groups of criminals and the risk of obtaining the opposite result by provoking conflicts in doing so.

The feeling of having to respect the rules in force is, fortunately, shared by a great majority of the members of society who thus repress their possible inclination to act as 'free riders'. Individual criminals make the choice to live on the fringes of the law. There is no a priori reason to think that they are any more inclined to respect the rules of an organization than those of a society. Lacking a foundation as strong as that from which society benefits from collectively, criminal organizations are particularly exposed to the opportunism of their members. To protect themselves, they may reinforce their membership rites. These latter, however, in spite of their sometimes spectacular nature (Sicilian Mafia), constitute a relatively fragile display, as the confessions of repentant members attest. The threat of violent sanctions against traitors can certainly dissuade those who might consider betrayal; but at the same time the pressure by terror imposed upon the members of an organization can lead some among them to see no other way out than to place themselves under the protection of the police. Thus, while criminal organizations seek to make their activity effective by instituting a system of common values that lubricates the functioning of the market, the brutal nature of this same value system creates conditions for defection, and thus produces an effect that contradicts its reason for existence. Here again, the organization must know how to arbitrate between the advantages derived from criminal rituals (which impose a real cost on defection) and the risk of seeing defections multiply because of the very existence of such bloody rituals. The struggle against criminal organizations requires great vigilance, notably in order to be in a position to prevent their becoming established and to take adequate measures before they are able to consolidate their control. It thus appears essential to identify auspicious configurations for criminal organizations and to specify the characteristics of their preferred sectors of activity. The observation can then be broadened by bringing out the broad lines of strategic action of criminal organizations. It is on these elements that the remainder of this section will endeavour to shed some light.

Independent criminals and criminal organizations

When criminal organizations exist, they do not pull all of the criminals into their ranks. What is it that determines an individual's choice to join an organization rather than to set up his own business and stay on the fringes (or vice versa)? What is it that determines why an organization includes a new member?

Membership is a choice which is likely to be strongly marked by irreversibility, and one can assume that the criminal will choose it only if the benefits he will derive are greater than the costs. However, in view of the high costs of joining and leaving the organization, together with the considerable amount of difficulty the independent criminal has in collecting enough information to assess his situation once he joins, this individual makes his choice under unfavourable conditions.

The organization, on the other hand, knows that by increasing its size, it grows weaker. It therefore does not necessarily want to welcome new members. A number of criminals will thus remain (through their own doing or that of the organization, or even due to lack of good contacts) on the fringes of organized crime.

Criminal organizations and independent criminals are thus going to be motivated to establish relationships. A significant part of organized crime activity will consist of supplying to independents, in exchange for payment, the assistance that allows them to conduct their activities successfully.

Production factors provided by the criminal organizations

Even if a number of criminals remain independent, they will nevertheless require from criminal organizations certain production factors that the criminal organizations have a comparative advantage in providing. Let us begin with a situation in which a number of criminals conduct business in the same market. To examine the conditions in which an individual criminal will appeal to a criminal organization, let us consider the example of the 'protection' market. Individual criminals want to be protected. To achieve this they need to buy the necessary complicity of the police and judicial authorities. Their choice is either to try to procure the requisite complicity themselves, or they go to a criminal organization to acquire it. In order for such an organization to exist, it is necessary that it be in a position to furnish the protection sought by petty criminals at a price lower than the cost they would incur by producing it themselves.[7]

When it is a question of supplying input necessary to production, the comparative advantage held by a criminal organizations (compared to individual criminals) is weaker the more specific the input.[8] Thus, criminal organizations will emerge in sectors of criminal activity that ensure the supply of input that are not very specific but are necessary to criminal enterprises. If the input required by the individual criminal is highly specific, that is to say, has value only for the criminal who wants to obtain it, the organization does not benefit from any efficiency of scale for supplying it. The organization is thus not any better placed to produce it than is the individual criminal.

For example, a criminal organization can invest extensively in the corruption of the police force. Under these conditions, the organization can offer the individual criminal the advantages of a corrupt police force at lower cost. Lacking the benefit of the same economies of scale, the individual criminal does not have the means to corrupt the police. It is therefore more advantageous for him to turn to the services of the large organization than to produce the 'corruption' input himself. As long as the corruption remains a sufficiently impersonal input, this strategy is effective. On the other hand, if the corruption becomes a strongly specific input, appealing to the criminal organization ceases to be efficient and self-production becomes more cost-effective.

Let us look at another example: assume that police patrols stop patrolling a wide area, but each police officer is responsible for patrolling a medium-sized zone. The criminal who operates within this zone must try to corrupt the police officer. A large organization cannot be of any use to him because the input that interests him is so specific that there is no possibility of producing it while benefiting from economies of scale. Consequently, the criminal organization has no economic reason to be involved because it does not offer an advantage in matters of cost.

Furthermore, in the case of an attempt to corrupt the customs service, the more hierarchical the customs structure – in the sense that it forbids a customs officer to refer to an independent authority or to the head of the hierarchy without going through his immediate superior – the more the criminal organization will try to corrupt higher level officials, relying on the fact that the honest elements will not be able to go directly to the top of the hierarchy without the knowledge of their immediate superiors. This approach is not accessible to the individual criminal, who cannot make such an investment pay off. He will, therefore, want to corrupt precisely the customs officer who confronts him, and hardly has any need for the organization to do that. On the other hand, if that proves to be impossible, he will appeal to the organization and will take advantage of the corruption established at a higher level.

Our analysis thus permits us to deduce an initial general rule: criminals will turn to a criminal organization relative to the specificity of the service the organization renders. This is, in fact, how the organization benefits from economies of scale. In other words, the less specific the criminal production factor that the individual criminal needs to promote his activity, the more he is tempted to turn to a criminal organization.

Loyalty or betrayal

If criminals use the services of a criminal organization when the factor of criminal production they seek is sufficiently unspecific, the exchange for them is often frustrated by the incentives of each of the parties to betray the other. When a single criminal buys protection for his activities from a criminal organization, opportunism on the part of the organization can take the form of furnishing a degree of protection inferior to that agreed by the two parties or of requiring additional unanticipated payments.

One can look at game theory to demonstrate, from a simple example (Dick, 1995), the impact of opportunist behaviour on the relations criminals maintain with large organizations. The independent criminal and the criminal organization can adopt one of two types of behaviour: loyalty or opportunism. Let us say the purchase of protection from a criminal organization allows an independent criminal to register a net gain of 5. The organization's net gain from the transaction is also valued at 5. If one of the partners does not respect this contract (the criminal organization does not supply the degree of protection it has guaranteed or the individual criminal underestimates his income to minimize his contribution to the organization), the first party to breach the contract realizes a net gain of 7, reducing the net gain of his partner to 2. If both partners behave in an opportunistic fashion, the net gain of each is valued at 4. We then obtain the following matrix of net gains (Table 1.7).

Table 1.7 Loyalty and opportunism in relations between independent criminals and criminal organizations

Individual criminal	Criminal organization	
	Loyalty	Opportunism
Loyalty	(5, 5)	(2, 7)
Opportunism	(7, 2)	(4, 4)

Note
The first number in parentheses in each case corresponds to the net gain of the individual criminal; the second to that of the organization.

The situation is akin to the 'prisoner's dilemma', the outcome of which is well known: as long as the individual criminal and the criminal organization have no way to guarantee the mutual fulfillment of the commitments undertaken, they will both decide to betray these commitments.[9] The individual criminal will abandon the idea of buying the protection that he wants from the organization and will try to produce it himself, and the criminal organization will see its reason to exist disappear.

Two elements qualify this conclusion, however. One is that an agent's strategic choice depends on the reprisals to which his behaviour could expose him. It is clear that the two parties being considered here do not have equal retaliation possibilities, and there is no doubt that the independent criminal will think twice before betraying an organization that has a reputation of not giving anyone the opportunity of betraying it twice. The other is that the incentives for betrayal are considerably reduced when the exchange has a chance of recurring.[10] If the exchange between the criminal and the organization is likely to be repeated, treachery is less likely, the less specific the input, at least as far as the individual criminal is concerned; the less specific the input, the greater cost savings he will realize in turning to the organization.

The importance of reputation

In studying relations between individual criminals and organizations, one must take into account the fact that each partner is incapable of observing the behaviour of the other. How can the individual criminal know if he is evading the police thanks to the protection from the criminal organization or simply by chance? How can the criminal organization know the exact amount the individual criminal is taking in? The uncertainty that prevails regarding the amount of resources involved and the results of actions of the two parties seriously weakens the trust necessary for successful contract fulfilment. In order to compensate for this, the criminal organization will be tempted to develop its reputation capital, for example, by regularly demonstrating its power in the form of executions widely covered in the media.

The risk of betrayal is greater, as has been seen, in the case of exchanges that are not repeated ('one shot'). It is thus tempting for the individual criminal to disappear with the spoils. The criminal organization must then invest in its reputation so as to limit the temptation for betrayal by occasional clients. It will therefore prefer to maintain relations with those who devote themselves to criminal activity involving a long-term presence on the terrain (drug dealing, pornography, prostitution, betting on horse races, etc.), rather than with amateurs looking for the 'hold-up of the century'.

In order to reduce the risk of being betrayed, robbed or having criminals use their services without paying for them, criminal organizations create

enterprises that enable them to precisely control the volume of their partners' activity, and to collect their percentage of the turnover at the same
time. Thus, it is more practical to force a bar or a restaurant to purchase
alcohol and foodstuffs supplied by the criminal organization at an elevated
price than to demand a percentage payment of the turnover. Among other
advantages, this method limits the risks of deception regarding sales
turnover. Similarly, dealers in pornographic videos will buy them from the
criminal organization, producers will rent filming equipment from agreed
providers, etc. The criminal, for his part, will prefer to pay the organization
for a service whose effect he can measure (arms purchases, for example)
rather than for a service (such as protection) that seems to him more like a
tax on his activities without observable compensation. By developing
laundry businesses (there is a ratio between the number of meals served
and the number of napkins brought in for washing) or food and alcohol
delivery services, the criminal organization can ascertain the actual amount
of sales and overcharge for their services so to collect their percentages.
That way they not only benefit from an effective monitoring system, but
they also launder the proceeds from their racketeering at the same time.

Criminal organizations and the legal economy

How does the existence of criminal organizations disrupt the functioning
of the economy? Contrary to the traditional view, the detrimental consequences of organized crime on the conduct of other economic activities
are not linked to its weight in the GDP – generally not very significant in
developed countries – but are a result of its penetration of the legal
economy and the distortions it creates.

The impact of the criminal economy

Despite some reservations justly voiced regarding calculation methods,
most of the estimates carried out attribute to the criminal economy a
range of less than 1 per cent of GDP in the countries studied (Rey, 1992;
Van de Werf and Van der Ven, 1996; Davies and Groom, 1998). If one
takes an interest in the potentially destabilizing effect of the criminal
economy, however, one cannot be content with an assessment of its size; it
is necessary to ask oneself what portion of it results from a more centralized activity, that is, emanates from organized crime.

  The limited size of the 'centralized' criminal economy must not lead
one to think that it ultimately exercises only negligible effects on the functioning of the legal economy. On the contrary, organized crime activities
are sources of important distortions. That does not keep us from viewing
criminal organizations as vulnerable that must devote a portion of their
resources to implementing protection strategies.

The indirect effects of the criminal economy

In fact, criminal organizations are not content to prosper in criminal markets; they also try to penetrate the legal economy. It is thus useful to become better acquainted with the reasons why criminal organizations divide their resources among different legal and illegal activities. The few existing studies on the subject show that organized crime takes an interest primarily in legal branches of the economy that have at least one of the following characteristics: obsolete technology, absence of large unrecoverable investments, strong share of demand emanating from the public sector, and location within regions where the definition of property rights is poorly established.

Conversely, criminal organizations cannot easily increase their market share in legal markets where the competitive process focuses on the accumulation of human capital and new technologies and where one observes frequent variations in the demand structure. They benefit from a real comparative advantage, on the other hand, in branches characterized by a weak opportunity cost of invested capital. Here they can establish monopolistic control over key essential inputs.

These characteristics of legal activities in which criminal organizations are involved have implications that are even more concrete if one takes into account the mobility of capital in the financial market. This is because the firms controlled by organized crime can easily be resold without loss of capital – because of the virtual absence of unrecoverable capital – so much so that the measures taken in a single country have a significant probability of bringing about movements of capital towards new countries where enforcement is weaker.

According to economic theory, an efficient allocation of resources results from a situation in which market forces play their part freely and in which the *risk-adjusted returns* on investment are equalized at the margin for all forms of economic activities. We know that such a situation is never attained in reality. The externalities and imperfections of the market have the effect of disrupting the allocation of resources and breaking up the theoretical correspondence between private efficiency and social efficiency. The destructive effects of the criminal economy add to the imperfections of the market and inflict distortions on the legal economy (Quirk, 1996). Examination of the impact of the distortions imposed by criminal organizations on the legal economy gives us more information about the degree of harm they cause in a way that is infinitely more satisfactory than assessments, unavoidably disputable, of their weight in the GDP:

- *Distortions of competition in production:* Since it has the possibility of acquiring significant margins on illegal activities, organized crime pulls down prices in legal activities and motivates competitors to adjust. Prices are then abnormally low compared to the costs of production, and the competing enterprises cannot long resist the pressure of this unfair competition. Globally, this technique amounts to accomplishing a kind of dumping thanks to subsidies that overlap illegal activities with legal activities. Ultimately, once competition is eliminated, organized crime finds itself in a position of monopoly over the legal activity targeted in this way (for example, the clothing industry, or catering).

- *Distortions of competition in the execution of contracts:* Companies are supposed to respect the law. The degree to which they can break it is more or less the same for everyone, except for those who benefit from the support of criminal organizations. By turning to an illegal and underpaid worker (in the case of building construction, for example), companies working in the lap of organized crime drive honest enterprises towards bankruptcy. Similarly, the recovery of debts by a supplier is more or less possible, depending on whether it is honest or has ties to organized crime. More generally, the capacity for recourse in case of broken contracts varies widely according to the character of the company.
- *Distortions of competition in access to credit:* By exerting pressure on a credit establishment or by controlling one or several such establishments, organized crime has at its disposal a source of preferential credit that will supply funds to several dummy companies destined to disappear or to declare bankruptcy. Insurance companies and/or society will then assume control of the outstanding payments or the banks will abandon their letters of credit.
- *Distortions of competition in access to profit opportunities:* It is always possible for organized crime to corner, first and foremost, new opportunities for profit in order to exploit them directly or to sell access to them. For example, in the development of a commercial zone, the awarding of leases can be accomplished freely or not. The free transfer of resources towards growth sectors is thus blocked by the existence of organized crime.
- *Distortions of the rules of confidence:* Organized crime concentrates its investments in certain sectors, notably real estate. It corrupts the systems that oversee the granting of credit and in this way permits the greater part of the credit to be concentrated in one sphere (for example, touristic real estate). By introducing dishonest practices into legal businesses, through the corruption of accounting experts, organized crime favours the emergence of speculative bubbles. It is difficult to isolate organized crime's exact share of responsibility in this affair. It is certain, on the other hand, that by distorting the information coming from accountants and from the price system, it plays a significant role in the sudden emergence of crises of confidence.
- *Distortions in the allocation of capital:* Due to the lack of hard evid-

ence, strong presumptions exist regarding organized crime's practice of blackmail in order to manipulate the exchange rate or the shares of companies listed on the stock exchange. By corrupting a politician who is sufficiently influential in the financial sphere, it is possible to encourage him to declare, for example, that the national currency is strongly overvalued or to publicly evoke the possibility of an imminent devaluation. The currency falls, and before the markets correct the information, the speculator can realize an easy gain. The same goes for stocks. The most flagrant case is that of manipulation by an armed political organization. By intensifying its actions against a particular economic sector (oil pipelines in Colombia, for example), such organizations provoke a drop in the share prices of the national enterprises whose activity is tied to this sector (engineering). Repurchasing them before the announcement of the (short-lived) cessation of hostilities is an excellent transaction; reselling them before recommencing the operation is another. This tactic, sometimes carried out by a racket directly linked to the firms involved, generates irrational capital movements within and towards the economy of a country.

• *Distortions in the granting of public subsidies:* As soon as a criminal organization has at its disposal a minimum number of legal intermediaries (companies, syndicates, corrupted elected officials, etc.), it will try to corner public subsidies, notably Community subsidies in the case of European Union countries. The further the source of payment (and thus the expertise) is from the territory, the more possible it is to embezzle it. Numerous cases of diverted agricultural subsidies have been recorded. To this must be added the windfall that natural disasters represent for organized crime. When international aid must flow to a country, the urgency does not allow implementation of serious evaluation mechanisms, and sometimes a significant portion of the aid is diverted from its intended ends.

Evaluation of the ultimate effect on the economy

The relative weight of the four main segments of criminal[11] activity in the total turnover informs us about the core business of the criminal organization under consideration. Once the principal activity of the organization is known, it becomes possible to speculate about its effects on the legal economy. For example, an organization specializing in drugs affects the rest of the economy indirectly by its reinvestment strategy, while another that devotes itself to extortion affects the economy more directly. However, the distortions brought about by the existence of organized crime are so diverse that it is extremely difficult to sum up their ultimate effect on the economy by a conventional accounting ratio.

Efficient distortions?

It is conceivable that distortions engendered by criminal organizations are 'very efficient'. In the case of corruption of government administration in a country where the State is particularly bureaucratic and ineffective, one cannot exclude the possibility that corruption reduces transaction costs and accelerates exchanges. Its consequences for the efficiency of the markets can thus be shown to be positive.[12] Analogous reasoning can be applied to the case of drug trafficking. At the price of often exorbitant perverse effects, drug trafficking sometimes plays a role of social modernization by sweeping up segments of society where the market was struggling to assert itself.

Criminal regulation

A second paradox merits highlighting. When an economy is totally corrupted by criminal activities, it is no longer possible to speak of distortions. In fact, the entire economy experiences a form of 'criminal' regulation that makes honest economic activity the exception and crime the rule. In such extreme situations, generally of short duration, the very idea of a 'negative' influence of criminal organizations on economic activity loses its meaning.

It thus emerges from the preceding paradoxes that criminal activity always distorts the structure of legal activities, most often by conflicting with the rules of the market and exploiting the proceeds of the situation it is protecting through violence and corruption. These distortions sometimes accelerate the implementation of modern market regulation, but always at the price of perverse effects that cannot be overcome.

Furthermore, the precise modes of the internal operation of organized crime will influence the extent of damage inflicted on the legal economy. We know that criminal organizations group individuals into a rather loose structure. In this way, the more centralized the organization, the greater will be the financial resources that can be deployed to alter the normal structure of the economy to the benefit of organized crime. Conversely, the less centralized the organization, the less important will be its attempts at distortions, but they will in this case be more numerous.

To a varying degree, depending on their nature and on the nature of the disputes involved, criminal organizations turn to violence to settle their conflicts. Violence produces negative externalities that affect, first of all, the life of the individual (insecurity), but also the proper functioning of the economy (paralysis of a transport system, ongoing violence in a neighbourhood, flight of businesses, re-allocation of household income within communities and neighbourhoods, etc.). The more violent the criminal organizations, the more inadequate the furnishing of the collective good that security constitutes, and the more the presence of these organizations is experienced as a threat.

And so, the importance of the distortions caused by organized crime must be viewed in relation to the degree of competition prevailing in the economy. In this way, organized crime develops even better if markets are less transparent and property rights are not well defined. Consequently, it will exercise (at a given size) less of a distorting influence in an economy in which the absence of competition is the rule and not the exception. This is why, paradoxically, the less competitive an economy, the better it can accommodate organized crime.

These few reflections illustrate that the gravity of the threat organized crime poses to society cannot be measured with the yardstick of GDP percentage generated by the criminal world. Travelling by circuitous routes, the activity of criminal organizations contributes to profoundly distorting the allocation of resources in the economy.

Conclusion

The organizational methods of drug dealers and the strategies of actors differ greatly from those of a classical firm. The challenge for economic analysis consists in interpreting this particularity not as the manifestation of the actors' criminal psychology, but rather as the result of their reactions to environment factors. The law plunges the markets into illegality; the actors therein evolve in a context marked by incomplete information, thus experiencing difficulties forged by rational strategies. With an incredible responsiveness, the whole criminal fabric adapts, as well as it can, to its environment. Exposed to high organizational costs for their criminal activity (risk of betrayal, violence, risk of imprisonment), criminals try to optimize their strategies. Some create criminal organizations, highly flexible networks that seem best adapted to their context. Others maintain independent forms of criminality. All impose a high cost on society.

2   Addictive consumption

Economic analysis is always based on hypotheses about an actor's behaviour in markets. If drug-addicted consumers react paradoxically to the price signals engendered by public policy, then it is the efficiency of the latter which can be questioned. A question therefore runs through this chapter, what are the consequences for the orientation of public policies on the addictive character of drug consumption? Do drug consumers have control over their choices? Should we consider them, in accordance with the canons of economic theory, as rational individuals making choices that are, certainly, bad for their health, but free choices all the same?

For some people, drug consumers are not responsible economic agents but individuals whose economic behaviour has become abnormal as a result of their affinity for drugs. This thesis rests on the idea that once he has had his first experience, the drug consumer would lose all willpower, since the addiction-causing substances that he has taken would drive him to consume more. According to this thesis, the 'drug-addicted' individual would respond not to price signals, but only to an irrepressible mechanistic need for consumption. This irrepressible need to consume would thus cause an increase in quantities demanded. Drug use under this thesis is similar to irrational demand behaviour that does not take into account either the harmful effects to health or the budgetary constraints that weigh heavily on every consumer in any case.

This thesis poses problems, because it repudiates the value that the act of consumption represents for the individual. In short, drug consumption disappears behind addiction. And yet, demand for drugs cannot be reduced to a choice that is imposed on a subject who is deprived of all free will. This is particularly the case because not all drug consumers have the same degree of addiction and because, moreover, with regard to harder drugs, some individuals have succeeded in managing their consumption, avoiding the snare of addiction.

We ought therefore to understand the motivations for an individual's initial choice in favour of drugs, and then describe how an individual, even though he has become a regular consumer, nevertheless preserves a palette of choices that he uses to try to optimize his drug consumption in an environment full of temptations, where the main variables are income, price, dependence, and the pleasure that drugs bring.

How are we to render an account of the division between the 'normal' and the 'pathological' in drug consumption? The difficulty lies in the following paradox: on the one hand, we want to analyse drug consumption with the help of traditional microeconomic tools because we reject the thesis of the irrational drug consumer; on the other, this consumption follows its own peculiar methods that cannot be avoided.

Price and consumption

Let us look at the reaction of drug consumers to an increase in drug prices. In general, the quantity of a good consumed declines with an increase in its price; the elasticity of demand to price is therefore negative. When elasticity is valued at -1, an increase in price by x per cent leads to a reduction in consumption by the same amount. Certain goods are characterized by weak elasticity, that is, between 0 and -1, reflecting the fact that consumers cannot do without them. Conversely, when elasticity is strong – that is, less than -1 – a minor positive variation in prices gives rise to a significant reduction in consumption. In which category of goods should we place drugs? Are all drugs characterized by the same elasticity? Do all consumers have identical reactions to drug prices?

Price elasticity of demand for drugs

The first authors to take an interest in drugs in the early 1970s, such as Little (1967), Koch and Grupp (1971, 1973), Eatherly (1974), and Clague (1973), held that drug demand was inelastic to an increase in prices. This hypothesis was perfectly representative of the ideas generally prevailing at that time about drug consumption. The face that dominated the drug scene was that of the drug addict who, confronted with a rise in the price of heroin, increased his level of criminality to obtain the income necessary to purchase an irreducible quantity of drugs. It quickly became apparent that the sensitivity of drug consumers to prices depends not only on variations in price but also on price levels before any increase takes place.

If prices are initially low, consumers present in the market are not the same as those who are there if prices are high. In the first case, there may be a good many occasional consumers, while in the second, the only ones left would mostly be drug addicts. Blair and Vogel (1973) propose taking this finding into account, suggesting that demand would be elastic at low prices and inelastic when prices rise. Elasticity would decline (in absolute value) with price, and the demand curve would be convex.

White and Luksetich (1983) contest this point and defend a thesis that is opposite to that of Blair and Vogel. According to White and Luksetich, elasticity would be very weak when prices are low and strong when prices are high (elasticity rising and demand curve concave). They also emphasize that there would exist a strong substitutability between heroin and other drugs when it becomes rare or too expensive. Previous results from Levine *et al.* (1976) support the White and Luksetich thesis (1983). According to these authors, the number of individuals disposed to pursue voluntary withdrawal programmes would increase in relation to the rise in the price of heroin. From a theoretical standpoint, these authors base their hypothesis on the following idea: Unless the pain is a discrete variable that changes instantly from 'zero pain' to 'unbearable suffering', addicts can space out their drug intake. Thus, a price increase should encourage a process of self-limitation. Conversely, unless one considers that consumption of an additional unit of heroin brings no increase in utility, a fall in price should stimulate consumption.

A number of original contributions began progressively to chip away at the earlier unanimity. Hadreas and Roumasset (1977) echoed observations that daily drug consumption by heroin addicts would be greater than what they 'really needed'. They thus invoked the idea of a possible elasticity of drug demand to price. These two authors proposed an original model in which elasticity and inelasticity of demand go together, in accordance with the capacity of dependent users to restrain their consumption (other than drugs) to meet the increase in heroin prices. Brown and Silverman (1974, 1975) and Silverman and Spruill (1977) produced the first measurements of elasticity of demand, which pointed in the same direction. Their work employed a statistical base set up for the study, presenting monthly data collected in Detroit between November 1970 and July 1973. Since (according to the authors) heroin consumption was not measurable, they had to reconstruct it using an elasticity indicator. This elasticity indicator was dependent on the purity of the heroin and its price during the preceding months. From this study, they found that elasticity, over the long term, would vary little according to the purity of heroin. When this purity is between 2.5 per cent and 10 per cent, a 10 per cent rise in prices would bring about a 2.5 per cent drop in consumption (i.e., price elasticity = -0.25).

The Becker school and elasticity of drug demand

The models developed by Becker and Murphy (1988), to which we will return later, gave rise to a series of empirical studies dealing with all types of consumption that cause dependence, including tobacco, alcohol, and gambling. Some of these studies fall within Beckerian themes and emphasize consumer rationality. Other contributions, not coming out of the group of convinced Beckerians, move in the same direction and firmly establish the elastic nature of drug demand. Thus, in a recent article, Caulkins (1990, 1994, 1995a, 1995b) proposes an estimation of the price elasticity of demand for heroin (between -1 and -1.5) that is very clearly higher (in absolute value) than the usual figures (-0.5). These results confirm findings obtained by Chaloupka and Saffer (1995) in testing the Becker model. They estimate the price elasticity of demand for cocaine to be between -0.72 and -1.1 and that of heroin to be between -1.8 and -1.6. Bretteville-Jensen and Sutton (1996) find a price elasticity of demand for heroin of -1.23 in a sample of non-dealer heroin users who participated in a needle exchange programme in Oslo, Norway. Grossman and Chaloupka (1998) predict that a 10 per cent reduction of the price of cocaine would increase consumption by young adults by almost 14 per cent over the long term.

Eleven US states decriminalized the possession of small amounts of marijuana between 1973 and 1978. Some studies find that this increased the use of marijuana, while others do not (Chaloupka *et al.*, 1999). These mixed results may arise from the fact that nearly every state liberalized its treatment of marijuana possession in the 1970s. Chaloupka *et al.* (1999) report that marijuana use and cocaine use by US high school seniors are inversely related to state fines for conviction of possession. These effects are weak most likely because the probability of apprehension and conviction is low.

Van Ours (1995), for his part, delivers a fascinating historical study that shows the presence of a certain price elasticity of demand for opium before the Second World War in what is now Indonesia: over the short term (-0.7) and the long term (-1). Liu, Liu and Chou (1996) report similar findings in a study of opium demand in the Japanese colony of Taiwan during the 1914–1942 period.

The preceding results concerning drugs must be compared with those regarding other substances such as tobacco and alcohol. We should note that the elasticity of drugs is generally higher (in absolute value) than that of other products. This is a consequence of the high level of drug prices, and it puts into relative terms the opinion that prices would have no effect on drug consumers. Studying cigarette consumption between 1955 and 1985, Becker *et al.* (1990) calculated that the price elasticity of demand over the long term was between -0.8 and -0.7, while elasticity over the short term was only -0.4. Chaloupka (1991) also establishes the existence of divergent elasticities over the short and long term. He confirms, moreover, that the poor are more sensitive to changes in cigarette prices. The conclusion of Chaloupka's work: a doubling of the tax on tobacco would bring about a 15 per cent increase in the price of cigarettes and a 4–6 per cent decline in consumption. Along the same lines, Lewit and Coate (1982) underscore that youths are also more sensitive than adults to price variations. As far as alcohol is concerned, elasticity would be -1.8, according to Cook and Tauchen (1982). According to Ornstein and Hanssen (1985), elasticity of demand for alcohol would be between -0.8 and -1; and near unity for beer.

How to model addiction?

Empirical studies show how sensitive drug consumers are to price. The reactions of drug consumers to market signals are therefore not unusual. Nevertheless, before concluding that drug consumers are just like other consumers, an additional aspect of their behaviour merits clarification.

In general, a consumer is prepared to devote to a purchase a sum of money more or less similar to that which he has spent in the past, so that therefore the demand line decreases with price. Drug consumption, on the contrary, engenders growing needs of addiction, so the sums devoted to this product often rise with the quantities previously consumed.

The hypothesis of non-convexity of preferences

Microeconomics considers that consumer preferences are convex. This means that the consumer prefers to consume a wide range of goods rather than concentrating his consumption on a sole product. It is tempting to consider that drug consumers constitute an exception. White and Luksetich (1983) and Lemennicier (1992) pursue this line, considering that such consumers prefer to focus their consumption on a sole product: drugs. Preferences of these consumers would therefore be concave: that is, the consumer would always choose a basket of extreme goods. We, for our part, do not subscribe to this hypothesis of concavity of drug consumer preferences. Empirical results indicate that elasticity of demand over the long term is stronger than over the short term, which demonstrates clearly the extent to which consumption of drugs, or addictive substances, is complementary over time. This finding of complementarity is expressed by a convexity turned towards the origin of the consumer indifference curve (see Figure 2.1).

In Figure 2.1 we find in abscissa the quantity of normal goods X and in ordinate the quantity of drug Y. The convex indifference curve indicates all the baskets (X, Y) – in other words, all combinations between a quantity of drug (Y) and a quantity of normal goods (X) – procuring for the agent a same utility U_1. The line AB represents all linear combinations $\alpha A + (1 - \alpha)B$ between the two baskets of goods, or all possible combinations of the two baskets A and B. All these combinations are situated on an indifference curve superior to U_1, for example, U_2, for the combination C, which indicates that the agents prefer baskets of mixed goods rather than baskets composed almost exclusively of a single type of goods. The concave indifference curve (Figure 2.2) indicates the contrary, as the mixed basket C is situated on a lower indifference curve than the points A and B. The consumers are thus not ready to substitute the normal goods in their basket for drugs. However, the position of point C shows that all combinations which increase the quantity of drugs in the basket at the expense of normal goods procures a superior utility to the consumer.

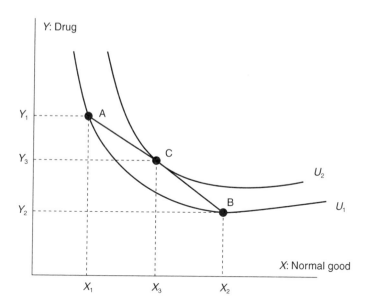

Figure 2.1 Convex preferences

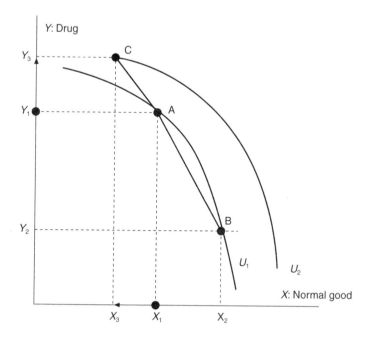

Figure 2.2 Concave preferences

From an analytical point of view, the debate on convexity of preferences relates to the degree of control over consumption that analysis ascribes to the drug consumer. We have shown that even in the case of heroin (and a fortiori for soft drugs), consumers do not lose all power to regulate their consumption and do not necessarily abandon all normal life (and purchases of goods other than drugs). The hypothesis of specialization in drug consumption corresponds only to a core of totally dependent consumers. We consider drugs to be much more of a 'good like other goods' the consumer has taken only for a short while, that is, described by a classically convex indifference curve. Since the effect of dependence is not immediate, the novice drug consumer is sensitive to price. Elasticity decreases only to the extent that dependence increases. All these reasons make us think that the hypothesis of concavity of preferences should not be retained.

The hypothesis of changes in taste

Since it is impossible to make concave preferences the explanation for an immoderate need for drugs, another path must be envisaged. Traditional microeconomics rests on a hypothesis called 'stability of tastes'. An individual is not supposed to modify his preferences. It is nevertheless tempting to think that a characteristic of drugs, as well as of tobacco, for that matter, is precisely to bring about a particular craving for the product as consumption is prolonged. In other words, alcohol and tobacco modify the tastes of those who consume them. Yesterday they were unaware of the need, today they cannot do without the product, and tomorrow they will definitively break off their consumption . . . only to take it up again several months later.

The model proposed by Stigler and Becker (1977) with the publication of their article entitled '*De Gustibus Non Est Disputandum*' lays the foundations of a new theory of the consumer, and owes a great deal to questions that drug consumer behaviour posed for traditional theory. The originality of the theses of Stigler and Becker consists of their demonstration of the fact that the search for an explanation for changes in individual attitudes towards consumption does not require abandoning the hypothesis of constancy of tastes.

This point is fundamental for these two authors, whose intent is to prove that price signals are sufficient to explain the consumption behaviour of individuals without the need to appeal to hypothesis whose ad hoc nature appears evident. Their objective is to show that all changes in consumer behaviour can be explained simply by variations in price and agents' income. That an individual begins to take drugs would thereby not be explained by a sudden taste for them, but by a change (in price and income) in the environment of the agent.

In the case of drugs, the marginal cost of drug use increases with age and with the duration of previous intoxication, because, in equal amounts, the effect of drugs declines and habituation increases. The increase of present 'euphoria' brought on by the consumption of heroin increases the marginal future cost necessary to achieve the same 'euphoria'. The effect of the euphoria of yesterday on the cost of future euphoria therefore ought to motivate users to reduce their consumption as the duration of intoxication increases. Such a mechanism is nevertheless thwarted by consumers' habituation to the product. A given quantity of drugs produces an increasingly weaker euphoria. Consequently, and provided that the consumers are insensitive to an increase in drug prices (inelasticity of demand), users must increase their consumption of heroin.

As long as demand is inelastic, the quantity of heroin consumed increases as its effect diminishes. Stigler and Becker emphasize therefore that heroin addiction, defined as an increase in quantities consumed, is the result and not the cause of inelasticity of demand. This is how, without evoking a change in tastes, Stigler and Becker explain why the quantity of heroin increases (instead of decreasing) as a function of previous consumption and how this increase is insensitive to a price increase.

The approach of Becker and Stigler not only permits dealing with drug consumption in a unified way within consumer theory, but it also provides a predictive model of the structure of demand. According to these authors, drug demand increases, independently of price, as a result of consumers' addiction. This prediction does not turn out to be very convincing, however, because we know that a consumer passes through phases of heavy consumption followed by periods of abstinence and sometimes phases of reasonable consumption.

The instability of demand for drugs

An individual often finds good reasons for wanting to stop taking drugs when he observes the situation of those around him who have started to abuse drugs. It is therefore the eminently foreseeable future consequences of present drug consumption that often motivate drug consumers to moderate their consumption. The theory of 'rational addiction' (Becker and Murphy, 1988, 1991) constitutes notable progress over Becker's previous work, in that it allows us to take into account fluctuations in demand for drugs, breaking with the previous prediction (Stigler and Becker, 1977) of increase in demand. Fluctuations in demand are generated by the behaviour of the consumer, who is constrained in regulating his consumption in order to mitigate the contradictory effects of the drugs.

The model of rational addiction

The contradictory nature of the effects of drugs becomes clear in distinguishing the two components of addiction: reinforcement and tolerance. It is assumed that the rational individual chooses a basket of goods in such a way as to satisfy his needs and to maximize the utility brought about by the consumption of the goods he has obtained. There are two types of goods, a 'normal' good $y(t)$, and a drug $c(t)$ that engenders secondary effects on the consumer. The extent of these secondary effects depends on prior consumption of drugs, which triggers the stockpiling of 'addiction capital' $s(t)$. The addiction capital shows the present negative effects of past drug consumption. The utility that an agent derives from his consumption depends on his consumption of drugs $c(t)$ and of ordinary goods $y(t)$, and on the level of addiction capital $s(t)$. In other words:

The term 'addiction' covers two distinct effects of drugs: reinforcement and tolerance. Tolerance, notated U_S, indicates that the effects of drugs diminish with the quantities consumed $U_S = \dfrac{\delta U}{\delta S} < 0$. The utility of the drugs decreases with the level of addiction. Tolerance is stronger to the extent that past consumption was significant. Present consumption diminishes the utility of future consumption by increasing the addiction capital $s(t)$.

Reinforcement, notated U_{CS}, indicates that the stronger the previous drug consumption, the stronger the present desire to consume drugs $\dfrac{dc(t)}{dS(t)} > 0$. Reinforcement implies that previous consumption increases the marginal utility of present consumption

The choices of the drug consumer are therefore constrained by perverse effects. On the one hand, he is motivated to consume more drugs (dependence), which will increase the marginal utility of his future drug consumption; and on the other hand, he is motivated to consume a smaller amount of drugs because present drug consumption increases his addiction capital and reduces his total future utility (reinforcement). Consumers, assumed to be rational, choose a level of present drug consumption $c(t)$ that constitutes the solution to the model, as a function of the following variables:

σ: the discounting rate. The closer this rate is to unity, the more the consumer depreciates the future.

U_{CS}: U_{CS}, the positive effect of dependence on total utility.

U_S: the negative effect of habituation on total utility.

δ: the rate of depreciation during periods of past consumption. When δ is near unity, the effects of drug consumption on future utility are strong.

This model teaches us three things about the behaviour of the most dependent drug consumers. The less individuals attach value to the future, that is, the higher their discounting rate (close to one), the more they will be inclined to accept a degree of habituation that is greater than the level of dependence. In concrete terms, this shows that the individual who does not attach importance to the future will consume more and more drugs in order to keep his immediate level of satisfaction constant. He will do so in spite of the increase in habituation whose future effects on his welfare will be greater than the beneficial effects of a weaker dependence, which itself leads to an increase in the future satisfaction brought about by taking drugs. The consumer who devalues his future is thus interested only in the immediate effect of drugs and is not concerned about the fact that tomorrow he will have to consume still more drugs to obtain the same benefit.

The same individuals who accord little value to the future will succumb more easily than others to drugs. Traditionally, economists agree in thinking that individuals attach more value to a dollar today than to a dollar tomorrow, meaning that their discounting rate is greater than zero. This devaluing of the future is generally explained by the uncertainty that hangs over it. It is therefore tempting to generalize this pattern by considering that all individuals depreciate the future. Becker and Mulligan (1997) are hardly convinced of this, claiming that some individuals devote time to developing strategies that reduce future uncertainty: for example, by buying a supplementary pension. In doing so, they secure their future, which thus assumes its whole value. Compromise between savings and consumption will vary from one individual to another as a function of the desire of each to realize such an investment. It is therefore just as rational for one individual to play the lottery as it is for another to take out life insurance. Becker and Mulligan hold that it is rational to play the lottery if one is not interested in buying life insurance that would totally secure the future but would diminish present satisfaction. To be sure, playing the lottery offers only a limited guarantee of gain, but it has only very little effect on income. By way of analogy, it emerges that where drugs are concerned, those who devalue the future have no reason, according to Becker, to deprive themselves of the utility that drugs bring them.

Not all individuals have equal resistance to drugs. The higher δ that is, the rate of depreciation in times of past consumption, the more an individual's present consumption of drugs is transformed into addiction capital, and the more it leaves traces negatively affecting his future utility. The more resistant an individual is to the effects of drugs, therefore, the lower is his δ and the greater his room to manoeuvre vis-à-vis drugs; that is, he can consume drugs longer than another individual before the negative effects on his future make themselves felt.

The model thus shows how consumers incorporate into their choices the effects of habituation brought about by drugs. This habituation leads the rational consumer to be content with an increase in present consumption that is limited precisely to a quantity sufficient to generate a positive effect greater than future unpleasant consequences that would be linked to an increase in dependence (and thus to an increase in the quantities of drugs ultimately required). In this way, Becker *et al.* (1991) take into account the fact that the drug user manages his career as a consumer.

Multiple stationary states

Each individual consumption trajectory of an addictive good leads the consumer towards a stationary state in which his consumption of drugs will remain constant. Such a state can be stable or unstable. In Figure 2.3, which describes a consumption of drugs in equilibrium, one finds on the abscissa past demand for drugs represented by the consumption capital and on the ordinate, present consumption. The line $c = \delta S$ expresses the levels of equilibrium of present consumption, where c is a function of past consumption, S, and the rate of natural detoxification, δ. For a given level of past consumption, S, present consumption c is all the greater, the weaker the rate of natural detoxification δ. The curve $c[S(t)]$ also describes the levels of present consumption as a function of past consumption, but it is a question in this case of values resulting from the process of dynamic intertemporal optimization by the consumers.

The values located at the intersection of the curves describe the stationary equilibriums where the optimizing behaviour of the consumers leads them to retain a level of present consumption compatible with their past consumption and their personal levels of resistance to drugs δ. These steady states (S_e^{*1}, c_e^{*1}) and (S_e^{*2}, c_e^{*2}) are not necessarily stable. We find that the stationary state at (S_e^{*1}, c_e^{*1}) is unstable. This is because, to the left of (S_e^{*1}, c_e^{*1}), $c(t) < \delta S(t)$, consumption capital is reduced, allowing the consumer to reduce his consumption and perhaps arrive at a stable abstinence. To the right of S_e^{*1}, $c(t) > \delta S(t)$, drug consumption increases under the effect of the growth in consumption capital to the point where the stationary state (S_e^{*2}, c_e^{*2}) is attained. This second stationary state is stable. For

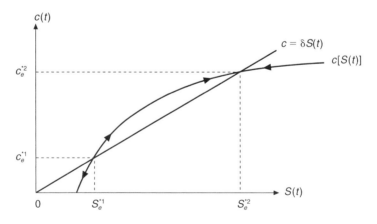

Figure 2.3 Stable drug consumption

the same reasons, the action of the consumption capital leads the consumer towards that state rather than distancing him from it, as in the preceding case.

Such a consumption path, made up of two kinds of steady states, allows us to represent normal addiction. Normal addiction is a rapid increase in drug consumption during a limited period. If the dependent economic agent who initially consumes c_e^{*1} has a particular experience that leads him to reduce his stock of addictive capital $S(t)$ to a level lower than that of the unstable stationary state S_e^{*1}, he will succeed in shifting from a high level of drug consumption to a lower level, perhaps even in some cases to abstinence. Indeed, when the consumption path is particularly vertical, the dependent economic agent can be induced to stop his consumption abruptly. This abrupt break is called 'cold turkey'.

Strong dependence is linked to a high degree of adjacent complementarity. We recall that goods are complementary when they are always consumed together in the same proportion and substitute for one another when the consumer is prepared to exchange in some proportion the goods he considers. A specific form of complementarity results from the potential addiction to a good. The specificity of the complementarity resides in the temporal dimension: past consumption increases future consumption. Adjacent complementarity exists when an increase in past consumption of an addictive good $S(t)$ increases U_c, the marginal utility of instant consumption. Thus, strong adjacent complementarity accompanies a high degree of dependence and a pronounced instability of equilibrium.

According to Figure 2.3, a high level of drug consumption can only be attained if the slope of the line $\delta S(t)$ is sufficiently great. It follows that an individual experiencing a strong dependence on drugs will only be able to cease his consumption by going 'cold turkey'. This abrupt break is a rational decision on the part of the economic agent, even though it leads temporarily to a very disagreeable state of withdrawal. The considerable temporary loss of utility due to drug demand is all the stronger, the stronger the dependence. It is rational to cease consumption of addictive goods suddenly because that way the substantial temporary loss will be counterbalanced by an even greater long-term gain.

The role of price

If one is situated in the vicinity of the steady state, the effect of a price reduction on the quantities demanded for consumption is reinforced over the course of time; that is, a permanent change in the price of an addictive good may have only a small initial effect on demand, but the effect grows over time until a new stationary state is reached.

The effect of a modification of current prices

As we find in Figure 2.4, the price effect between the unstable steady states is greater than that between stable steady states (Janod 2003). In Figure 2.4, $c_A[S]$ represents drug consumption for price P_1, while $c_B[S]$ represents drug consumption following a price reduction from P_1 to P_2. Given that a price reduction leads to an increase in the consumption path, $c_A[S]$ is located below $c_B[S]$. The effect on the level of consumption varies depending on the amount allocated $[S(t),c(t)]$ at the moment of the price reduction.

If the drug consumer finds himself at a point $[S_1,c_1]$ on the consumption path $c_A[S]$ located between a stable and an unstable steady state, that is, between S_{eA}^{*1} and S_{eA}^{*2}, at the moment the price reduction intervenes, drug consumption rises initially from c_1 to c_2, then progressively over the course of time to c_{eB}^{*2}, in conformity with Figure 2.5.

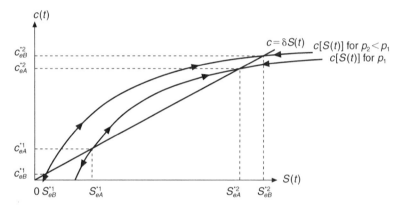

Figure 2.4 Effect of a price reduction on drug consumption

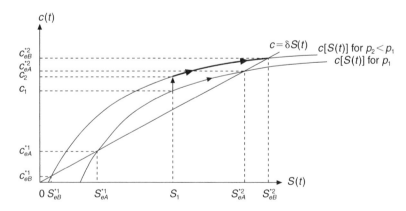

Figure 2.5 Effect of a price reduction on consumption located between the stable and unstable steady states

Drug consumers who are initially situated between the two unstable steady states S_{eA}^{*1} and S_{eB}^{*1} turn towards abstinence in the absence of a price modification as an exogenous shock. If a price reduction intervenes, however, their levels of drug consumption shift to the right of the unstable stationary state S_{eB}^{*1}. Their levels of consumption will then draw closer together and progressively attain a stable stationary state $[S_{eB}^{*2}, c_{eB}^{*2}]$, as Figure 2.6 shows.

Drug consumers located initially below S_{eA}^{*2} increase their consumption over the short term, then reduce it to the point where they totally abandon drugs. Drug consumers located initially to the left of S_{eA}^{*2} remain dependent but the stable level of consumption attained is distinctly higher.

According to the mechanisms described, modifications in drug consumption induced by a reduction in prices are much greater over the long term than over the short term. Conversely, an increase in prices allows a reduction in the level of drugs consumed, even to the point of quitting the drug market. An increase in prices can occur, for example, in the wake of an increase in penalties for drug offences, since the penalties incurred raise the price of drugs on the illegal market. This reasoning is based on the hypothesis that all drug consumers react to price modifications; in this way, demand for drugs is never inelastic.

Effects of future price modifications

According to Becker and Murphy (1988), past price modifications, just as modifications in future prices, influence current consumption of drugs. While past changes in drug prices modify the level of consumption capital stock, changes in future prices modify the level of present consumption and thus the capital stock of future consumption. These authors demonstrate, moreover, that the effect of a change in future prices is all the

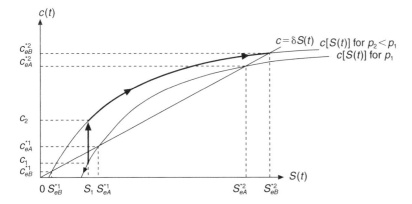

Figure 2.6 Effect of a price reduction on consumption located between two unstable steady states

greater to the extent that it is anticipated early, because then modifications in the level of consumption are undertaken earlier. They also point out that a permanent increase in the price of the addictive good reduces present consumption of drugs more sharply than would a one-time price increase. That the economic agent takes into account the variations in future prices underscores the rational nature of addiction.

The Becker and Murphy model has been severely criticized. The authors have been reproached for having constructed a model that denies the existence of a phenomenon not desired in drugs. Indeed, in the Becker and Murphy model, individuals are 'happy addicts' who choose to become addicted, without doubts and without regret, after a careful examination of the consumption alternatives available to them and following a simple calculation of optimization. And yet heroin addicts, for example, often maintain that they have not chosen their addiction. At the heart of this discussion lies the thorny question of temporal consistency[1] of agents' choices.

The temporal consistency of choices

Understanding how an individual begins and then interrupts his drug consumption constitutes a very important question whose answer has a significant effect on public policy recommendations. Let us start with a simple example. Every individual has found himself at some point faced with the following dilemma: the desire to eat an additional piece of cake and the fear of regretting it tomorrow. Representing the behaviour of a drug consumer poses the same type of problem. Take the example of a potential drug consumer before he makes the choice at $t = 0$ between consuming drugs and not consuming them. If he does not consume them, then at the moment $t = 1$ he finds himself *ceteris paribus* [all things being equal], faced with the same choice and the same preferences $P(0)$. One supposes that he will also not consume them in this new period (Figure 2.7).

On the other hand, if he does consume drugs, he will again find himself at $t = 1$ with preferences $P(1)$ different from $P(0)$, and he will once again have the choice of consuming (choice a) or not consuming (choice b). The consumer can therefore change his preferences. What interests us here is the choice of the consumer over the two periods together. Let us assume that an individual would like to use drugs recreationally (path a) but that he is susceptible to becoming hooked on drugs (path b) and would therefore be better off abstaining (path c). If the individual is 'myopic', he will follow path b. If he is rational, he will anticipate the change in his preferences and will be able to choose abstinence. This second choice is said to be temporally consistent, in the sense that a myopic individual initially choosing to consume drugs recreationally will deviate from this choice to become a permanent user. The rational individual, in contrast, will never deviate (in a certain environment) from his initial choice, having foreseen

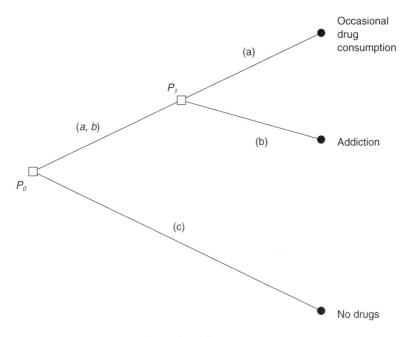

Figure 2.7 Intertemporal inconsistencies

Note
Four solutions:
1 Myopic behaviour: according to preferences (a, b) then (b): Addiction
2 Sophisticated behaviour: temporally sub-optimal choice (c): no drugs
3 Pe-commitment: the subject narrows his range of choice by eliminating (b), (a, b) then (a):
   occasional drug absorption
4 Changing preferences P_1 to P'_1 in such a way that $P'_1 b \geqslant (a, b)$ and then (a): occasional
   drug consumption.

all the consequences. One readily observes that neither of the two solutions describes perfectly the behaviour of the drug consumer. If the consumer is myopic, how can we explain that he sometimes wants to leave the world of drugs and that to do so, he must be capable of sensitivity to his future? If the consumer is temporally consistent, how do we explain that some people begin to consume drugs and then want to stop?

The inconsistency of drug consumers

The simplest model of drug consumer behaviour considered the drug consumer to be myopic, or incapable of foreseeing the future consequences of his present actions. A more sophisticated version considers that two facets of the personality enter into opposition: one that wants to stop taking drugs and the other wanting to consume them.

Consumer myopia

The individual chooses to consume drugs, doubtless for recreational purposes, then regrets it but is unable to break his habit. His behaviour is then sub-optimal (Pollak, 1970). This model postulates that individuals are myopic and that past consumption influences present preferences in a deterministic way through the formation of a set of habits. The intertemporal utility function of the consumer is written:

$$U^x(X_t) = \sum_x^T \alpha_t \log(x_t - b_t), \text{ with } \alpha_k < 1, \text{ and } (x_t - b_t) > 0$$

In this function, the goods consumed by the user in period t are represented by x_t, but only a portion of this consumption produces utility. The term b_t represents the portion of the consumption that brings no utility to the present moment. This non-utility portion of consumption is linked to the consumer's habit, which is formed according to the following process: $b_t = b^* + \beta x_{t-1}$. The first element of this expression represents a fixed quantity of consumption linked to maintaining the basic necessities of life; the other element is linked to psychological needs: consumption is a source of utility only if it exceeds a necessary level defined as the sum of an individual's basic needs weighted by a factor of individual depreciation. The habit is at once physiological and psychological, and the variable of individual sensitivity to the habit is captured by the variable β memory of the process of forming the habit. The process of forming the habit is myopic, since at no time does the individual take into account the fact that his habits can end up depreciating his future financial resources. At no time is he able to regret his choices. Such an approach is hardly satisfactory because it does not explain why drug consumers may want to stop taking drugs. If they are myopic, the immediate positive effects of the drugs prevail over the subsequent negative effects. In a word, the heroin consumer described by the myopia models, imagining the effects of withdrawal, is incapable of refusing a dose.

Two selves models

In order to explain why drug consumers often make choices that they regret, a whole series of authors have looked into the hypothesis of an intrapsychic conflict between two 'selves' that they say inhabit the drug consumer. Thomas Schelling (1976) considers that drug consumers are not 'happy addicts', as Becker and Murphy would have it, but individuals dominated by their preferences, over which they have no control and which they know can lead them to self-destruct. Winston (1980) tried to model this type of strategy by taking up the idea of intrapsychic conflict. According to him, the individual has orders of preferences that are identical from one period to another, but within the same period, he must arbitrate between long-term and short-term orders of preferences. Over the short term, the individual has two orders of preferences. In one, he is more inclined to consume drugs than in the other, to the point that under this order of preferences, the product can become a 'totalitarian' good. Under the other order, the individual is more inclined to pay attention to his health. The individual can make a decision that satisfies him and regret it a minute later, because it has harmful consequences over the long term.

Formally, if t is the length of the life of the individual, U and U^* two functions of instantaneous utility, with U^* corresponding to an order of preference in which drug consumption is strongly desired, the long-term utility function is written:

$$V = \left(\frac{n}{t}\right).U(M,Z) + \left(1 - \frac{n}{t}\right).U^*(M,Z)$$

where M is the psychotropic substance, Z other goods, and n the number of periods, exogenous and specific to the individual, during which the individual is less attracted by drugs. The conflict can arise from the fact that at every moment the utility function of individuals is V over the long term and U or U' over the short term. At any given moment, the individual can have myopic behaviour and optimize the value of U or of U' or have rational behaviour and seek to maximize V. Thus, there exists the possibility of temporal dissonance between what he would prefer for the short term and what he would prefer for the long term. The individual decides to consume or not by comparing the gains in utility of consumption and of abstinence.

This model furnishes a form of explanation of the entry into and exit from drug consumption for each individual. It all depends on the order of preference that dominates the short term (with drugs or without). The explanation is ad hoc to say the least, because nothing explains how to determine the frequency $\frac{n}{t}$ at which drugs either dominate an individual's life or, on the contrary, lose their influence, since it is set exogenously.

If the intrapsychic conflict does not constitute a solution that allows representation of drug consumers' choices, one can speculate that such consumers might make decisions today that would prevent them from changing their minds tomorrow. We observe, for example, that drug consumers sometimes implement strategies in an attempt to take advantage of their lucid moments to put into place mechanisms to prevent them from falling back into their habit. Along the same idea, in the case of gambling, there exists in France the possibility for a gambler to have himself barred from gambling. He will then be turned away at the door of casinos and will have to surmount a number of administrative hurdles to retract his decision. Modelling this type of attitude takes us away from the two selves models and reveals the idea that an individual can rationally exploit a moment of lucidity to make an investment that will in the future enable him to avoid the drawbacks of his habitual behaviour (drugs, gambling). We recall here the image of Ulysses and his sirens. According to Elster (1986), by having himself chained to the mast, Ulysses anticipates rationally the change in his preferences and chooses an optimal strategy that will avoid the snare set by the sirens. The problem, as underscored by Hammond (1976b), is that this strategy does not correspond to any intertemporal system of preferences over the two periods. Moreover, Ulysses, tied to the base of the mast, regrets not being able to yield to the charms of the sirens, just as the heroin addict who has thrown away his reserve dose in a fit of willpower regrets his gesture. And yet, there is no absolute and general reason to favour current preferences over future preferences when they are in conflict.

Intertemporal consistency

If one views the case of Ulysses and the sirens once again with the eyes of an economist, one will note that Ulysses' strategy requires an investment.[2] Ulysses demands of his sailors that they chain him, which requires an expenditure of time and energy. In fact, Ulysses' strategy can be analysed as temporally consistent. He sacrifices today the resources necessary to survive tomorrow, and in this way optimizes his intertemporal strategy. Once chained, he is incapable of any action, and nothing in his behaviour indicates that he is making choices that are inconsistent with those of the preceding period, precisely because he has made an investment in order not to be able to make them. Becker and Murphy adopt this point of view in their model of rational addiction. They impose an additional condition of rationality on consumer preferences with respect to the traditional neoclassical model: intertemporal preferences must satisfy the condition of reversion to past choices.

Under this new hypothesis – that is, if the individual is rational and consistent in his intertemporal choices – how can we explain the abrupt reorientations in his consumption trajectory: complete changes in his way of life? Such breaks appear as sharp deviations from a consistent consumption trajectory, that is, violations of the principle of temporal consistency of choices. As we have seen, temporal preferences of agents are continuous in the Becker and Murphy model, so that changes in the consumption trajectory are explained by the interplay between present and future prices of drugs. The heroin consumer who decides to wean himself abruptly arbitrates between the present benefits of drugs, which he judges from that moment to be small, and the benefits of a healthy life. For Becker and Murphy, it is not a change in preference for the present (an individual who would cease to diminish the future) that explains the change in behaviour, but the fact that the vagaries of life offer more or less important satisfactions. With a rate of depreciation for the future identical at ages 20 and 30 (imperative of temporal consistency), the individual can decide to stop taking drugs at 30 if someone suddenly offers him a good situation. Even if he disregards this promise, if its fulfilment is sufficiently close, it brings a gain in utility that is greater than his drug consumption.

This approach is theoretically very consistent but makes entry into and exit from drug consumption exclusively dependent on exogenous data (variation in prices and sudden events). Thus, there is one last research path that can be explored. Between temporal inconsistency and consistency, can one productively envisage the existence of discontinuity?

Temporal discontinuities

Some authors have suggested introducing a kind of discontinuity of temporal preferences of agents. This involves taking into account the fact that a young man can strongly devalue the future and therefore have a propensity to choose drugs rationally that is stronger than that of this same person when he is older and has a family to support.

The Ainslie (1992) theory of intertemporal choices differs from the Becker–Murphy theory in basically two points: in the form of the discount function and in the notion of the fixed discount rate. The shape of Ainslie's temporal discount function is hyperbolic rather than exponential: discounting would be steeper at short delays of availability of the addictive good, and additional equal increments of delay produce progressively less additional discounting. Moreover, the relative value of two alternatives available at fixed times can switch, based solely on the addition or subtraction of an equal delay to both alternatives. Given thus the form of the discount function, an alternative that was inferior from a distance may become preferable when its availability becomes immediate. Hyperbolic discounting leads consequently to regular and systematic inconsistencies and changes in preferences (Monterosso and Ainslie, 1999).

According to Monterosso and Ainslie (1999), the following formula is fit to represent the hyperbolic discounting:

$$v_d = \frac{V}{(1+kd)}$$

In which:

v_d: the present discounted value of a delayed reward;
V: the objective value of the delayed reward; k: an empirically derived constant proportional to the degree of discounting (i.e. sensitivity to the delay); and d: the delay duration. Thus the larger the delay, the smaller the present value.[3]

Orphanides and Zervos (1994), faithful to the Beckerian approach, do not challenge the idea of temporal consistency: the individual does not change his preference for the present, but this preference can change under the effect of a random variable and of the past experience the individual has had with drugs. In their model, the parameter of temporal preference depends positively on the consumption stock S_t on one hand, and on a variable of the random state F_t, or $a = (a/S_t, F_t)$ on the other hand. The random variable F_t can assume several values according to a Markov process. Technically, this approach is more satisfactory than that of Becker and Murphy because it substitutes, in place of the explanation of changes in consumption patterns by external accidents, an endogenous explanation founded on the discontinuity of preferences, while at the same time subscribing formally to the imperative of temporal consistency. Hence, it is not changes in the individual that bring about a change in their preferences for the present but external changes that change the preference for the present and therefore the individual. However, the explanation by discontinuity of preference for the present is introduced exogenously and randomly, which reduces its explanatory reach.[4]

Event nodes

The idea of temporal discontinuity gave rise to descriptive modelling of event nodes (Gérard-Varet, 1992; Masson, 1995). Nodes based on events in the life cycle modify the situation of the individual. They are of three types: some are programmed nodes, resulting from a decision by the agent; others are accidental and represent chance events; while still others are informational nodes. The key hypothesis consists in making the temporal preference dependent on age t of the position attained in traversing the event nodes. The temporal preference α is written $\alpha(p_j,t)$, where p_j represents one event node in the set of these nodes and t the age of the individual. The rate of depreciation of the future increases in the case of an unfortunate event (widowhood, unemployment, etc.) and diminishes after a happy event. These discontinuities in the temporal preference parameter considerably enlarge the representation of the range of behaviours open to the drug consumer during the course of his life. The agent no longer relates his choices only to the time remaining until death, which steadily diminishes as he ages. The horizon also registers the accordion-like movements at the occurrence of a happy event, and this all the more so as his temporal preference presents a significant leap of discontinuity. Before the event, the horizon is limited by a fateful expiration date; after the event, everything takes place as if date were extended until it progressively closes up at the approach to the next node.

The imperfection of the analytical tools of economic science is doubtless of an order similar to that of the other sciences that likewise stammer out their explanations of the entry into and exit from drug consumption.

Conclusion

Since the body of work carried out by economists to analyse and represent addictive consumption is incomplete, it is not useful to return to this collection of contributions that we have tried to present in a logical order of presentation. One comment, somewhat out of order, seems to us nevertheless important. Across all the models evoked, one finds a fracture whose consequences are essential to conducting public policy. Under rational addiction theory (Becker and Murphy), decentralized allocation is Pareto-efficient without taxes or corrective public policies. This is true even with some form of uncertainty; Orphanides and Zervos develop a model in which agents differ in their susceptibility to developing a strong consumption habit, and may acquire their susceptibility only by consuming the good. There is some room for regret, but in some sense even regret is perfectly forecast: agents know *ex ante* the true probability that they may regret their choice in the future. Again individual decisions are *ex ante* optimal, and rational addiction does not justify taxes or public policies on drugs, from an efficiency point of view. In contrast, a situation in which government intervention may enhance welfare is one in which agents fail to correctly evaluate the probability distribution of future events, or when they are myopic. In this case, an appropriate tax or public policy may be needed to implement Pareto-efficient allocation. This assumption may justify paternalistic policies in favour of public intervention in the consumption of habit-forming goods, such as drugs or tobacco and alcohol.

Part II

The welfare economics of illegal drugs

3 Economics of prohibition

Introduction

Can economic analysis help define the outline of a good drug policy? In the sphere of drugs, where ideology and moral judgements are omnipresent, it is worth knowing what kind of policy an economic approach based on research into policy effectiveness would recommend: that is, minimization of the social costs generated by drug consumption and trafficking, or the sum of the increased negative externalities and utility procured for those who consume it.[1] Taking an interest, admittedly in rather abstract terms, in the form of an optimal drug policy allows us to indirectly bring to light the economic cost (sometimes exorbitant) of any policy deviating from this norm. In concrete terms, society must be aware that by deviating from optimal drug policy it incurs a waste of resources.

If the objective of economic effectiveness seems too restrictive for policy-makers and society as a whole, it is still possible to choose another direction. The relevance of normative analysis nevertheless remains perfectly intact because it represents a sort of witness pointing out the social cost of a choice. Unfortunately, a quick review of the literature shows that although mainstream normative analysis is fine for evaluating the marginal effects of drug policy (new treatment or inroads in criminal policy), it is incapable of clearly indicating which of the two main regimes of drug policy (prohibition or legalization) should be favoured. The school of analysis called 'law and economics' initiated by Coase (1937) presents an interesting approach that differs from traditional normative analysis. Basically, it states that criminal law forbids transactions that call the inalienability of rights into question. Transactions such as drug deals or the sale of human organs are so appalling that they are neither Pareto-improving nor improving in the sense laid out by Hicks-Kaldor,[2] because they shock the majority of individuals more than they improve the lot of the parties who engage in them. Thus, criminal law can be considered a transaction cost whose level is deliberately set very high in order to eliminate certain exchanges such as the drug trade, and not simply to ensure that these exchanges are conducted efficiently. Criminal law, therefore, reflects the idea that if certain transactions are offensive, then the transactions suggested by Coase to gain the neutrality of those who feel offended are equally offensive. The 'law and economics' approach thus leads to the unambiguous conclusion that the key to the choice between prohibition and legalization is in the hands of the citizen: as long as most of them stigmatize drug consumption, prohibition will remain the most worthy regime. North's (1990) demonstration allows us to better understand why, for example, the cannabis regime is seriously discussed, at least in Europe, where everything leads to the belief that the externalities engendered by the implementation of the law are superior to those experienced by those who stigmatize consumption. The 'law and economics' approach is, however, not entirely satisfactory as it deprives economic analysis of any predictive potential. Finally, we will see that unfortunately we must content ourselves with asking economists to evaluate the marginal changes of public policy rather than radical reform.

General equilibrium analysis is very general

Normative economic analysis rests on several value judgements, the application of which can seem to be disputable. The principle of 'consumer sovereignty' excludes the weighting of utilities according to the value that could be attributed to them by those who consider themselves the elite in society. The only thing that counts, from a purely utilitarian point of view, is the quantity of pleasure procured from a good, not its quality as evaluated by an outside observer, regardless of its merits and virtues. 'Rational behaviour' is the second postulate. From a purely individualistic perspective, no one is better placed than the individual to know what is best for him. We must assume that each of the choices he makes represents the best solution for him to maximize his satisfaction. Normative economic analysis recognizes, however, that cases exist in which the consumer cannot behave in conformity with these postulates, and consequently, it may be necessary to protect him from himself.

Irrationality?

Nonetheless, state drug regulation can be justified as consistent with the normative theory, if it can be shown that drug consumption departs from one of the two basic hypotheses on which this theory is based: 'sovereignty of the consumer' (the individual is the best judge of his welfare) and 'rationality' (individuals do what they prefer). Are drug consumers ignorant or irrational? An affirmative response to either of these questions would work in favour of public intervention and drug interdiction.

All the same, we should also consider the existence of what Musgrave (1954) refers to as 'merit goods', to which public authorities control access (directly or indirectly). These goods manifest characteristics that make reliance on the market to ensure their allocation seem inappropriate. Public intervention in this case consists in imposing on individuals different choices from those that they would make without constraints. The intervention compels the consumption of goods to which agents would not spontaneously devote sufficient resources (vaccination, insurance, education), even though they generate positive externalities. Conversely, public authorities can curb or interdict consumption of products whose risks are more apparent to them than to the individuals (drugs, alcohol, pornography, etc.). The reduction of consumption in these cases should lead not to a diminution in the level of welfare, but on the contrary, to an increase in that level. This indicates that the demand curve is, in certain cases, a tool that is not appropriate for measuring the utility of certain products. Along these lines, one can argue that consumer preference as revealed by demand curves is myopic. Addiction causes demand curves to shift over. The consumer short-sightedly maximizes only his current utility and not his intertemporal utility.

For the most hard-line proponents of the rationality hypothesis, ascribing to drug consumers a form of irrationality is absolutely absurd. From their viewpoint, it is out of the question that state intervention could be justified with respect to individual free choice. Some more moderate authors have shown that adhering to the idea of consumer rationality, on the contrary, does not prevent giving an accurate accounting of the behaviour of drug consumers. Incidentally, a good number of empirical findings back up proponents of the rationality thesis. It appears clear that consumers are not 'possessed' by drugs, as some accounts in the early 1960s tended to make people believe. The various studies devoted to drug consumers, coming from ethno-sociologists not likely to succumb to the charms of the restrictive postulates of mainstream economic analysis (Williams, 1990; Bourgois 1996), emphasize the capacity of users to regulate their consumption. This is not to say that they are capable of stopping it, but they can at least limit it.

Non-sovereignty of the consumer?

If the argument of consumer irrationality cannot be invoked in favour of prohibition, what about that of ignorance? If drug consumers are ill informed about the dangers of drugs, their personal assessment of their welfare can lead them to make bad decisions. This is a good reason to reject the principle of consumer sovereignty. This 'paternalistic' approach underscores the difference between preferences as revealed by the market and the reality of individual welfare, when the preferences expressed are distorted by ignorance. The information an individual has at his disposal at a given moment about the goods he consumes, or plans to consume, is never perfect.

If information is a collective good, individuals are tempted to procure a less than optimal quantity of it. This finding does not necessarily imply that the State must seek to modify spontaneous consumption choices using authoritarian means. It ought to suffice for the State to make directly available to individuals all of the forms of information; education on the harmful effects of drugs, then, would be enough to make them adjust their choices. But this is not the way the State intervenes in practice, since it prefers purely and simply to prohibit drugs. Justifying this interdiction in normative terms requires coming up with something other than the collective nature of the good called information.

The counter-argument to this is that individuals are not sufficiently motivated to become acquainted with all the information that can be given to them free of charge. In practical terms, one can judge that the average individual lacks this prior knowledge on the possible utility of specific information about a good. Thus, he might very likely not take advantage of the means offered to him to better understand the characteristics of the goods he is considering purchasing. The individual may also not wish to commit enough time to learning the information. Taking into consideration all of these factors, it is plausible that an individual would prefer to have his options limited directly rather than having to bear the costs involved in having to find things out for himself. Knowing that welfare economics is founded not on respect for freedom but on concern for the Paretian welfare of individuals, it is possible to justify, by the theory of the optimum, State intervention that protects the consumer from himself. In the case of drugs, however, it is impossible to believe that drug consumers are completely unaware of the risks they run. On the other hand, knowing whether they have an exact idea of the risks is tricky!

The very nature of the information that should be disseminated about drugs raises complex issues. Heroin consumption is undeniably harmful to health, but is this due mainly to the psycho-pharmaceutical nature of the product or to the illegal manner in which it is consumed? The problems that drugs pose to society greatly exceed the hardships endured by the consumers. This is why the social cost of drugs is calculated by calculating the aggregate damage inflicted by drugs. Some of the destructive effects are linked directly to drug use and in particular to ensuing dependency. Others, often the most serious, are not a direct result of drug consumption, but accompany it. These involve, in particular, the violence surrounding the criminal activities involved in drug distribution. However paradoxical it may seem, the violence associated with the sale of drugs, just as in the case of the development of a significant criminal economy, is a result not of the psycho-pharmaceutical effects of the products consumed but rather of the repressive public intervention that follows the decision to ban drugs. One can imagine, kidding aside, that the prohibition of chocolate or tobacco would spur the development of an illegal market as violent as the drug market.

Thus the information that drug consumers have at their disposal is not entirely insignificant, but it is, on the other hand, incomplete and often biased. It is impossible, however, for the State to dispense free of charge enough information (the content of which remains problematic) to induce consumers to abandon drugs. Drug interdiction pure and simple thus finds its normative justification in the imperfection of consumer information, rather than in their supposed irrationality. Nonetheless, the fact that economic theory could legitimize interdiction does not mean at all that this is desirable.

Unpredictables moves

If drug prohibition can be theoretically grounded on the lack of consumer information, what is society's interest in banning drugs? There is no doubt that society has every right to question whether it would not prefer to allow free drug use and thus relieve itself of the cost generated by a ban that is too costly to enforce. The subject of drug legalization brings together very different advocates, including radicals concerned with the individual rights of drug consumers, liberals hostile to public repression (Ostrowski, 1990), and pragmatics like the Nobel Prize winner for economics Friedman (1991) and Nadelman (1994) who maintain that the benefits of legalization would be greater than the social costs of prohibition. But in order to prevail, each camp would have to demonstrate the veracity of the following assertions:

- Advocates of prohibition would have to prove that: (1) the consumption of drugs would increase after legalization; (2) the harm caused by this increased consumption would not be offset by the appearance of substitutes and legal drugs that are safer and without secondary effects on health; (3) the harm caused by this increased consumption would not be compensated by a reduction in the consumption of other products dangerous to health such as alcohol or tobacco; and, finally, (4) the harm generated by this increased consumption and not compensated by 2 and 3 would exceed the harm caused here and now by the perverse effects of prohibition.
- For their part, advocates of abolishing prohibition would have to demonstrate that: (1) interdiction would have no restrictive impact on the level of drug consumption; (2) abolishing prohibition would not increase illicit drug usage; (3) interdiction would displace consumption of illicit drugs towards drugs that are legal but dangerous; (4) and finally, the perverse negative effects of prohibition would overcome the beneficial effects that accompany a reduction in drug consumption.

Unfortunately, the normal model (cost–benefit) used by economists for this kind of demonstration is not applicable here, since it deals with the spontaneous behaviour of individuals posing a problem that is difficult to observe and predict with any precision. Neither of the two theses (prohibition, legalization) can be proven and no complete studies assessing the social costs of drugs under one regime or the other have been undertaken. No one knows, in the case of legalization, what would be the level of consumption, the extent of the effects of substitution between currently illicit drugs and legal ones (tobacco and alcohol), the social costs of drugs, and, a fortiori, the outcome of all these problems combined. Even recognizing that the greater share of the damage generated by drugs is a result of public intervention, the total cost of banning consumption still does not unequivocally lead to a clear recommendation for legalization. There is no guarantee that the social cost would diminish with the legalization of drugs, and everything gives the impression that such a calculation is impossible. Economic analysis can shed light on each of these aspects, but is scarcely in a position to treat them definitively.[3] For this reason, we consider the economic discussion on the global merit of prohibition and legalization to be incomplete and probably destined to remain so.

Partial equilibrium analysis is more partial

Hence, taking into account the whole set of effects on social welfare introduced by an eventual legislation of drugs amounts to a sort of 'mission impossible'. However, using partial equilibrium analysis, an approach that does not consider the impact of changes observed in the drug market on other markets (alcohol, crime, psychotropes, etc.), it is possible to observe the localized consequences of drug liberalization on the level of consumption. The swcope of this reasoning is obviously limited. It is no longer the impact of a new policy on welfare in general we are talking about, but only its consequences on the level of consumption in the drug market. The interest of such an analysis for the policy-maker is more limited, but it does have the merit of opening up a debate on the question of whether or not drug consumers are atypical beings, at least from the point of view of economic theory. This means discussing how these consumers adapt their consumption habits in relation to price movement. This will lead us to examine the degree of price elasticity of demand, and the eventual convex nature of drug consumer preferences.

Back to Capone's time

An examination of the precedent of alcohol prohibition during the 1920s and 1930s presents an instructive case study for a discussion of the comparative merits of prohibiting and legalizing drugs. In 1917, the US Congress promulgated a resolution forbidding consumption of alcohol during time of war. This ban became permanent with the passage of the 18th Amendment to the Constitution (January 1920) and was not abolished

until fourteen years later, by the 21st Amendment (December ⬛
the exception of the work of Warburton (1932), no studies have a⬛
to provide an estimate of alcohol consumption during Prohibition.⬛
burton compensated for the absence of statistics on consumption by rec⬛
stituting them with the help of other measures, such as the level of
agricultural production, the number of arrests for public drunkenness, and
the number of deaths tied to alcohol consumption. This writer concluded
that alcohol consumption per capita during prohibition stabilized at
between 65 per cent and 71 per cent of its previous level (in 1925 and 1929,
respectively).

Miron and Zwiebel (1991) tried to verify Warburton's analysis. To
estimate alcohol consumption, the authors retained the following variables: the number of deaths from cirrhosis of the liver, the number of
deaths linked to alcoholism, the number of first-time psychiatric hospital-
izations tied to alcohol, and the number of arrests for intoxication while
driving. According to these authors, alcohol consumption during Prohibition clearly declined at the beginning of Prohibition, then climbed back to
60 per cent or 70 per cent of its previous level. Finally, abolishing Prohibition did not bring about an immediate climb in consumption. In addition
to their initial finding, Miron and Zwiebel offer several comments on the
impact of the rise in alcohol prices during Prohibition. On the one hand,
they claim that the prices of alcohol increased three- or four-fold during
Prohibition; on the other hand, they observe a decrease in consumption
that is modest (between 20 per cent and 30 per cent) compared to the
price increase.

Knowing that alcohol consumption is relatively elastic with regard to
price, why does alcohol consumption not decline in the same proportion
that prices increase? Miron and Zwiebel advance an explanation: prohibition surrounds alcohol with an aura of mystery that renders it attractive.
Alcohol prohibition thus alters the demand curve, displacing it upwards,
which would explain why the price effect does not play as great a role as
expected in limiting consumption.

Equilibrium on an illegal market

The example of alcohol prohibition underlines the difficulties of predicting
how individuals react to a change in the legal status of drugs. By banning
the consumption and trade of drugs, prohibition gives rise to an illegal
market whose equilibrium differs from that observed in a legal market.
Let us take as a starting point a situation in which the drug is legal merchandise not subject to any particular taxation. In technical terms, drug
prohibition causes displacement of the supply curve upwards under
the effect of the tax that prohibition imposes. If repression is directed
against consumers, the demand curve is displaced downward under the
effects of repression. It is not even necessary that this be accompanied by

The ban alone stigmatizes those who continue to
ration is economically interpreted as a growth in
, which explains the movement of the curve down-
gure 3.1 that the equilibrium before drug prohibi-
a price P_1 higher than after prohibition P_2 and a
aged on the market q_1 greater than q_2. In any case
duction in quantity of drug exchanged depends on
ovement of these two curves.
at repression affects drug suppliers more harshly
than consum... , he displacement of the demand curve is less important than that of the supply curve. In fact, it is not simply whether enforcement against sellers is harsher than against users, but also how elastic
demand and supply are to the associated legal risks. A given enforcement
level against buyers may have much more of an effect than the same level
aimed at sellers. Unless the demand is clearly less elastic[4] than the supply,
the price of drugs rises and the demand for drugs falls with prohibition.

Thus, the degree of price elasticity of drug demand constitutes one of
the poles around which the discussion of eventual merits of prohibition is
organized. Although abundant empirical literature exists, most notably,
Grossman and Chaloupka (1998) suggest that the drug demand price is
fairly elastic, while Miron and Zwiebel (1995) consider that the weak elasticity of demand to prices and the banalization of drugs would pull the
demand curve down, making – in the case of drug legalization – an explosion in consumption unlikely. In Figure 3.2, an initial equilibrium on the
drug market is established for a quantity of drugs sold q_1 and a price P_1.
Drug prohibition displaces the supply curve S_1 to S_2. A new equilibrium is

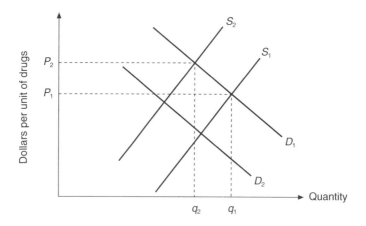

Figure 3.1 Prohibition effects on the drug market

Note
$(P_1\ q_1)$ 5 price and quantity consumed before prohibition
$(P_2\ q_2)$ 5 price and quantity consumed after prohibition

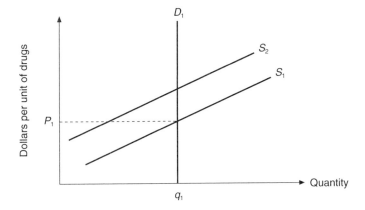

Figure 3.2 Prohibition with inelastic demand

thus reached for a quantity of drugs sold identical to the circumstances prevailing before interdiction but at a higher price p_2. Thus, as was the case with alcohol during prohibition, interdiction would render drugs attractive, particularly for young people looking to rebel against the social order. The positive effect of a price reduction on consumption and the negative effect of the disappearance of the 'publicity' of interdiction should cancel each other out.

Preference's concavity

White and Luksetitch (1983) and Lemennicier (1992), a French economist, also think that liberalization would have only a weak impact on demand. But their reasoning is based on the hypothesis that drug consumers would be characterized by concave preferences. Microeconomics theory generally considers consumer preferences to be convex. Basically, this means that the consumer prefers to consume a wide range of goods rather than concentrate consumption on a single commodity.[5] It is tempting to consider that drug consumers constitute an exception by holding the view that they prefer to concentrate their consumption on a sole commodity. The nature of drug consumption implies that the preferences of such consumers would thus be concave; that is to say, the consumer would always choose a much more limited basket of goods.

It is true that empirical literature underlines the fact that drugs dominate the expenditure pattern of heroin addicts, but this observation does not necessarily validate the thesis of concave preferences. The fact that a drug consumer would sacrifice his food, for example, to buy drugs – in other words, between two baskets of goods, a good meal and heroin, he would always prefer a maximum of heroin and no meals – only points out that the quantity of heroin at his disposal is insufficient, and thus the two baskets do not have the same utility. In order to have concave preferences, we must start with two baskets having the same utility and verify whether the consumer does not prefer mixed baskets. If we offer a heroin addict twice his monthly consumption and we propose to exchange part of this for food, there is no doubt that he will accept the exchange. Empirical observations on behaviour of drug consumers also point out that rather than the costly need for drugs, their budget is tight and they satisfy their needs following an order of priority. It is not merely because an individual with low revenue would start to buy drink before food that his preferences are concave; there is a point at which he would no longer exchange water for food. We now represent consumption by an individual with concave preference in Figure 3.3, where the ordinate measures monthly consumption of drugs and the abscissa measures the consumption of other goods. The budgetary constraint is represented by the line (ab). In Figure 3.3, we start from point (a) where the individual consumes no drugs. The price reduction motivates him to discover this product and he quickly consumes drugs to excess. His consumption goes from zero to quantity (b). The 'participation effect' (discovery of the product after the lowering of the price) and the 'substitution effect' (change of the basket of goods consumed following the price reduction of one of them) combine to bring about an abusive consumption of drugs. That is the characteristic of concave preferences, with the individual specializing in drug consumption.

Let us now take the case of another individual who already consumes

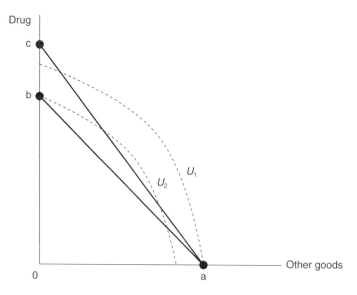

Figure 3.3 Drug consumption with concave preferences

drugs in quantity (b). The price reduction leads towards increased consumption of drugs (c), but this is a consequence solely of the increase in his real income, an increase that is a result of price reduction. If one maintains either real income or satisfaction constant, the price reduction is without effect on consumption. The 'substitution effect' is nil. In the case of concave preferences, one must separate those who are already in the market and those who are not yet there. Consumers already present in the market are insensitive to price. Demand is inelastic. Therefore, if one is interested only in users already in the market, a policy of prohibition fails, because the increase in drug prices that results from this policy is without effect on drug consumption. What is true of an increase is true of a reduction. If drug consumers have strictly concave preferences, one can draw the following conclusion: legalization of drugs would not lead to an increase in demand by consumers as a consequence of a price reduction.

We should also note that a rise in drug consumption will nevertheless be observed as a result of the increase in the drug consumer's real income following the price reduction. This effect is by definition weighted by a budgetary coefficient of one, since the drug consumer devotes the entirety of his budget to this product. The impact of the income effect on elasticity of drugs is thus maximum. It is clear, however, that drug demand is inelastic for users, according to the canons of economic theory, since it is precisely the price effect that one is seeking to measure, everything else being equal and, in particular, real income (or satisfaction) remaining constant. The group of consumers already on the market and already dependent cannot be considered as an obstacle to legalization since they are by definition insensitive to variations in relative prices.

Concavity and legalization

Let us consider that drug consumers can be divided into three groups of individuals. The first is composed of individuals who will never consume drugs, regardless of price. They are thus insensitive to the legal regime to which drugs are subjected. Whether prohibition or legalization, their consumption is nil. The second group comprises individuals who already consume drugs in spite of the ban. Their preferences are concave, and they do not divide up their income on a diversified basket of goods. On the contrary, they prefer to concentrate their expenditures on a sole commodity: in this case, drugs. In the case of liberalization, they will take advantage of the drop in prices to increase their consumption. This effect is due solely to the drug consumers' increased real income. The 'substitution effect' among the goods is nil since the preferences are concave. The third group is composed of those who do not consume drugs but who do not demand an absolute ban on consumption. It is vital to know whether this group will turn towards drugs in the case of liberalization and lowering of prices. Under the hypothesis that these individuals have concave preferences, there always exists a drug price–quantity combination that will motivate them to try drugs, and then to devote their entire income to drugs.

Armed with this approach, advocates of liberalization follow the theory that the dealers distribute drugs free of charge to attract new customers, knowing that once hooked, they will pay full price. Hence, the 'participation effect' is thus integrally captured by the traffickers' marketing strategy. In Figure 3.4, an individual does not consume drugs; the dealers offer him quantity (ab), which is worth (bc) on the illegal market. The consumer finds that this price–quantity combination improves his satisfaction, and he finally consumes an excessive quantity of drugs (oc). He goes from being a non-participant to becoming dependent. Those who can be tempted to consume drugs will necessarily do so, in spite of prohibition, the day they encounter a dealer. The dealers' strategy would thus explain why the demand for drugs increases in spite of prohibition.

Liberalization of drugs would thus bring about an increase only in the quantity of drugs consumed, not the number of consumers. The current consumers of drugs would take more of them, but no one would take advantage of the drop in prices to become initiated to drugs since that would have already been done, under prohibition, by way of the distribution of free drugs by the dealers. Better still, liberalization could even constitute a regime capable of limiting drug consumption. The state could implement a strategy of price discrimination aimed at dissuading non-consumers from trying drugs. By making drugs expensive for non-dependents and providing them at low prices for dependent consumers, the social cost of drugs would be minimized and the number of consumers stabilized.

Can the hypothesis of concave preferences seriously be used in defence of drugs? This original approach poses several problems. For one thing, the consistency of the level of consumption after the lifting of prohibition

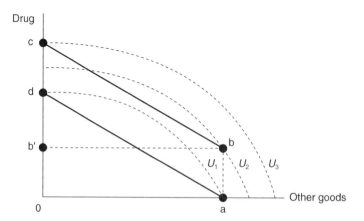

Figure 3.4 The participation effect

rests on the belief that the totality of the 'participation effect' is tapped by traffickers in spite of interdiction. However, it seems hardly credible to us that marketing by dealers is sufficiently aggressive that they can get everyone who is likely to do so to try drugs. For another thing, the discussion turns on the concavity of drug consumer preferences. This hypothesis suits only a small minority of drug consumers, addicts who are totally dependent on the product and who devote their entire income to it. In any situation, individuals who do not yet consume drugs, even if they do not face a strong ban on them, still have no reason to have concave preferences.

With convex preferences, the high prices brought about by prohibition effectively chase away potential new consumers, and free distribution of drugs by dealers does not allow them to attract new initiates to drugs on a long-term basis. The argument of the advocates of prohibition must thus be formulated as follows: following the legalization of the drug trade, an excessive increase in demand will be observed because there will be a more or less massive entry of new consumers into the market. What prohibitionists fear is the 'participation effect'. Moreover, it is for this reason that demand for drugs does not increase uncontrollably under prohibition, contrary to the forecast of some abolitionists.

Prohibition and crime: which is the chicken and which is the egg?

It seems impossible to test the opportunity for drug legalization in general equilibrium. The partial equilibrium approach is simpler, but contents itself with the discussion of the level of consumption and not of collective welfare. However, the impact of drugs on the crime rate is a central question in all discussions of public policy orientation. Let us then leave the reassuring framework of partial equilibrium and try to comprehend the link existing between crime and prohibition. Prohibition fosters the development of illegal activity. If there is a conflict, the participants in the criminal economy cannot turn to the judicial system to defend themselves. The marginal cost of recourse to violence is therefore less when the market is illegal than on a free market to the extent that, once the leap into illegality has been accomplished by an agent who becomes a criminal, the recourse to violence does not constitute a true additional step but is a complementary activity.

Prohibition and crime profitability

Prohibition thus encourages criminal agents to form themselves into criminal organizations. These organizations employ violence to discourage small-scale traffickers and the temptation to betray members of the organization. In legal business, a company well established in the market loses money when it lowers its prices to meet those of a small competitor. Its losses are proportional to its share of the market. In illegal markets, competition might be regulated by violence. So, the small trafficker is very vulnerable. A criminal organization thus restores its supremacy at lower cost in an illegal market than in a free market. Without attaching more meaning to this finding than it deserves, we are forced to recognize that drug prohibition generates violence and gives a boost to 'organized crime' activities.

Some others, such as Friedman (1991), take this reasoning even further. For him, the cost curve of the severity of penalties as a function of the number of crimes is concave. In other words, starting from a given degree of criminal activity, an individual knows that it is useless to moderate his behaviour since such moderation would not have the effect of reducing substantially the penalties he incurs. Thus the law, rather than limiting the number of infractions committed, has an incentive effect on agents by pushing them towards recourse to violence so as to avoid being caught. In this way, violence results from the interdiction of drugs and not from the consumption of the product.

Friedman (1991) backs up this thesis by showing the existence, since 1910, of a positive correlation between the death rate in the United States and the relentlessness with which the government has enforced the drug ban. However, recent statistics do not confirm Friedman's (1990, 2000) thesis. Data contradicts his hypothesis. Drug enforcement has become tougher but homicide rates have been falling. There is no doubt that any prohibited substance in persistent demand constitutes an opportunity for criminal activity. On the other hand, the thesis based on the idea that repression increases crime profitability and the level of criminal activity does not appear founded. The hypothesis according to which the cost curve of the severity of penalties as a function of the number of crimes is concave is an interesting short cut, but it is disproved by empirical observation and theoretically unconvincing. Actually, this hypothesis implies considering that there are no sanctions strong enough to counterbalance crime.

Needs of drug and supply of crimes

A more balanced view of crime supply can be illustrated by Cooter and Ulen's models (1996). In Figure 3.5, the demand curve D_A (the demand for an illegal drug by those already addicted) is inelastic. If we suppose that the supply curve is initially S_1, the equilibrium price and quantity are then p_1 and q_1. The total amount spent by drug consumers is the rectangle $oq_1E_1p_1$. If we make the simplistic assumption that drug addicts pay for all of their drugs by committing crime, then the total expenditure by drug consumers comes from committing crimes in the amount $oq_1E_1p_1$. Now suppose that the government raises the expected punishment for using

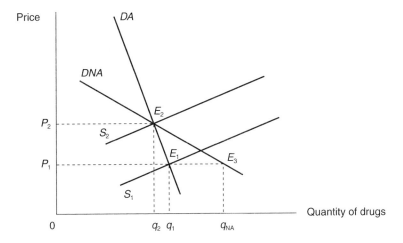

Figure 3.5 Crime and drug prices

addictive drugs, and that the result of this policy is reduction in the supply of the drug, causing the supply curve to shift to S_2. The new equilibrium price and quantity are p_2 and q_2. Because of the inelasticity of demand, the reduction in the quantity of the illegal drug is small.

When demand is inelastic, an increase in price causes an increase in the consumer's total expenditure for the commodity. In Figure 3.5, when the price of drugs rises to p_2, the total expenditure of drug consumers increases to the amount p_2q_2, to the rectangle $oq_2E_1p_2$. Harsher punishment causes more crime. If this analysis is correct, increasing law enforcement may in fact increase the number of crimes. This analysis does not rely, as Friedman's does, on the assumption of concavity of crime supply, but on the inelasticity of drug demand. This assumption is not very realistic, except perhaps for the more addicted drug users who cannot permanently moderate their consumption. Let us introduce the non-addicts' demand, which may be elastic, as D_{NA} in Figure 3.5. Non-addicts respond to change in the price of illegal drugs. The same increase in price that induces addicts to engage in more crime dissuades non-addicts from consuming the drugs. If non-addicts are initially consuming Q_{NA} when the price is p_1, the increase in price to p_2 causes non-addicts to reduce their demand to q_2. Thus the policy of lessening expected punishment for selling illegal drugs to addicts also lowers the price for non-addicts. Because this latter group has an elastic demand, this lower price could induce more experimentation with drugs, possibly leading to more addiction. If this were to happen, then the policy of reducing the price of illegal drugs might reduce the social cost of crime by addicts, but it might also increase the social cost of drug use by non-addicts. The social cost of experimentation by non-addicts can be avoided if the authorities can maintain a policy of price discrimination for addictive drugs. Addicts would pay a low price, and non-addicts would pay more.

The difficulties experienced in trying to understand the link between crime and drug prohibition come no doubt from the somewhat diffuse framework of the normative approach. Normally, such approaches are more like artificial frameworks within which to place problems than policies designed to resolve them. In the former case, the hypothesis according to which drug addicts obtain the whole of their revenue for drug purchases from criminal activity is the key to its reasoning. Empirical studies deny this affirmation and point out the importance in the revenue of drug consumers, including legal aid to the most addicted, undeclared work, prostitution, and resale of drugs, which, to one degree or another, belongs to the category of victimless crime (although the prostitute could be seen as the first victim of prostitution) and not criminality committed against society. In other words, the social cost of consumer criminal behaviour should be re-examined in more detailed terms than those which suit the necessarily very synthetic representations of illegal market dynamics. At the end of this rapid review of normative economic literature, it appears that the question of benefits in the comparison between the regimes of prohibition and legalization remains unsettled. This question seems impossible to resolve in the context of a comparison of levels of welfare respectively obtained in one or the other of the two theoretical reference situations. It is, however, frustrating to conclude by conceding that the science of economy cannot support one regime rather than the other. This is why we attempt an alternative path of analysis. The idea is simple: perhaps we should base our prescriptions in matters of drug policy, and not on the static comparison of welfare, by trying to verify if the market is a market in which the actors can internalize for themselves, without public intervention, the externalities they create. If the answer is yes, and by following a perspective inspired by Coase (1937) and the school of law and economics reclaiming it, liberalization of drugs would then have a solid foundation.

Law and economics: consensus, dear consensus!

We have seen that traditional economic analysis does not permit us to solve the puzzle of drug interdiction, but only allows us to rationally assess each of its elements. In fact, the microeconomic tools that we have deployed will be more useful to a discussion of the impact of the marginal variations in drug policies than in determining which of the two main models (prohibition, legalization) should prevail. If one wishes to definitively settle this question from the point of view of economic analysis, it is necessary to reconsider the question from a fresh point of view, such as that suggested by law and economics.

A Coasian perspective

What, from the perspective of law and economics, are the reasons that would support interdiction of a product or an activity? If we suppose that drug consumption and trade are among the activities that improve the welfare of the seller and the buyer, does the law authorize this kind of exchange? When drugs are sold, we are in the presence of a voluntary transfer of property, money for merchandise. When this transfer is consensual, the risk of inefficiency is low because the parties are engaged in interaction.

It can therefore seem paradoxical for the law to forbid certain exchanges (drug trade, prostitution, sale of human organs). Obviously, however, the problem posed by drugs cannot be confined to defending the rights of the consumer and the seller. The consumption and sale of drugs generate externalities that affect third parties. Even if some of the externalities generated by drugs are frequently linked to their interdiction, one still must not forget that certain externalities are due to characteristics of the product and to its mode of utilization.[6]

Dealing with the question of the appropriateness of banning drugs thus requires taking into account the harm drug exchanges cause to those who do not participate in them. Even if the two parties improve their circumstances in the course of a drug exchange, they diminish the welfare of those who may have to suffer the consequences of consumption and trafficking (victims of the violence or the illnesses fostered by drug trafficking and consumption). Applying the Pareto criterion, the exchange is inefficient, but it can be efficient if a criterion less demanding such as that of Hicks-Kaldor is applied.

The Coase theorem[7] constitutes an invaluable tool for determining which party it is whose rights should be protected by the law when a conflict breaks out between two parties, such as the players in the drug market on the one hand and ordinary citizens on the other.

Let us consider two laws that serve to protect, in turn, the rights of drug consumers and the rights of non-consumers. The first law permits consumption of drugs, but calls for compensation of victims in cases where drug consumption generates negative consequences for third parties. The second law decrees that the drug consumer deserves to be penalized whether or not he is, in fact, inflicting harm to third parties.

According to the Coase theorem, if the parties – in this case the persons implicated in the consumption and trafficking of drugs, on the one hand, and the victims, on the other – can negotiate freely and without transaction costs,[8] it matters little which of the two laws are adopted. In fact, if one retains the first law, the victims of the drugs will see their damages compensated, and if one retains the second law, those who like drugs will buy out from potential victims the right of the consumer. In both cases, those who want to consume drugs will do so, and will internalize the costs that they incur by the prices they pay. The Coase approach thus leads, at first glance, to a recommendation of a drug policy that excludes interdiction in all cases, leaving it to the parties involved to settle the question of externalities.

This cursory reading of the Coase theorem only works when the parties can negotiate without transaction costs. In the case of drugs, it should be acknowledged that the negotiation between the buyers and sellers of drugs, on the one hand, and citizens, on the other, to determine who is injuring whom can be costly. But in the presence of transaction costs, the Coase theorem recommends assigning the rights to the party that attaches the greatest value to them. Thus, if drug consumers attach a higher value to the right to drugs than non-consumers attach to the additional security that drug interdiction brings, it is appropriate to adopt the first law: that is to say, the freedom to consume drugs accompanied by an obligation of compensation if the consumer's behaviour causes third parties to incur risks. Conversely, if the majority of the population that does not consume drugs set a higher value on the right to security than the minority of consumers of drugs value their freedom, it is appropriate to sanction the players in the drug market. This involves an eminently political choice that reflects the opinion that public policy-makers, themselves the arbiters between freedom and security, are making.

Determining which party attaches the greatest value to rights is thus not an easy task, save for relying on the preferences of the public policy-maker. Otherwise, there exists no simple formula allowing us to compare the subjective assessments the parties make of their rights, particularly when transaction costs are high and are borne asymmetrically by the two parties. Calabresi (1970) has offered a kind of back-up strategy that would indirectly achieve the wealth maximization goal. This strategy calls for assigning the right to the party from whom it could be transferred less expensively. If it turns out to be an incorrect assignment, the chances that there will be a market correction are higher than if the incorrect assignment were made to the other party.

A law imposing sanctions on the players in the drug market could thus be justified if it turned out that the transaction costs accompanying the implementation of a law allowing drugs were higher than those generated by the opposite choice. It all depends, therefore, on the behaviour of the individuals in the market. Let us imagine that drugs are prohibited, and that the law is well accepted by the population. The consumption of illegal drugs would be weak, and the transaction costs of implementing the criminal law would be low. The law would thus find rather solid economic justification. It is enough for a sufficiently large portion of the population to consume drugs, however, to make the transaction costs increase. The interdiction law then loses its foundation. This framework of analysis is useful in explaining why institutional systems that the laws of a country constitute must evolve when the behaviour of agents render them ineffective. The movement in favour of decriminalization or legalization of cannabis that affects a number of countries is a good illustration of a situation in which it is possible for the transaction costs associated with prohibition to become higher than those that liberalization would engender. This brings to mind again the idea developed by North (1990) that slow incremental changes in behaviour can lead suddenly to a positive change in the institutional system in an effort to economize on transaction costs.

The protection of rights

Once the rights have been assigned to one or the other of the parties, and assuming, to deal with reality, that we know that it is a law forbidding drugs, it is advisable to choose a procedure that guarantees that the rights of non-consumers, whom the law protects, will not be violated.

The proposition, set forth by Calabresi and Melamed (1972), is that entitlement can be protected by liability rules, property rules, or a rule of inalienability. Liability rules are used when a person is permitted to encroach upon the rights of another and then compensate him. A property rule, on the other hand, is one under which a party must have permission from the affected party before taking or using the other party's entitlement. Finally, in some cases, the rule is that entitlement cannot be sold or exchanged, as is the case with the inalienability rule.

According to the authors, when transaction costs are low, the rule best adapted to defending the rights of individuals is that of property, because if an error is committed and the law inadvertently assigns the rights to the wrong party, the market will succeed in correcting this situation. Conversely, when the transaction costs are high, it is advisable to apply a liability rule. This permits compensating possible victims, whereas trying to impose a return to the situation prevailing before the violation of the rights of one of the parties turns out to be extremely costly.

In the drug market, the transaction costs accompanying a negotiated settlement of conflicts that pit consumers and non-consumers against each other would be substantial. In fact, the number of participants in the negotiations between consumers and non-consumers of drugs would be considerable and the uncertainty as to the amount of damages affecting the one group and the extent of liability of the other would be very high. Thus, since the transaction costs are high in the case of the drug sales, the lawmakers ought to rely on a liability rule. Moreover, this is a criminal law that is going to guarantee the rights of non-consumers, and yet it is similar to a property rule, since it forbids all transgressions even in return for compensation for damages. The principle of Calabresi and Melamed therefore seems to be proved wrong in the case of drugs.

It appears logical, moreover, not to count on a liability rule to guarantee the rights of non-consumers of drugs. In fact, it is hard to see how, under a liability rule, the victims would be compensated. How would we identify those who are victims of the sale of drugs? The cost of a system for identification would be high and the risk of strategic behaviour huge. Everyone would have an interest in claiming himself as a victim. Finally, one can consider that the gains of the beneficiaries would never be enough to compensate the victims.

If the liability rule proves to be inapplicable, then it is a particular form of the rule of property that must be applied in the case of drugs, in this case the third rule evoked by Calabresi and Melamed: inalienability. According to this principle, it is advisable, for example, to forbid individuals to sell certain of their organs, even if such a transaction seems to represent a Pareto improvement. Calabresi and Melamed suggest that such a transaction is so shocking that it is neither Pareto-improving nor improving in the sense of Hicks-Kaldor, because it shocks the majority of individuals more than it improves the lot of the parties who engage in it. By way of analogy, some people consider – but this is an eminently subjective consideration – that the rights of non-consumers of drugs to live in a world without drugs are inalienable and that criminal law ought therefore to guarantee this. Indeed, the rule of inalienability constitutes a particular form of the rule of property that leads to designating as criminal the activity of those who threaten the inalienability of those rights.

Criminal law forbids certain transactions that would call into question the inalienability of rights. It can thus be considered as a transaction cost whose level is deliberately set very high in order to eliminate certain exchanges such as the drug trade, and not simply to ensure that these exchanges are conducted efficiently. Criminal law therefore simply reflects the idea that if certain transactions are offensive, then the transactions suggested by Coase to gain the neutrality of those who feel offended are equally offensive.

Conclusion

We end this discussion of the good based on the interdiction of drugs with mixed feelings. The conventional normative approach provides some excellent instruments for a discussion of the marginal variations of a public drug policy. We will use them again elsewhere. It is impossible, on the other hand, to use this set of tools successfully to analyse the complexity of the interactions between the different effects, hence the impossibility of reaching a conclusion as to the superiority of the prohibition model or the legalization model. We experience the same dissatisfaction, to a lesser extent, with respect to law and economics. Emerging from this school is the idea that prohibition of all drugs, or of at least some of them, has an economic foundation only if the laws are not the subject of massive transgressions. Finally, the laws must adapt to the perception of drugs held by the individuals who compose society. As long as this perception is preponderantly negative, forbidding drugs allows the protection of consumers from themselves, which amounts to declaring the human body inalienable by the will of the one who inhabits it. Thus, where drugs are concerned, everything rests on the social consensus, a consensus that is unstable and elusive.

4   Optimal public intervention

Protecting individuals from themselves is a legitimate reason, in the eyes of economic theory, to justify banning drugs. Nonetheless, public policy-makers have not looked to economists to make a decision for or against enforcement of drug prohibition. Anti-drug enforcement is driven by factors other than the enthusiastic search for economic efficiency. History, moral standards and several more or less accurate descriptions of the effects of drugs on individuals and society as a whole play a much more important role than economists do.

Economic theory and governments of many countries may be in agreement on banning drugs, yet they continue to circulate illegally. Our perspective is very different from the previous one. The question no longer involves deciding whether we should prohibit or legalize drugs, but determining which public policy should be retained within an institutional framework where prohibition is a fact. The perspective certainly remains theoretical but the approach is more realistic. So, to state the situation from a normative point of view, governments should therefore implement public policies aimed at maximizing social welfare, i.e. minimizing the social cost of drugs.[1] Another way to put the problem is to state that government should design policies aimed at the internalization of externalities created by illegal drugs. To help accomplish this economic analysis it is particularly important to provide useful tools, because the question of externalities is almost as old as the science of economics itself.

Notwithstanding this lengthy practice of treating externalities, normative economic analysis experiences real difficulties in playing its role of supporting decision-making. The reason for this is that conventional economic analysis ties the reduction of social costs to intermediate objectives. Classical analysis of correcting externalities is inspired by the work of Pigou (1920) and the study of crime economics developed by Becker (1968), both of which aim at minimizing social costs. The former proposes accomplishing this by bringing society to an optimal level of consumption of illegal drugs. The latter suggests attaining this result by reducing criminal activity to its optimal level. Nothing proves that the orientation of a public policy which permits attaining optimal level of one or the other of these variables (consumption and crime) guarantees maximization of collective well-being, or in other words, minimization of the social costs of drugs. All of the difficulty where drugs are concerned stems from the fact that the level of social cost – that is, the severity of the harm inflicted on society by drugs – does not depend exclusively either on the level of consumption or on the level of illegal market activity; the means of suppression can themselves affect welfare in more than the trivial sense of tax distortion.

This chapter has two objectives. One is the discussion of the legitimacy of the normative objectives applied generally by economic theory to illegal activity. Our approach is then fairly critical, for it rejects the idea that attaining a so-called optimal level of drug consumption or crime constitutes a guarantee of seeing public policy minimize the social costs related to drugs. The other is that the following developments explore the different interactions between prices and behaviour, that are characteristic of illegal markets. The lessons are not negligible, if the objective is to draw from economic theory good reasons to question public policies designed without considering elementary market characteristics. Or, if it is to elaborate a new drug policy, it is necessary to be more familiar with the reactions of agents to price. Following the example of a toolbox where all the tools are present and neatly arranged, it is still necessary to specify in the rest of this book, how to use them. Without clear directions on how to use them, even the best tools are useless.

The optimal level of consumption: a missed target

To consider public anti-drug policy as a means of arriving at an optimal level of drug consumption is a common error explained by the fact that it is the most direct application, but also the least well thought out, of standard microeconomics in the area of illegal drugs. In the domain of public policy, confusing the end (minimization of the social cost of drugs) and one of the means can have particularly ambiguous effects: consumption reduction is regrettable but frequent. One is thus forced to notice that many governments fix the objective, in the worst case, at consumption-zero, and in the best case at optimal level. Even though one is sceptical about such an objective, the methods recommended by economic theory to attain it should be discussed in detail. After having specified that which should be understood by 'optimal drug consumption', we will discuss each of the three solutions: Coase's voluntary negotiation, Pigou's taxation, and the modification of the agent's preferences.

Internalizing the externalities

Let us apply the economic model of market functioning to the case of drugs and assume that drugs are legal and circulate in a competitive

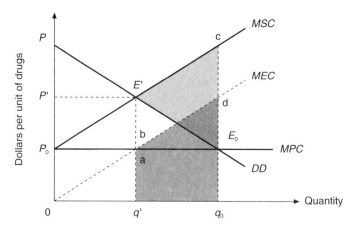

Figure 4.1 Externality in a legal market

market as illustrated by Figure 4.1. At the equilibrium, the price that represents the marginal value for a consumer of one additional unit of drugs is equal to the marginal private cost (*MPC*). This solution is not Pareto optimal, since the marginal valuation by the consumer (*DD*) is lower than the social cost (*MSC*), that is, than the sum of marginal private cost and marginal external cost, represented by point *C*. The socially optimal level of consumption is q', because it corresponds to the intersection of the demand curve *DD* and the marginal social cost (*MSC*). The benefit of moving from q_0 to q' is represented by the (hatched) zone $E'E_0c$, whose surface is equal to the amount where the social cost exceeds private demand for a given price.

To remedy this situation, microeconomic texts propose two main alternative solutions: the Coase solution and the Pigou solution. When externalities disrupt the market, economists generally propose either favouring negotiation among the perpetrators of the harm to find a solution that allows them to compensate the victims for the harm and to pursue their activity (Coase solution), or taxing the merchandise that gives rise to the externality in order to reduce consumption to its optimal level (Pigou solution).

The Coase solution

Assume that drug lovers hold a 'property right for drug consumption' and that these rights are respected. The non-consumer victims of the externalities produced by the drugs can buy a sufficient quantity of this right to reduce the quantity consumed to q'. The non-consumers would thus pay a sum equal to the zone $q'bdq_0$ (equivalent to $aE'cE_0$), and the consumers would receive the benefit of accepting a payment higher than $aE'E_0$, from which comes the room for negotiation between the two parties. Conversely, if the non-consumers initially benefited from property rights, they would profit from paying the sum P_0fE'a to attain the right to consume q' units of drugs, while the consumers would acquire the benefits of accepting an amount greater than the surface area obq' (or P_0E'a), giving rise once again to room for negotiation. As we have already pointed out in Chapter 1, this solution is very abstract. Among other things, it is very difficult to envisage the practical conditions under which a non-consumer of drugs who is a victim of a viral illness and a drug consumer who may have transmitted it to him could negotiate their rights. The Coase solution runs up against problems related to the difficulties of identifying the parties, of asymmetry of information and harm assessment.

The Pigou solution

Following the work of Pigou, the conventional economic approach generally suggests that externalities be corrected by imposing a tax. For the time being, we will set aside the question of determining what such a tax represents in the case of an illegal product and represent the Pigou solution graphically.

In Figure 4.1, the tax would be equal to the segment aE'. It is of secondary importance whether this tax is levied on the consumer or the producer, so, in order to facilitate the graphic demonstration let us assume that it is levied on the producer. The tax affecting each unit of drugs sold increases the price of P_0 to P'. The line *MPC* is displaced upward and a new equilibrium is established at E' for a quantity sold q'. The social gain ($E'cE_0$) is equal to the reduction of harm (surface area $aE'cE_0$) – reduction of the consumer surplus ($P_0P'E'E_0$) plus the product of the tax ($P_0P'E'$a).

Niskanen (1962), in a study of alcohol consumption, held that the Pigou correction of externalities ought to permit satisfaction of two conditions, that of optimality and that of equity. First, the tax rate ought to be set at a level such that the price paid (faced) by the consumer reflects the real marginal cost (private cost plus external cost) of his consumption. In this way, the tax would reduce consumption to its optimal level and would minimize the consumer's bad allocation of resources between drugs and other products. This condition is indispensable to achieve an optimum because it guarantees a complete internalization of external costs by the market.

Second, total tax revenue ought to be equal to the total social cost of consumption. That way, consumers would pay exactly what their choice costs society. This second condition permits a reduction of the inequality between drug consumers and non-consumers. It is not essential to achieve an optimum but reflects the objective of equity.

The pursuit of optimality requires that the rate imposed on each unit of drugs consumed be equal to the marginal social cost of the quantity of drugs consumed. But, as Figure 4.1 shows, the marginal external cost

(*MEC*) increases with consumption, which is logical since drugs are of greater concern when use is pervasive. One should note, however, that the tax rate is only equal to the marginal external cost for the last unit of drugs consumed. For all the other units, the tax rate is higher than the marginal external cost. The tax rate that permits consumption reduction to q' corresponds to a total external cost represented by obq' (or $P_0E'a$). The revenue generated by this tax is equal to the surface area $P_0P'E'a$. Thus, the taxes paid are twice as high as the total external cost.

The Pigou taxation of drugs therefore permits achievement of a social optimum but at the expense of equity and, as it happens, of drug consumers. An optimal and equitable policy would require a variable tax where each unit consumed is taxed at a level equal to the total external cost, which is impossible to implement.

A mathematical approach

In a world composed of n_1 non-drug-consuming individuals and of n_2 firms who exchange m goods. Among these goods, some are drugs and engender externalities. We note:

c_{ij}	the consumption of merchandise i by the consumer j ($i = 1, \ldots, m$) and j ($i, \ldots, n_1$)
q_{ik}	the production of merchandise i by the producer k ($k = 1, \ldots, n_2$)
r_1	the total quantity of goods available
$U^j(c_{1j}, c_{2j}, \ldots, c_{mj}, E_j)$	the utility function of the consumer j incurs an externality E_j due to the presence of drug traffic,
$F^k(q_{1k}, q_{2k}, \ldots, q_{mk}, E_k)$	the production function of firm k emitting externality E_k as a joint product. We suppose that the only 'polluting' enterprises are the dealers whose activity creates an externality. The entirety of production is then defined by $F^k(q_{1k} \ldots, q_{mk}, E_k) \leq 0$ or $q_{ik} \leq 0$ when merchandise i is used as input by firm k and $q_{ik} \geq 0$ is one of its outputs.

We suppose that the utility functions representing the system of consumer preferences are endowed with the usual properties.

The externalities emitted by the dealers are linked to the externalities absorbed by the victims as per the relation:

$$\forall_j \, E_j = \sum_k E_k$$

The search for a Pareto optimum comes back to the maximization of the utility of an ordinary agent; agent 1 under the constraint that the other

agents do not incur losses of well-being and under technological constraints and availability of resources.

$$
\left\{
\begin{array}{l}
\max U^1\,(c_{11},c_{21},\ldots,c_{m1},E_1 \\
\quad U^j(c_{1j},c_{2j},c_{2j},\ldots,c_{mj},E_j = \overline{U^j}\ \forall j = 2,\ldots,n_1\ (\lambda_j) \\
\quad F^k(q_{1k},q_{2k},\ldots,q_{mk},E_k = 0\ \forall k = 1,\ldots,n_2\ (\lambda_k) \\[2mm]
sc.\ \ \sum_j c_{ij} - \sum_k q_{ik} < r_i\ \forall i = 1,\ldots,m\ (\mu_i) \\[3mm]
\quad E_j = \alpha_j \sum_k E_k\ \ \alpha_j = 1\ \forall \alpha_j\ or\ \sum_j \alpha_j = 1
\end{array}
\right\}
$$

The Lagrangian of this programme is written:

$$
1 = U^1(c_{11},c_{21},\ldots,c_{m1},\sum_k E_k) + \sum_j \lambda_j\left[U^j(c_{1j},c_{2j},\ldots,c_{mj},\sum_k E_k) - \overline{U^j}\right]
$$
$$
- \sum_k \lambda_k(F^k(q_{1k},q_{2k},\ldots,q_{mk},E_k) - \sum_i u_i\left(\sum_j c_{ij} - \sum_k q_{ik} - r_i\right)
$$

where the λ_j, λ_k, μ_i are the Lagrange multipliers associated with the different constraints.

$$
\frac{\partial 1}{\partial c_{ij}} = \lambda_j\,\frac{\partial U^j}{\partial c_{ij}} - \mu_j = 0
$$

$$
\frac{\partial 1}{\partial q_{ik}} = \lambda_k\,\frac{\partial F^k}{\partial q_{ik}} - \mu_i = 0
$$

$$
\frac{\partial 1}{\partial E_k} = \sum_j \lambda_j \partial_j \frac{\partial U^j}{\partial E_j} - \lambda_k \frac{\partial F^k}{\partial E_k} = 0
$$

The last condition expresses the fact that at optimum the marginal cost of
the reduction of externalities be equal, for each dealer, to the marginal
damage he creates.

From a Pigouvian point of view, it would be possible to correct the
externalities by establishig a tax t on the dealers' production. From that
moment on, the latter would have to maximize their profit by following
the programme:

$$
\max_{\{q_{1k}, q_{2k}, \ldots, q_{mk}, E_k\}} \Pi^k\,(q_{1k}, q_{2k}, \ldots, q_{mk}, E_k) = \sum_{i=1}^{m} p_i q_{ik} - t_k E_k
$$

$$
sc.
$$
$$
F^k\,(q_{1k}, q_{2k}, \ldots, q_{mk}, E_k) = 0
$$

where the conditions of first order:

$$\begin{cases} p_i = v_k \dfrac{\partial F^k}{\partial q_{ik}} \\[2ex] t_k = -v_k \dfrac{\partial F^k}{\partial E_k} \end{cases}$$

It then follows that in order to have a connection between the social and private optimums the tax must be fixed in such a way as to:

$$t_k = -\sum_j \lambda_j \alpha_j \frac{\partial U_j}{\partial E_j} \mid E_j = E_j^* \text{ with } \frac{\partial U_j}{\partial E_j} \le 0$$

The optimal unit tax which should be imposed on each dealer then corresponds to the sum of marginal damage created by his externality, evaluated at optimum and expressed in monetary terms via the inverse of marginal utility of revenue.

Specificity of an illegal market

The Pigou model must now be adapted to the case of the drug market (Boyum, 1992). In an illegal market, the tax is not actually collected by the State. We will consider, therefore, that suppression constitutes a tax that increases the effective marginal private cost P to P'. This is because suppression increases the time spent looking for drugs and the disutility of arrest or victimization. Consumer surplus diminishes by a quantity represented by the surface area $P_0 P' E' E_0$ (Figure 4.1). The harm is reduced by an amount equivalent to the surface area $q'bdq_0$ (or $aE'cE_0$). The variation in welfare is equal to $E'cE_0 - P_0 P' E'a$.

The two major differences from the legal market are linked. On the one hand, in a legal market the Pigou tax is imposed (in theory) without cost and brings in money for the State. In an illegal market, suppression is costly to implement and brings in no money for the State. The conditions of optimality are thus slightly modified in an illegal market.

At the optimum, suppression ought to be set at such a level that the price faced by the consumer reflects the true marginal cost (private cost plus external cost) of his consumption. In this way, suppression would internalize the externalities and would reduce consumption to its optimal level. The cost of an optimal suppressive public policy would therefore be such that the last dollar spent on suppression would generate an equivalent reduction in the social cost of drugs; that is, the marginal cost of suppression would be equal to the marginal benefit expressed in terms of marginal reduction of social cost.

Note that the standard model exposed is in partial contradiction with the very foundations of prohibitionist choice. We have seen that prohibition finds its justification in the desire to protect the consumer from himself. This paternalistic vision is in contradiction with the definition of equilibrium which states that it is normal for the consumer to internalize these costs. This legitimate approach to drug consumption only seems to be a problem as long as the externalities are not internalized, while prohibition is based on an absolute rejection of drug consumption independent of those who assume the cost. This debate thus reveals that the basis and methods of public policy are in opposition. Another problem arises, if, in addition to optimality, the public policy-maker pursues an objective of equity, as Niskanen (1962) formulated it; in this case, he should set a suppression level proportional to the consumption level. Yet, in practical terms, the gradation of sanctions incurred by the consumers only partially satisfies this requirement of proportionality. Moreover, on the contrary, the least seasoned consumer is sometimes the one whose probability of arrest is greatest, which contradicts the theoretical recommendation.

Even if the policy-maker is content to pursue only the optimality objective, difficulties remain. In concrete terms, the policy-maker should be in a position to implement a suppression policy that would create a cost sufficient to compel the participants in the drug market to modify their behaviour and curb their drug consumption to an optimal level.

Another major problem lies in the fact that nothing proves that social cost actually diminishes with an increase in suppression, as the Pigou model requires. Indeed, we can on the contrary, consider that the condition of illegality and precariousness into which consumers are plunged increases with suppression, thus engendering a sharp increase (instead of a reduction) in social cost. Where drugs are concerned, the externalities are not linked in a one-to-one correspondence to the level of consumption. In contrast with the case of pollution, which, according to economic analysis, increases with the quantity produced, the externalities tied to drugs stem from the psychotherapeutic properties of the products and increase with the quantity consumed. In addition, they result from the conditions of implementing the law, which affects social cost in a complex manner. In some cases, the increase in suppression leads to a reduction in consumption (and thus in social cost), and in other cases it provokes, for example, a substitution of methods of consuming heroin from inhalation to injection and therefore an increase in social cost.

Therefore, if the suppression policy contributes to an increase in external social cost (crime, increase in communicable diseases, etc.), the tax imposed on consumers by suppression gives rise to an increase in crime and small-scale trafficking to finance consumption. As a result, the tax is not paid by the drug consumer or by the producer; rather, it is transferred to society as a whole, and therefore does not lead to a reduction in drug consumption.

Repressive public intervention can thus be a factor in the increase in social cost, notwithstanding any reduction or stabilization of quantities consumed that it induces. It is therefore plausible that the expenditure incurred in implementing a public policy can in fact be higher than the benefits created by a reduced consumption, and can render useless the efforts undertaken, unless there is a proportional reduction in social cost.

These different observations lead us to conclude that the socially optimal level of drug consumption is difficult for economists to calculate, and that even the question of what measures to take to approach this optimal level is infinitely more complex to determine in an illegal drug market than in a the traditional one. Public intervention based on the 'optimal correction of externalities' is therefore, in the end, too imprecise to form a serious base for public policy. It is impossible to reliably determine the total amount of resources we would need to devote to suppression of drug consumption and trafficking using the equalization rule of the marginal benefit of consumption reduction and the marginal cost of measures employed.

Modification of consumer preferences

Technically drug prohibition consists in trying to move to the right the consumer demand line. Another strategy is possible: attempt to provoke this movement to the right, trying to modify the economic agents' preferences. The objective is still that of attaining the optimal consumption level, but the method of achieving this differs. This reminds us that suppression does not constitute the only means for obtaining a so-called optimal level of drug consumption. Other approaches, resting partly on the hope of modifying agent preferences such as treatment and prevention, are possible.

First, treatment does not fall exactly within the same analytical framework as suppression, because it is concerned not only with reducing drug consumption but also with treating the consequences of consumption. Treatments can sometimes aim at abstinence and sometimes rehabilitation without any clear objective concerning consumption level. For some reason, treatment policy is more directly aimed at the minimization of drug social cost, which is a more tangible improvement.

Second, drug prevention programmes are aimed at discouraging drug use (primary prevention). Secondary prevention is persuading occasional users from becoming regular users; it therefore has an effect on consumption similar to that of suppression. These programmes are aimed at modifying agent preferences by increasing their knowledge in such a way that the demand curve shifts. In Figure 4.2, the line DD describes consumer demand for drugs before an educational programme is implemented, and the line DD', after its implementation. DD intersects the consumer's marginal private cost (MCC) at E_0; thus the quantity consumed is q_0. For this quantity of drug, the marginal external cost (MEC) is added to the marginal private cost to obtain the marginal social cost (MSC). When individual preferences are modified by the anti-drug programme, the new

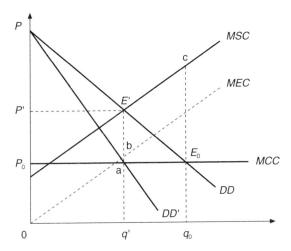

Figure 4.2 Preference shaping and optimal condition

quantity consumed q' corresponds to the social optimum defined by the intersection of DD' and MCC. The social gain ($E'cE_0$) is equal to the reduction of harm (surface area defined by $aE'cE_0$) – the reduction of the consumer surplus ($P_0fE_0 - P_0fa$).

The optimal allocation of public expenditure where drugs are concerned would require that the policy-maker invests in educational programmes to the point where the marginal reduction of social cost becomes lower than the marginal cost of the educational programme. At the equilibrium, no reallocation of expenditures between suppression and prevention is possible since each dollar is being spent efficiently.

Again, the implementation of such a policy is complex. Some public programmes that combat drugs through education do not appear as directly targeting drugs. When a town conducts a campaign to promote sports, it is influencing the behaviour of potential or actual drug consumers. Yet, these expenditures are not counted as public expenditures devoted to the drug problem. In fact, only secondary prevention, that is, measures centred on current drug users, shows up as being clearly drug-oriented. Without being able to clearly identify the resources actually devoted to the fight against drugs through prevention, economic analysis is not of much use in determining the optimal amount of these expenditures.

The search for the optimal amount of public expenditure required for reaching an optimal level of drug consumption proves to be futile. The tools of economic analysis do, however, constitute a framework that is well adapted to the study of interactions among policies and behaviour of drug market participants. We must not, however, expect that these tools will allow us to provide precise instructions regarding the amount and manner of public expenditure for prevention and suppression. Taxation of other externalities is already very imprecise, but in the case of drugs, illegality further complicates the task. Anyway, the very idea that the pursuit of collective welfare can be accomplished exclusively by attaining a given level of drug consumption proves to be a particularly simplistic view of the problem drugs pose for society. Indeed, several levels of social cost can accompany a given level of consumption, depending on the form public intervention assumes. The level of consumption thus turns out to be a manifestly bad indicator for discussing the effect of public policy on collective welfare.

Crime economics: another wrong objective

Since reduction of consumption constitutes only a very imperfect means of reducing the social cost of drugs, the next strategy available is that of reducing the crimes that constitute violations of the drug laws. It is indeed tempting to consider that offences against drug laws might be brought to a level that would correspond to the minimization of the social cost of crime. The difference between the two approaches (optimal consumption and optimal sanction) lies in the fact that in the first case, improvement in welfare is accomplished by reducing drug consumption, and in the second, by reducing the level of criminality. This second approach was developed by Becker (1968), among others.

These authors consider that an individual engages in criminal activity as the result of a rational calculation. The level of criminality therefore depends on the equilibrium existing between positive and negative incentives to commit crimes. Although the term did not exist at all at the time, the Becker's approach (1968) falls within the category of the 'Principal–agent' model. The criminal is the agent for whom the crimes and offences constitute an optimal response to both positive (gain) and negative (sanction) incentives, the latter being determined by the government (the principal). The government selects the number of penalties imposed on arrested criminals, while the amount of resources devoted to the fight against crime determines the probability of arrest. We note that the fact that Becker favours public action focused on sanction rather than on the probability of arrest does not mean that he considers the latter as fixed but rather that he observes, with good reason, that it is less costly for society to increase sanctions than to increase the probability of detecting criminal activities.

Several empirical articles attempt to corroborate the Beckerian thesis that raising penalties reduces criminal activity (Ehrlich, 1975; Witte, 1980; Layson, 1985; Grogger, 1991). On the other hand, other contributions try to invalidate it (Myers, 1983; Cover and Thistle, 1988; Cornwell and Trumbull, 1994). The surveys by Pyle (1983) and Cameron (1988) provide a good overview of this literature. In order to confine ourselves to recent publications, we note that Marvell and Moody (1994) estimate that a 10 per cent increase in the prison population reduces crime by 1.6 per cent; Spelman's (1994) results confirm this finding. For his part, Levitt (1995) establishes that a 10 per cent rise in the number of detainees reduces crime by 4–6 per cent. Let us also mention the very controversial contribution of Zedlwski (1987). This author asks himself whether imprisonment pays 'at the margin'. His study shows that the benefits of imprisonment exceed costs of imprisonment by 17 to 1. The validity of all these studies hinges on how they theorize the number of crimes attributed to each criminal imprisoned. Zedlwski considers that each prisoner committed about 18 crimes a year. For an average number of crimes that is clearly lower (12–15), the cost–benefit ratio of imprisonment is always greater than one but falls below that for more occasional criminals (Dilulio and Piehl, 1991). It is also necessary to consider other forms of punishment likely to lower the cost of suppression (house arrest, electronic surveillance, etc.).

Choosing an effective policy

The law forbids trafficking and consumption of drugs, and sanctions those who do not respect it; it remains to be determined whether the policy-maker ought to pursue the objective of completely eradicating all forms of drug consumption, or, on the contrary, of tolerating a certain level. To simplify our presentation and remove the delicate problems posed by the addictive nature of drugs, we will devote our presentation of the theories of crime economics to drug trafficking rather than to consumption.

The optimal level of criminality

Infractions of drug laws are a source of externalities. The role of the law is to dissuade individuals from violating these laws in a manner that is sufficiently effective that the level of residual criminality corresponds to the theoretically 'optimal' level. In Figure 4.3, the ordinates measure the costs and benefits, and the abscissa, the frequency of criminal activity consisting of violation of the drug laws. The line *MB* describes the marginal benefit that an additional criminal action brings to its perpetrator. One assumes that the marginal benefit to the trafficker declines with the frequency of his acts, therefore, *MB* is falling. The second line represented on the graph, *SC*, describes the marginal cost imposed on society by drug traffickers. This cost is equal to the probability that an additional legal violation causes harm to society multiplied by the extent of this harm. The more the frequency of crime increases, the more the social cost grows; the line *SC* therefore rises.

As long as legal violations are fairly infrequent, the social cost imposed on society is lower than the benefit that drug traffickers derive from them.

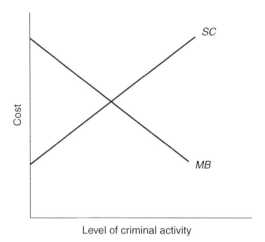

Figure 4.3 Social cost of crime

Indeed, the traffickers impose an involuntary transfer onto society. The line *MB* describes the value of what traffickers levy on society and the line *SC* indicates the value for society of their levy. As long as *MB* is lower than *SC*, the collective welfare rises with the frequency of legal violations. This is because the benefit the traffickers draw from their activity exceeds the social cost that they impose on other citizens. When the *SC* curve passes above the *MB* curve, the optimal level of crime q is exceeded.[2] Below a frequency q, violations of drug laws bring in more for their perpetrators than they cost society. For theoreticians of the economics of crime these violations are therefore socially 'positive'. The objective of public policy must therefore be to reduce trafficking to its most efficient level: that is to say to the level at which the social cost becomes higher than the benefit to traffickers.

Optimal sanctions

How can criminal policy arrive at offering incentives to individuals to renounce their criminality? The economics of crime considers that the sanctions (prison and fines) constitute a cost that, multiplied by the probability of arrest, must be sufficient to dissuade the traffickers and not engender an implementation cost higher than the social benefit that the society as a whole draws from the reduction in trafficking.

Let q be the optimal frequency at which one must tolerate drug trafficking. Unfortunately, traffickers are insensitive to the social cost that they impose on society and behave as if the line SC_1 gave the social cost, so they increase the frequency of trafficking to q_1. The marginal benefit for the traffickers of a frequency of q_1 is lower than the social cost. Everything functions as if traffickers were insensitive to the harm they cause. Before examining how to modify the perception that they have of their behaviour, it is worthwhile to understand the source of this distorted perception. The answer can be broken down into several parts.

First, even though the traffickers engender a social cost, only some of them are arrested. In fact, individuals do not react as a function of the harm their behaviour inflicts on others, but rather as a function of how this harm can affect them, as in their being arrested. Second, since the offender can be indifferent to the harm caused to others, the economic role of criminal policy is therefore to propose a sanction that permits individuals to measure the exact harm that their behaviour engenders, not through the biased perception they have of the fate of others but through the more lucid perception they have of the harm their behaviour is causing themselves. In this sense, the criminal policy forces individuals to internalize the externalities they engender. In Figure 4.4, we can observe that imposing a sanction on traffickers displaces the social cost curve from SC_1 to SC, an amount equal to the vertical distance between the curves, or segment AB. In theory, suppression permits reduction of deviant behaviour to its optimal level q.[3] Thanks to this reasoning, economic analysis advocates increasing the anticipated fine to the point where the gain from suppression exceeds its cost. This process is interrupted when the last offence avoided costs more to avoid than the net harm it would have caused.

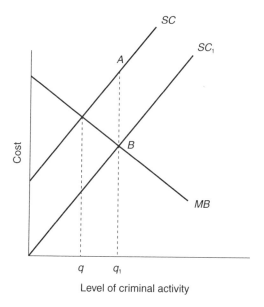

Figure 4.4 Optimal level of crime

104 The welfare economics of illegal drugs

Formally, risk-neutral individuals choose whether to commit an act that benefits the actor by b and harms the rest of society by h. The policy-maker does not know any individual's b but knows the distribution of parties by type described by a uniform distribution with support $[0.1]$ and a cumulative distribution b. It is hypothesized that $h>1$, so that the offences are not socially beneficial. The social planner chooses a fine or a length of imprisonment f, the probability of detection and conviction p is constant, and c is a cost parameter indicating expenditure for suppression. The objective function to be maximized is the sum of the individual's benefits minus the harm caused by his acts and enforcement costs. One can assume that the sanction is without cost to impose and collect. Risk-neutral individuals commit an offence if and only if $b=pf$. Given the individual's decision to be honest or dishonest, the social utility is $W = \dfrac{1}{pf}(b-h)\ db - c.$

The social planner maximizes the welfare function in f (severity of punishment). When the sanction is a fine, f^* cannot exceed F, the wealth of the agent. The optimal fine is maximum, and the probability of detection satisfies $p^*F = h - c/F.$[4] The expected sanction $pf^* = h$ is equal to the harm. Individuals commit crimes only if their gain exceeds their sanction, which is the first order of behaviour. This initial result is interesting: it shows that the optimal sanction – that is, the sanction (taking into account the suppression budget) that maximizes society's welfare – is greater than the harm created.[5] Since increasing the probability of detection is expensive, it is preferable to increase the sanctions. To be sure, this reasoning has limitations; indeed, one could be tempted to recommend proposing a probability of detection of almost zero and an infinite sanction. Obviously, fine collection is limited by the wealth of the potential criminals and the prison term by life expectancy. Sanctions in the form of fines therefore cannot exceed the seizable portion of their wealth; the mechanism thus reaches its limit. The maximum feasible sanction is F, which can be interpreted as the maximum wealth of the individual. One should therefore take into account that they will not be able to pay more than F, and as a consequence, increase the probability of arresting them. To do this the policy-maker can increase public expenditure for suppression. The expenditure for detection and conviction to arrive at a probability p are represented by cp, where $c>O$ is a cost parameter. Under these conditions, the social planner maximizes the welfare function in f (severity of punishment) and p (probability of punishment) subject to $O=f=F$. The optimal fine is the maximum fine. The optimal probability of detection and conviction satisfies $p^*F = h-c/F.$

The policy-maker must therefore increase public expenditure for suppression to the point where it permits attaining the optimal probability of crime detection: that is, when the marginal crime benefit reduction engendered by the suppression is equal to the marginal suppression cost. In other words, it is not necessary to spend more for suppression at the margin than that which will improve collective welfare.

Implementation difficulties

The Beckerian approach sets the rules that are supposed to enable society to maximize its welfare in the fight against crime. To attain the optimum, society has only to increase its expenditure for crime control to the point where the marginal dollar spent (adjusted by the 'welfare loss' to collect the same dollar by taxation) produces a marginal reduction in the social cost of equivalent crime. Society should therefore allocate to crime a sum of expenditures such that the marginal cost of the expenditures does not exceed the discounted marginal benefit. This calculation requires the collection of data that is difficult to generate, such as the positive variation of the social cost engendered by the increase in the number of crimes. In the absence of being able to carry out such a marginal calculation, most of the empirical studies are content to evaluate the average cost of crime and compare it with expenditure devoted to reducing it. Such simplification deprives these empirical studies of the microeconomic foundation that constitutes the originality of the Becker thesis, and considerably limits their reach.

Are traffickers 'risk lovers'?

An individual is described as a 'risk lover' if he has a weak preference for the present and feels ready to question it for gains whose expected utility is lower than expected gain. Stated another way, between the certitude of honest pay of $10 and the probability of one chance in two of a successful drug delivery that brings $20, an individual neutral to risk hesitates and a 'risk lover' accepts. The fact that individuals are 'risk lovers' makes it obligatory to increase sanctions to achieve a dissuasive effect of criminal policy identical to that in a population neutral to risk. In absolute terms, let us assume that a guaranteed penalty of one year in prison $p = 1$ punishing trafficking is equivalent to a penalty of 20 years with a probability of 20 per cent. If the risk in itself does not constitute a source of disutility for the individual, then the individual being less severe than the first will perceive the second solution. This indicates that some individuals ('risk lovers') will violate laws more easily than anticipated, as they do not integrate the disutility of risk into their calculation. Moreover, as Shavell and Polinsky (2000) point out, the disutility associated with risk for those who violate the law constitutes a cost. The cost for someone who breaks the law must be subtracted from the expected sanction because in this way society can save on the expense of suppression. In other words, traffickers who are 'risk lovers' would have to be sentenced more severely than others because they renounce crime only for a higher-than-normal risk and thus do not achieve any economy for society. Becker himself pointed out in his 1968 article that if certain individuals were 'risk lovers', a 1 per cent increase in the probability of being arrested would have a more significant preventive effect than an identical increase in the severity of the penalty.

These few observations prompt us to wonder about the behaviour of drug traffickers. One must guard against misinterpreting the notion of 'risk lover', since it indicates nothing about the psychological relationship that individuals have with risk, but rather describes their relationship with money. It is plausible to simultaneously love paragliding and to conclude that in these conditions the individual is 'risk adverse' without being particularly prudent. Thus there is no basis for considering that traffickers are 'risk lovers'. It is also plausible that a number of them prefer to cancel a transaction rather than run even a very slight risk of losing money. They would thus be somewhat 'risk adverse'. We do not have sufficient data on which to base a particularly severe punitive policy against drug traffickers based on their behavioural characteristics and the recommendations of crime economics.

A similar complication focuses on the question of determining whether, if we suppose that drug traffickers of a certain level are wealthier than the average criminal, it would be normal to impose higher than normal fines on them. Indeed, when individuals possess differing incomes, the effect of a potential fine is not the same for all. Moreover, if money has a marginal utility that declines with the wealth of individuals,[6] then the same combination of fine and probability 'costs' less for a wealthy person than for a poor one. And yet, some individuals can be more sensitive to the stigmatizing effect of a criminal sanction than others, and this stigmatizing effect can depend on whether the combination of sanctions is composed of a fine or a prison term. From a theoretical point of view, these observations suggest that the same sanction-probability combining does not have the same effect on two different individuals. In other words, it is impossible to efficiently impose the same cost on two different persons to compel them to internalize their externalities. 'Risk adverse' individuals are less tempted to commit crimes than others. On the other hand, reducing the sanction-probability combination in order to incorporate this finding implies that individuals who are less 'risk adverse' and have no reputation to protect can engage in criminal activities when such activity would not be acceptable to others.[7] Discovering the optimal level of dissuasion is therefore particularly complex.

Average and marginal dissuasion

In some circumstances, a trafficker may face the choice of committing one criminal act or several. For example, he can be content with importing drugs, or with importing them and protecting them by firing at the police. To discourage traffickers from resorting to the most serious crimes, it is advisable that sanctions increase with the seriousness of the crime; we thus speak of 'marginal dissuasion'. Moreover, everything else being equal, according to crime economics, it is socially beneficial for marginal dissuasion to succeed in curbing those for whom average dissuasion has not prevented criminal activity, or from choosing methods of activity that are very harmful to society. It would thus be advisable that sanctions increase relative to the harm engendered, which would imply that the majority of other sanctions are not maximum sanctions. One thus observes a conflict between the general imperative of dissuasion and that of marginal dissuasion. The intention to permit the possibility of raising sanctions in increments can lead to a situation where the average sanction is lower than the harm caused.

The economics of crime suggest an escape from this dilemma by suggesting to public authorities that they increase enforcement agency budgets in order to increase the likelihood of crime detection. In fact, it would be worthwhile to be able to specifically increase the probability of crime detection for those crimes that are accompanied by *modi operandi* causing the most harm. Up to now we have generally used the assumption that the probability of crime detection was fixed, or identical regardless of the crime. This idea conforms to the fact that a policeman in charge of traffic control can discover a significant quantity of drugs during a routine traffic stop. From this standpoint, the general rule that states that it is desirable to reduce the probability of detection and to increase sanctions can be challenged. To be sure, reducing the probability of detection does reduce the cost of maintaining the legal system. But the probability of detection for the most serious crimes would be decreased to the same extent as minor offences. It is therefore probable that the social loss due to the substantial harm caused by serious crimes more than offsets the benefits of budgetary savings. Thus, two paths open up. Either we must forget about reducing the probability of crime detection and assume the expenditure that such a policy involves, or we must specialize suppression by targeting a particular type of offence. When applied to the case of drug trafficking, this dilemma implies the need for a better analysis of the harm caused by this type of crime. If it proves to have a high social cost, then a powerful economic argument can be made to justify the specialization of suppression agencies. Not only would this be cost effective, but it would also permit achieving the same level of dissuasion by making only the means of detecting a particular form of criminality more severe, rather than increasing the average penalty (Shavell, 1992).

Can one predict the reaction of agents to incentives?

The economics of crime do not have the total support of specialists in criminality. Several objections have in particular been raised as to the basis of the behavioural hypotheses employed by this school. The case of part-time criminals, frequent among small-scale drug dealers (Reuter, 1991), constitutes a typical example of the questions raised. Indeed, when a criminal engages in an illegal activity, the interplay of positive and negative incentives can be disrupted by conflicts between the two sources of income, and a substitution of one by the other. As with the mechanism well known in macroeconomics of 'real cash balance', the increase in suppression can paradoxically lead a 'risk loving' criminal to increase the time he devotes to his criminal activity in order to keep his criminal income constant (Ehrlich, 1981, 1996).

Witte and Tauchen (1994) found that the majority of criminal offences are not premeditated. Therefore, they say we have to reject the Beckerian thesis that says that individuals choose the amount of time they grant to their criminal activities, substituting instead the idea that individuals set 'a level of criminal activity'. The profile of the penalties to minimize social cost must therefore be reconsidered by taking this aspect into account. Even more problematic, Witte and Tauchen maintain that only individuals who are capable of planning for the future can fear prison. But criminals are generally not capable of this, which would render them almost impervious to modifications of incentive parameters and would weaken the central thesis of crime economics. These two authors also point out that one must consider the non-monetary gains of crime: for instance, the pleasure obtained from violence that increases crime benefit and thus operates in favour of increasing the penalties. Dilulio (1996), for his part, points out that incarceration can be perceived as a promotion for some gang members, which also has the effect of disrupting a determination of the optimal level of prison terms aimed at discouraging crime. Finally, crime economics do not take into account the agents' strategic behaviour, and in particular, their capacity to organize for the purpose of responding as a group to the challenges of authorities. In the case of drug trafficking, Moore (1973), who studied the methods of heroin distribution on the New York market, stresses that the illegality of the transactions affects opportunity costs that confront the agents. In his view, the behaviour of agents is explained not by their reaction to cost variations provoked by new tactics of law enforcement, but by their strategic choices aimed, above all, at ensuring that transactions run smoothly.

Moore emphasizes that drug traffickers' utility depends not only on their profits, but also on their capacity to overcome the risks inherent in their trade. When the market is subjected to an increase in suppression, it is mastery over incertitude and not profit maximization that constitutes the principle of market reorganization. If one pursues such an analysis, the system of cost incentives advocated by crime economics would prove incapable of properly steering the agents' behaviour. Nothing allows us to predict whether the increased cost inflicted on candidates for a criminal career effectively contributes to limiting their activities. This latter perspective, taken up again by 'neo-institutionalists' such as Turvani

(1994), will not fail to bring new developments. Along the lines of a similar idea, Akerlof and Yellen (1994) propose taking into consideration the population's reaction to the increase in police pressure on underprivileged neighbourhoods, which once again has the effect of complicating the interplay of incentives that are supposed to induce a reduction in criminal behaviour.

Last but not least, it is worth returning once more to the objective set by Becker for criminal policy: minimizing the social cost of crime. This objective can appear to be rather limited and offer no guarantee of the respect of equity among individuals, of basic liberties, or of human rights that would issue from implementation of Becker's recommendations. In an area as sensitive as criminal justice, this aspect of crime economics, which, by the way, is appropriate for all normative policy, explains the contentiousness of the controversy. The narrowness of the normative objective of minimizing social cost is particularly difficult to accept when it is applied to the periphery of the market economy (crime, family). Ehrlich (1996) noted, in defence of crime economics, that it is always possible to widen the function of social welfare to include other objectives (reduction of the risk of miscarriages of justice, humanism, etc.). Such a broadening would allow us to consider the more complex preferences. On the other hand, by distancing himself from the precepts of welfare economics, he deprives the theory of some of its normative power, which thus requires an evaluation in concrete terms. It would be particularly beneficial to know if the addition of an objective complementary to economic efficiency reflects the preferences of the policy-makers, of society, or of its elected representatives.

Conclusion

The different normative approaches (optimal consumption and optimal sanction) agree on one point: the pursuit of efficiency does not lead to a recommendation to eradicate trafficking and drug consumption. This is directly affirmed by the Pigou approach, which argues that an optimal level of drugs ought to exist on the market, and indirectly by the school of crime economics, which recommends not attempting to reduce criminality below its optimal level and thus to let drugs circulate. The difficulties arise when it comes to determining a public policy that allows us to realize one of these objectives.

The public policy-maker can allot a more or less significant sum to suppression (and to prevention) in the drug market. But he is playing a game of billiards. In this game a ball that strikes the same point on the cushion twice in a row is not directed twice at the same objective if the player puts a different spin on it. The policy-maker is in the same situation. Once the amount of public expenditure has been set, he knows that depending on how it is divided up among the large agencies and the methods of implementation practised, the effects on the level of drugs in circulation will vary. According to Pigou, or Becker, the idea of reducing illegal drug market activity to its optimal level runs into serious difficulties of implementation that do not allow a precise definition of the outline of public policies necessary to accomplish the normative objective of efficiency. Incidentally, the very idea that the pursuit of collective welfare can be exclusively accomplished by attaining a given level of drug consumption or of crime turns out to be a particularly simplistic approach to the problem posed by drugs to society, since an identical level of consumption or of lawbreaking can be accompanied by several levels of social cost.

In spite of the limitations we have mentioned, the tools for normative economic analysis still turn out to be extremely useful to illustrate the interaction between agent behaviour in the drug market and their environment, particularly in terms of price and incentives provided by the law and its implementation. Several elements must still be improved in order to make economics a truly operational tool as far as public policy choices are concerned; we will attempt to move in this direction by more concretely evaluating the policies actually implemented in the sphere of drugs.

5   A new design for drug policy

Introduction

Drug policy cannot be reduced to the search for a hypothetical optimal consumption level any more than it can an efficient crime level. What is the normative objective that should be established in public drug policy? There is no need to be very innovative in answering this question, as economists systematically make efficiency the objective. The search for efficiency seems shocking when applied to the area of social policy: it is, however, intertwined with the objective of minimizing the social cost of drugs, and thus solidly establishes the basis for those policies aimed at harm reduction.

Minimization of drug's social cost is thus the objective of drug policy, but we still need to define and measure this celebrated social cost. Health economics, and particularly studies on 'cost of illness', permit such a calculation. Reassuring because they put a figure on a problem, these studies are not unanimously accepted. To measure social drug cost, it is necessary to give a monetary value to lives lost due to consumption and drug traffic.

How do we assign a price to human life? How do we rate the pain and suffering felt by people close to the victims? Aside from these technical problems, to make an operational instrument of the concept of social cost, it is still necessary to disaggregate the formula in order to consider the contradictory effects of a measure on the total aggregate. Therein lies one of the greatest difficulties in the matter of drugs: one public action can simultaneously cause an increase in certain elements of social cost and a decrease in others. Therefore, not only is the total result undetermined, but more importantly, some social groups benefit from the public policy while others suffer from it.

This last remark provides us with the transition necessary to raise a question that reflects the economic framework of public policy: who are the winners and losers when a policy is adopted? We know that the objective of economic efficiency may be attained by an infinite number of allocations of social resources. Effectively, a multitude of repartitions will permit maximization of the level of wealth, but each of these leads to a certain distribution of resources, situated between two goals: a totally egalitarian distribution and fundamentally non-egalitarian one. More specifically, to illustrate, if we limit ourselves to the examination of arbitration between two groups of individuals – the non-consumers of drugs and the drug consumers – the heart of the problem in the creation of drug policy consists in knowing whether the principal beneficiaries of the policy should be the first or the second group. In practice, many groups of actors have a vested interest in drug policy, and thus the public policy-maker must subtly negotiate the fact that any public action relating to social cost, even a neutral one, benefits certain groups and penalizes others. Second, the same public action may affect external factors generated by drugs and thus the social cost in two directions. So, in the best scenario, total social cost will decrease (or else the measure must be rejected), but, once again, there will be beneficiaries and victims of this public action. We should then calmly accept the fact that public policy is not only a vector of efficiency, but also a powerful force in regulating the distribution of wealth.

Harm minimization and efficiency

Public discussion about public drug policy is often somewhat evasive as far as objectives are concerned. Inversely, pure economic theory affirms rather directly that the objective of public policy should always be the search for economic efficiency, and most often contents itself with testing whether the means used are appropriate to this end. This approach often makes the members of neighbouring disciplines smile. The political analysts always point out, and rightly so, that if the objectives of public policy are generally so vague and so malleable it is precisely because, contrary to what economists wish, the objectives have developed simultaneously with the means to achieve them. This naïvete of normative analysis is obvious. This branch of economics is simply interested in describing that which would be the 'right' decision in an abstract world, but one guided by economic imperative. Thus it is not the naïvete of this approach that should be criticized, but rather its object, and we do not do that. On the other hand, the positive current of economic analysis is spared, as its preoccupations more directly rejoin those of other social sciences. Their partisans ask themselves directly about modalities, upon which the decisions are actually made in the real world. However, the real world is generally compared to an abstract world where economic efficiency reigns, which tends to bring the two branches of the discipline closer together in order to put out the critics' fire. Despite its fairly abstract nature, the normative approach has, at least in our eyes, one essential virtue: it forces the economist to discover and clearly state the public policy-maker's implicit objective, which the latter generally avoids doing, and this permits the comparison of the legitimacy of this objective in the light of simple economic efficiency.

Drug prohibition complicates the economic design of public policy. If we try to adhere to the traditional tenets of microeconomics and recommend following the objective of economic efficiency, we must not forget to point out that this does not constitute a first but a second-best optimum. This fundamental difference, to which we will return, indicates that drug policy attempts to reach economic efficiency within a framework distorted by an institutional limitation: drug prohibition. Once the framework of public policy is clarified (second best politics and economic efficiency objective), it then remains to evaluate the methods which should be used by the policy-maker in order to achieve this. We must then be capable of selecting the public policy which seems to be best adapted to achieving the objectives. The criterion used to choose between two policies is therefore decisive. We will illustrate this by using the criterion known as Hicks-Kaldor, the economic evaluation of public policy will lead to weighing public action by the gauge of its capacity to reduce social costs.

First-best or second-best optimum?

The drug market functions, as one would expect, following rules which are rather far removed from those of pure and perfect competition. It is only when the conditions of existence of the former (atomicity of supply and demand, free entry and exit on the market, product homogeneity, perfect information) are reunited that optimalization is spontaneously achieved by market forces alone. In more technical terms, it is what the first theorem of the economy of well-being indicates in confirming that 'all competitive equilibrium is an optimum of Pareto'. So, if the markets function competitively, the maximum of social well-being is achieved without public intervention. The fact that pure and perfect competition does not reign on the drug market does not, however, constitute a real surprise, and does not leave the economic analyst without a response. Public policy serves precisely to correct the imperfections of the market. Obviously, with drugs, as elsewhere, the first question that comes to mind is whether the best corrective public policy for market imperfections would not be simply to restore the competitive conditions.

The issue of whether to correct a distortion at its source or rather to correct its consequences through regulation is constantly debated within the economic profession. Following the first option would mean bringing the drug market as close as possible to the model of perfect competition. This would mean doing away with any form of drug prohibition and legalizing drugs. Then, all that would be left would be to ensure, as in any other sector of activity, that monopolies or barriers to entry do not restrain competition. We have already examined the question of prohibition (Chapter 3) and we have shown that it was impossible to rigorously compare the merits, in terms of well-being, of two extreme models: legalization and prohibition. We are therefore more inclined to adopt the second option and to examine the possibilities of improving the well-being of the collectivity in a pragmatic framework in which drugs are prohibited. This means correcting imbalances with legislation rather than supporting an advance towards the free market. We therefore recommend the adoption of public policies, called 'second best', which consist of looking for an optimal allocation of resources under the constraints of non-competitive behaviour. This last term designates all institutional constraints other than the initial distribution of wealth between individuals, or any form of distortion of competition, State tutorial intervention, public legislation, taxation, subsidies or transfers.

Pareto vs Hicks-Kaldor

To reach a second-best optimum, the public policy-maker has at his disposal a large enough palette of means (supply side enforcement, demand side enforcement, treatment, etc.). The economic analyst usually recommends submitting all the public policy-maker's potential actions to the Pareto test. If the measure being considered satisfies the Pareto criteria, it is because it improves collective well-being and moves closer to economic efficiency. The easiest way to relate the various efficiency concepts is to consider two particular individuals, A and B, who have utility functions $U_A(w_A)$ and $U_B(w_B)$ that are increasing in their wealth levels, w_A and w_B. Suppose further that w_A and w_B are function variable of γ, which may be thought of as a particular allocation of resources or assignment of rights. Thus, $w_A = W_A(\gamma)$ and $w_B = W_B(\gamma)$. The social problem is to choose γ efficiently. Under the Pareto efficiency concept, an action γ should be chosen to maximize the utility of U_A of one individual, say person A, subject to the constraint that the other individual, person B, achieves a minimum level utility. Formally, we can write this problem as:[1]

$$\text{maximize } U_A\left(w_A(\gamma)\right) \text{ subject to } U_B\left(w_B(\gamma)\right) \geq U_B^0 \tag{5.1}$$

The solution to this problem defines a utility possibility frontier (UPF) that gives the maximum level of U_A for all possible choices of U_B. The UPF arising from (5.1) is depicted by the curve labelled AB in Figure 5.1.

If the utility of person B is limited to level C, then the set of Pareto points superior to C is found on the segment CD. Alternatively, if the utility of person A is fixed in C, then the Pareto superior points are found on the segment CE. The ECD zone on the chart describes therefore all the Pareto points superior to C. In this zone, the two parties are at least as well off as in C. However, point F, which is not part of the Pareto points superior to C, still belongs to the Pareto-efficient points. There lies the main weakness of the Pareto concept. Although C is not Pareto-efficient and F is, it is impossible to compare (rank) these two points. Indeed, we cannot use either of the Pareto concepts to rank any two points where one

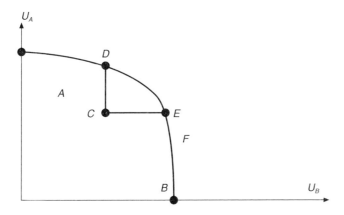

Figure 5.1 The utility possibility frontier (UPF)

party prefers one of the points and the other party prefers the other point. All points situated on the UPF are therefore incomparable. Unfortunately, most of the interesting questions in economics are constituted by propositions of public policy which permit passing between incomparable points (i.e. there are both winners and losers).[2]

The Hicks-Kaldor criteria permit us to precisely classify public policies as functions of their capacity to approach economic efficiency, even when the Pareto criteria is impractical. Let us consider points D and E in Figure 5.1. The two points are Pareto-efficient, but are not comparable as individual A is better off at point D, and individual B is better off at point E. The Hicks-Kaldor criteria class these points by asking if one is potentially superior to the other, from the Pareto point of view. If we examine the case of movement of E towards D, we ask ourselves if person A gains enough from the change to compensate B for his losses in such a way that the two parties find themselves better off after exchange. If the answer is yes, then the change D towards E is efficient in the Hicks-Kaldor sense without A compensating B. The Hicks-Kaldor criteria are generally the ones retained to discuss the efficiency of public policies. We can certainly blame it for a few things, but this does not prevent it from being the public economist's main tool.[3]

It is interesting to note a somewhat surprising result that arises with the choice of the Hicks-Kaldor criteria to evaluate public policy. Following the demonstration of Miceli (1997), we can easily show that retaining only the policies which satisfy the Hicks-Kaldor criteria creates a maximization of aggregate wealth and thus a minimization of social cost. This is interesting, as it establishes that in matters of public drug policy, the search for economic efficiency is combined with the minimization of social drug cost. It is amusing to note that outside of the economists' circle, the quest for economic efficiency – the objective of public policy in an area such as drugs, where social and sanitary preoccupations intersect – does not necessarily receive the immediate support of other social sciences. In return, the objective of minimization of social cost seems to constitute a more attractive target when in fact it is actually a reformulation of the notion of efficiency. Rewriting Equation (5.1) in the following form can illustrate this:

$$\text{maximize } U_A\ (w_A(\gamma) - T) \text{ subject to } U_B\ (w_B(\gamma) + T) \geq U^0_B \tag{5.2}$$

Where y is a reallocation, T a potential transfer of A to B (or the contrary if T is negative), and UB is the initial utility of B. In writing the Lagrangian and by choosing optimal y and T we obtain first class conditions:

$$\frac{\partial w_A}{\partial \gamma}\ U'_A(w_A(\gamma) - T) + \frac{\partial w_A}{\partial \gamma}\ U'_B(w_B(\gamma) + T) = 0 \tag{5.3}$$

$$-U'_A + \lambda U'_B = 0 \tag{5.4}$$

By substituting Equations (5.4) in (5.3) we obtain:

$$\partial w_A/\partial \gamma + \partial w_B/\partial \gamma = 0$$

which is a first-order condition for the choice of γ which maximizes $W_A(\gamma) + w_B(\gamma)$. In consequence, the economic analyst who favours retaining only the satisfactory measures of the Hicks-Kaldor criteria, will in fact recommend only those measures that increase collective well-being while minimizing the social cost, in other words, by limiting the incorrect allocation of resources. Thus, economic efficiency and reduction of social cost of drugs go together.

Social cost calculation

Evaluation of the social costs of substance abuse belongs to the classification of cost-of-illness studies (COI). Superficially a COI study involves combining an epidemiological database with financial information in order to generate an amount valued in monetary terms which purports to say something about the costs to society of a particular disease. At the heart of the economist's approach is the idea that all relevant costs are 'opportunity costs': that is, an activity (such as an illness) prevents resources from being used for some other purpose and is thus an opportunity lost. Thus COI studies are based on the supposition that if the illness did not exist, then the resources used by a society for treatment and other related purposes could be deployed elsewhere.

Table 5.1 presents the results of major COI drug studies. We present the results for illicit drugs simultaneously with those for legal drugs, as the

Table 5.1 Social costs of drugs (as % of GDP)

Study	Country	Studied year	Alcohol	Tobacco	Illicit drugs	Total costs in % of GDP[1]
Single et al. (1998)	Canada	1992	1.1	1.4	0.2	2.7
Rice et al. (1990)	USA	1980	1.7	1.4	1.1	4.2
NIDA (1998)	USA	1992	2	–	1	–
Collins and Laspley (1996)	Australia	1992	1	2.4	0.4	3.8
Fazey and Stevenson (1990)	UK	1988	–	–	0.4	–
Institut Suisse (1990)	Switzerland	1988	–	–	0.2	–
Jeanrenaud et al. (1998)[2]	Switzerland	1995	–	2.7 (1.3)	–	–
Rosa et al. (1996)	France	1995	–	0.26	–	–
Kopp et al. (2002)	France	1997	1.4	1.1	0.16	2.7

Notes
1 The total cost includes all the direct and the indirect costs, as specified by the author of the study, unless otherwise indicated.
2 This study includes all the intangible costs. The percentage without intangible costs is in brackets.

studies usually treat these two areas together. Illegal drugs represent about one-tenth of a GNP point and obviously come in well before tobacco and alcohol, which is normal due to their inferior level of consumption. The social cost of illegal drugs appears abnormally high in the USA, confirming the importance of the drug epidemic this country has witnessed. This is also due to the fact that the American study is the only one to include the cost of crimes linked to traffic and consumption. A more detailed interpretation of the results is difficult, because the calculation methods differ greatly from one study to another. For example, the Jeanrenaud *et al.* (1998) study includes intangible costs, or a monetary evaluation of the suffering of the relatives of the victims of drugs, while the other studies do not.

Peculiar interest

The public policy-maker therefore has numerous public policy tools to favour one solution over another. In the case of drugs, an identical level of national wealth (i.e. social cost) may be achieved with policies that require sacrifices of the non-drug consumers to improve the lot of the consumers, or the opposite. This question has been touched on by public discussion, in a fairly idealized form, when certain politicians asked if it was suitable to consider the drug consumers as delinquents or patients. Economic analysis does not provide a direct solution to this problem, but it allows us to lay out the terms in a clearer manner. This, in itself, represents progress.

Social choice and public policy

Traditionally public economics has provided a practical framework for rigorously, if somewhat simplistically, treating these problems. For pedagogical reasons, let us go back to the complexity of the public policy-maker's choice, to an exercise of maximization of a function of collective well-being W with the constraint of a barrier of possible utility (UPS).

First, let us examine the function of collective well-being. In a world of n individuals and r goods, we call the function of collective well-being $W = W[U_1(x_i), U_n(x_i), \ldots U_n(x_i)]$ where each $U_i(x_i)$ is the level of utility that the consumption from basket $x_i = (x_i^1, \ldots, x_i = (x_i^j, \ldots, x_i = (x_i^r)$ allows an individual i to reach. The shape of the function W will indicate the way in which the public policy-maker weighs the importance of different individuals in the society. The different functions can appear mathematically as particular forms, depending on the value given to parameter α which represents a vector of n dimension and serves to weigh the usefulness in function of its level, of the general function:

$$\begin{cases} W = \dfrac{1}{\alpha_i} \sum_i^n (U_i)\alpha & \text{if: } a \neq 0 \\[2ex] W = \log U_i & \text{if: } a = 0 \end{cases}$$

The value held by the parameter α translates numerically the value judgement indicating the sensitivity to inequality of the public policy-maker.

If $\alpha > 1$, the public policy-maker manifests a clear preference for inequality. We will therefore exclude this case. If $\alpha = 1$, we notice $\dfrac{\partial W}{\partial U_i} = 1$, which signifies that all the individual utility variations have an identical value in whatever initial level of utility of the individual is considered.

In this case, the function of collective well-being can be written as $\sum_i^n u_i$, which means we are dealing with the grandeur which classic utility, that of Bentham, recommends maximizing. Each individual, rich or poor, weighs equally in the function of collective well-being: taking into account the exclusion of a case where $\alpha > 1$, this 'sensitivity' to inequality is the weakest of those considered. Graphically, a function of collective well-being corresponding to this case is represented as forming an angle of 45° with the axes (see Figure 5.2).

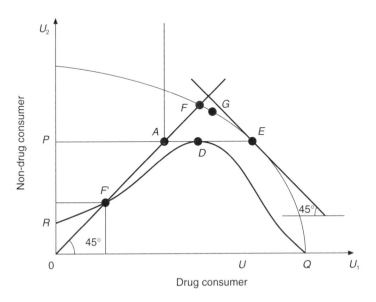

Figure 5.2 Ethical choice and public policy

If $\alpha \in [-\infty, 1] \setminus 0$, we notice that $\dfrac{\partial W}{\partial U_i}$ is a decreasing function of the

utility of each individual, which means that the variation of utility of an individual counts most when his level of utility is weak. This time, the poor are over-weighted in the function of collective well-being which will lead to, between two Paretian optimums, retaining that one which is most favourable to the poor. As α decreases, the aversion to inequality increases. This growing aversion for inequality translates graphically by more and more convex functions of collective well-being.

If α tends towards less infinity, the function of social justice is written $W = \min(U_1, \ldots, U_n)$. The weighted index given to usefulness is such that only the individual whose level of well-being is weakest counts, which corresponds to the prescription of the philosopher Rawls (1971). Graphically, OF, bisector of the right angle, represents equality of the utility. Once we are to the left or to the right of this angle, the level of well-being of one of the two individuals is weaker than the other. From a point such as A, the distribution of utility which corresponds to an increase in well-being of one of these individuals is ethically equivalent, as the well-being of the more favoured one does not count.

Losers and winners

Let us examine now the form of the 'utility possibility frontier' (UPF). With the classical concave individual utility functions, the possible set of utilities is convex. Any point situated on this border is a Pareto optimum. The only constraints imposed on the public policy-maker are the resources and the technology available within the economy. Suppose that the first individual is a consumer of drugs and the second is not. In the absence of any intervention, the first-best optimum is at point E. This point is doubly remarkable. On the one hand it corresponds to the tangency point between a line cutting the abscissa at $45°$ and the border of first-best possible utilities. It therefore indicates that, in the absence of any public intervention, and when the public policy-maker adopts a utilitarian conception of collective well-being *à la* 'Bentham', it is this one, from among all the optimums which constitutes the first-best border, which will be reached.

In this situation, the public policy-maker might eventually regret that the individual 1 (drug consumer) has a more enviable situation than the non-consumer does, as in E his utility is superior. He can then overweigh, in the function of collective well-being, the non-drug consumer. The function becomes convex and the new optimum, still first best, is situated for example in G. Thus, the State will reach, thanks to these transfers between individuals who compose society, a less unfavourable optimum for non-consumers. Technically, such a policy is practically impossible to put into practice. For complex reasons, to which we do not revert, the only form of acceptable transfer destined to re-establish the harmony between the two groups of individuals is of the type 'lump sum tax': this type of transfer being the only one that does not modify the conditions of consumer choice. Concretely, it requires that the consumers pay a 'tax per capita', which is unfeasible.

The possibility then remains for the State, if it considers that the non-consumers are excessively disadvantaged at point E when compared to the consumers, to prohibit drugs and restrict their use, which corresponds to a particular form of tax on drug consumers. A new constraint weighs now on the public policy-maker: drugs are illegal. The policy-maker cannot then fix as an attainable optimum any other than a second-best optimum.

Graphically, the new border, second best, represented by the curve QR, describes the level of utility of the two individuals, as little by little the tax grows with repression. In following this curve from Q, we observe that in the beginning the utility of the drug consumer diminishes but that of the non-consumer increases more than proportionally. From D the well-being of the two consumers decrease. Repression harms both of the individuals.

Observe that the different second best solutions bring less utility to consumers than those of first best. It would then apparently be possible to increase the well-being of the two individuals by eliminating the prohibition. The first-best border of the possible utilities graphically represents the respective levels of attainable utility by the two agents, through merchant exchanges. So, the externalities which affect individuals, consumers and non-consumers of drugs, do not intervene in the drawing of the border because, by definition, an externality is a variation of utility which has no monetary counter-part. It is precisely due to this fact that the public policy-maker is aware of, the existence of these external factors that he decides to prohibit drugs. The decision to situate public action on the first-best border rather than on the second, or the inverse, reflects the importance that the policy-maker accords to external factors accompanying one or the other of the two extreme regimes of legalization and prohibition. Being unable to decide between the two, as explained in Chapter 3, we place it within the only framework we know: that of prohibition.

Remaining within the framework of second-best policies, the objective of the public policy-maker can be, for example, to obtain absolute equality of utilities between the two representative individuals: consumer and non-consumer. He will then attempt, by limiting the repressive tax sufficiently, point F', at the intersection between the second best border and the bisector of the base angle. Under these conditions, the well-being of the consumer and non-consumer would be identical. If the public policy-maker adopts a position which is inspired by the philosopher Rawls (1971), he will prefer the point D where it is no longer possible to increase the utility of the most unhappy individual, individual 2, the non-consumer. The last notable point is found in R which closes the second-best border in a configuration where the utility of the drug consumer is nil as he is the object of very strong repression.

This simplified presentation of the public policy-maker's choices allows us to clarify the implicit value judgements that accompany discussions of drug policies. Simply being able to express classic theory, such as that of Rawls or Bentham, enables us to understand, in both cases, the groups of actors who will benefit from the public policy and those who will suffer. Once again, in matters of drugs, to admit that behind the collective interest, the interests of individuals may be better served by one policy than another, already constitutes, in our eyes, an important step. More so, independently of methodological problems, MacCoun and Reuter (1999) question the utility of the results. Suppose, he suggests, that in the USA the figure for drugs was, for instance, twice as high as that of alcohol, instead of two-thirds as high. What would we learn of significance either scientifically or in terms of policy? Without sharing all of his reserves, we agree that the calculation of social cost gives only an aggregate value on a macroeconomic level of the cost of the consequences of drugs. The following discussion specifies the interest in disaggregating the social cost in order to make it a better-adapted tool for the evaluation of drug policy.

Desegregation of the social cost

Considering public drug policy must minimize social cost, let us now discuss how to consider the complex effects of one measure on public policy. The difficulty of this task is explained by the particularity of the drug policy: one public action increases certain external factors and reduces others so the total effect on social cost is therefore undetermined, and the division of the cost between the different individuals is very sensitive to the type of measure. For example, let us take the case of a syringe exchange programme. The expected results are an improvement in the health of drug consumers and a reduction in the spread of contagious diseases. It is, however, not impossible that this programme would create an increase in drug consumption and favour initiation to injected drugs due to the reduction of risk in contracting a disease such as HIV or hepatitis. The total effect of the programme on collective well-being and the distribution of externalities on the different groups of actors must be absolutely specified before definitively judging such a public initiative.

The notion of social cost must thus be de-aggregated in order to specify the meaning and volume of variations created by public policies. The fact that one policy can increase certain elements of social cost and reduce others is explained by the fact that some categories of externalities are primarily attributable to drug prohibition and its enforcement (e.g. criminal justice system cost, intrusiveness, black market violence). Other externalities appear to be intrinsic properties of a drug and the pharmacological effects of its use irrespective of the regime in which the drug is used. Thus, all else being equal, a change in public policy might, for example, reduce the amount of external factors attributable to prohibition, while retaining the more intrinsic harm of drug use. Of course, everything else is not likely to be equal. Thus a policy change might reduce the harmfulness of the use of a drug yet increase the prevalence and intensity of its use. This is why MacCoun *et al.* (1996) and then MacCoun and Reuter (2001) suggest decomposing the social cost in order to be able to examine the variations in the opposite direction of each of the components. We use here their suggestion while adopting a slightly different notion. Classifying from 1 to *n* different sources of external factors linked to drugs (HIV, violence, legal costs, etc.), we state:

$$SC = \sum_{i=1}^{n} X_i = \sum_{i=1}^{n} (p.f.x_i)$$

with:
SC = cumulative social cost
p = rate of prevalence from 0 to 100
f = frequency of drug use measured by the number of grams consumed by period
X_i = type of external factor created by the drug
x_i = harm by gram of drug consumed for each type *i* created by the drug

This formula allows us to privilege the examination of the contradictory modalities which cause the social cost to reach a certain level rather than to focus excessively on discussion of the latter. It is then possible to examine each public policy from the perspective of its consequences on the prevalence (number of users), the intensity (average consumption per user), and the number of external factors by unit consumed, or 'harm by unit' in the terminology of the authors. MacCoun and Reuter then continue with an intensive survey of public policies, listing their various anticipated effects. The breakthrough of this research is that it strips the theoretical legitimacy from public policy whose exclusive objective is the reduction of consumption. We clearly see that the reduction in the rate of prevalence can be accompanied by a compensating variation (in the opposite direction) of harm by gram of drug consumed, thus creating an increase in social cost (Table 5.2).

The value of the work of MacCoun and Reuter is undeniable and it certainly represents the most advanced expression of our knowledge of drug policy. It would thus be instructive to return to some of the theoretical stakes brought to light by this approach. When evaluating a public policy, in addition to the question of its objective, a second theoretical problem arises. Effectively, it is one thing to prove that the goal of minimizing social cost is the only one compatible with the necessity of efficiency, but it

Table 5.2 Social cost and public policy change

Drug	Public policy	Use	Harm	Distributive issues	Major uncertainties
Cocaine	De-penalization	Little or no increase in prevalence; minor increase in intensity	Possible increase in impaired functioning and crime, decrease in criminal justice costs	Users benefit more than non-users	Little directly relevant evidence
	Adult market	Increased prevalence; increased intensity	Increase in addiction, health care costs, impaired functioning; decrease in economic crime, criminal justice costs/harm, and intrusiveness	Users benefit more than non-users; inner cities may benefit more than middle class	Little directly relevant evidence
Heroin	De-penalization	Same as cocaine de-penalization	Same as cocaine de-penalization	Similar to cocaine adult market	Same as cocaine de-penalization
	Adult market	Increased prevalence; decrease in intensity	Similar to cocaine adult market, but also decreases in drug-related illness and disease transmission	Similar to cocaine adult market	Little directly relevant evidence

Source: MacCoun and Reuter (2002).

is quite another to resolve the problem created by the multitude of possible solutions. The question is familiar to public economists. A large number of allocations of resources exist that allow us to obtain efficiency.[4]

Should we favour the well-being of the drug users or of the non-drug users?

A redundant problem persists in matters of public policy, even when the objective is clear: in the search for economic efficiency, the solutions are many. Theory establishes that for each economic states there are an infinite number of possibilities for distributing wealth in a Pareto-optimal manner (see Table 5.1). The second step of the economist's work consists therefore in suggesting that the public policy-maker indicates his conception of the notion of social justice clearly and retains the optimum which corresponds to this conception. This question, apparently somewhat abstract, is illustrated in the discussion of the following questions, opened up by the conclusions drawn by MacCoun and Reuter (2001).

First, must the objective pursued by public policy always be the minimization of total social cost? The question of knowing whether there exists a conflict between the reduction of total social cost and the reduction of average harm per user warrants examination. In certain cases a policy moves average and total harm in opposite directions. There will then be a trade-off. MacCoun and Reuter (2001) indicate, and rightly so, that the choice between average and total harm minimization depends on the weight one attributes to harm to current users vs harm to non-users (and potential users). For current users, reforms that reduce average harm will reduce personal risk, irrespective of what happens to anyone else. More generally, when average harm reduction and total harm reduction are in conflict, the choice of a criterion carries costs that the policy-maker should acknowledge. In order to endorse policies that might decrease average harm and increase total harm, we should believe that the present user's reduction in suffering would justify the harm to be suffered by a new user and those around him. To endorse public policies that might decrease total harm and increase average harm, we should accept that some users would suffer harm that could have been avoided. Is this reasonable?

Second, the question of choice between the objective of minimizing the total social cost or that of harm per user leads to a more global problem: that of the distribution of social cost among the different groups of individuals. The public policy-maker is confronted with a problem of 'trade-off' well known to public economists. Let us take an example suggested by MacCoun and Reuter (2001), again concerning the measures that would lead to a de-penalization of drugs. According to the authors, those regime changes that promise substantial reduction in black markets confer large gross benefits on inner-city communities, even if they may also increase the level of drug use and addiction. Elimination of the black market confers lesser aggregate benefits on the middle class and quite modest benefits per capita; those benefits to the middle class may appear minor in comparison to the costs of increased risk of drug involvement of a family member. Is this a reasonable trade-off?

Should we take into account the benefits of drugs?

If individuals consume drugs, we could think that they consider – rightly or wrongly so – that they derive benefits from them. Is it then not unfair to only consider in the policy discussion the social cost of drugs and not their benefit, at least in the eyes of the consumers? We will see that the question proves to be without real impact in the case of illegal drugs, especially harder and more expensive drugs such as heroin and cocaine. In approaching the question, we should keep in mind that in the cases of the tobacco-producing United States and wine-producing France, as commentators do not miss pointing out, tobacco on the one hand and alcohol on the other yield more than they cost. The next question is to know how to make the assessment, for the collectivity, of an activity (automobile traffic or drugs) which brings benefits but also creates externalities.

Therefore we must compare, on the one hand, the usefulness of drugs, in other words the satisfaction individuals get from their consumption, and on the other, the cost of this consumption for the collectivity: that is to say, the cost of the purchase of products increased by the externalities linked to drugs. Generally speaking, the utility of the consumption of a product or service, or the use of a lasting possession – as considered by the consumer/user – is at least equal to the price they pay for this consumption or use. In reality, it is greater, as a certain number of consumers would be prepared to pay more than they actually do. If the consumer surplus, meaning the difference between what the individuals pay to consume tobacco, alcohol or illegal drugs and the price that they are prepared to pay, is superior to the social cost engendered then the drugs are socially beneficial.

This calculation is of course unethical, but it conforms to the principles of modern economic calculation. It is the same as saying that if individuals find satisfaction superior to costs created, then the activity is socially beneficial. Obviously, we will observe that the beneficiaries of drugs and the victims of externalities are not necessarily the same individuals. This does not problematize the efficiency of drug markets, but raises questions of equity and social justice that should produce accompanying social policies.

Figure 5.3 represents the demand curve (the straight line D) and offer (the straight line S) of a product, in this case a legal drug (alcohol or tobacco) or an illegal one, in function of its unit price (by litre of alcohol, gram of tobacco, cannabis, heroin, etc.). If the price, which allows the determination of quantities exchanged at point B (equalization of supply and demand), is equal to P, then the consumption of drug is equal to Q.

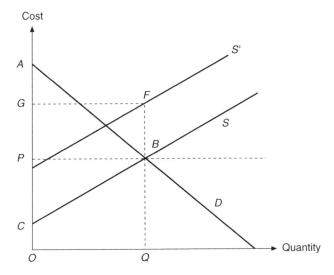

Figure 5.3 Social cost versus consumer surplus

The users pay $(OP \times OQ)$, or $OPQB$. But for all consumers (except the last, the marginal consumer), the utility of the consumption of a drug is superior to P, as they were willing to pay more than P, i.e. their reservation prices are higher than the price P, these prices being represented by all the points of segment AB of the straight demand line D. Thus they benefit from a real gain, but are variable according to consumer. Area PAB measures the surplus. For its part, the producer's surplus, i.e. the benefit from the production and sale of drugs, is represented by the area PBC. This is explained by the fact that all the producers (except the last, the marginal producer) were prepared to produce and sell quantities of drugs for prices inferior to P, these prices being represented by all points of the segment CB of the straight supply line S.

Finally, if the total utility of the 'production-consumption' of a product or service is measured by the surface $OABQ$, the collective well-being gained from this 'production-consumption' is represented by the sum of the consumer surplus (PAB) and the producer (PBC), or the area CAB. The surface $OCBQ$ represents the resources involved in the production of a quantity Q of product or service, i.e. the costs of production, broadly speaking, i.e. including the costs of research and development, commercialization, etc. of a quantity Q of product or service.

We will keep for the purpose of our calculation only the consumer surplus, leaving aside the producer's surplus. In fact, in a situation where legal drugs, (alcohol and tobacco) and illegal drugs were not produced, the resources used to produce these would be allocated to other activities which would generate an equivalent gain for the producers. Thus, there only remains the consumer surplus linked to the consumption of legal and illegal drugs.

It thus follows, then, to bring together the utility of legal and illegal drugs (consumer surplus) and the disutilities, or negative externalities (the social cost), associated with these drugs. We are speaking here of comparable concepts. The utility of a product or service, as we have valued it, represents the increase in well-being created by the consumption of this same product or service. The negative externalities generated by the consumption of this same product or service represent symmetrically the estimated decrease in well-being created by this same consumption. This can, and must, be subtracted from the total. Graphically, the space between the straight line S and the line S' represents the externality or the social cost of the drug. For a market in equilibrium with a quantity Q, the externality is equal to the surface $GFBF$ which should be compared with the consumer surplus PAB. To our knowledge, such a calculation has been carried out only in the case of France. The result is that contrary to hasty interpretations which compare, for example, the social cost of alcohol to the turnover of the *branche alcool* or the taxes charged to them, without regard to the most elementary economic calculation, the social cost of alcohol exceeds its benefit (Kopp and Fenoglio, 2003).[5]

In the case of illegal drugs, the price of these was already high. With the consumer surplus being weak, it is thus more than probable that the externality largely wins out over the utility.

Conclusion

To calibrate a public drug policy from a normative approach in which the objectives are established prior to the method is apparently an inaccessible dream. We are obliged to note that the actions of most public drug agencies in the world are so poorly coordinated that we could doubt the existence of any drug policy at all. We thus read between the lines by interpreting the muddle of often contradictory initiatives taken here and there. The guiding strategy is often developed ex-post facto, meaning it takes shape to justify existing action rather than to support it. Even more importantly, the few really centralized elements of public policy can often be thought of as an intense communication activity, the objective of which is more the re-election of the current administration than the implementation of a harmonious policy.

Part III
Drugs, crime and the law

6 Drug law enforcement

Introduction

The conventional approach for reducing externalities is based on the hypothesis that repression increases the price paid by the consumer for drugs and is thus a motivation to reduce consumption. Action aimed at demand constitutes the key to all anti-drug policies having a reduction in consumption as their objective, but effectiveness depends crucially on the degree of elasticity of demand of drug consumers: that is, on the consumer reaction to price. We will see that not only the particularities of price–demand elasticity can intervene and thwart the expected effectiveness of the repressive policy, but also that the organizational methods of drug supply can also play a negative role in reduction of consumption policy. Briefly, from the supply side and the demand side, there are valid reasons to think that an increase in repression does not necessarily engender a decrease in consumption.

Drug policy is the result of a combination of several instruments, particularly repression and treatment. How can we optimally combine these two instruments? Economic analysis supplies the goals, and the observation of implemented policies emphasizes how far governments are from reaching them. It is interesting to note that American drug policy is, without doubt, a classic case of sub-optimal lock-in where the resources used are insufficient and the use of the different instruments is badly measured. A multiple equilibrium approach explains why a sub-optimal public policy can continue for a long time, simply because small marginal modifications would aggravate even more the inefficiency, and the major measures required are too far from the reality experienced by the average citizen for him to make demands. A high degree of chance intervenes in proximity to the points around which two radically different strategies can become dominant.

Supply side enforcement

When repression centres on drug suppliers, it is supposed to provoke a price rise in street prices for drugs and a reduction in consumption. Leaving aside for the moment the eventual adverse consequences of a price rise, particularly the risk of seeing the user methods transformed in the direction of user precariousness, thus causing an increase in social cost, implementing the sequence repression–price–rise–decreased–consumption depends critically upon both the dealers' reaction to environmental changes and changes in the nature of consumer demand. Thus, on one hand, it is necessary to verify whether repression increases the risk run by the dealers, how they perceive this risk, and finally how they react. On the other hand, the dealers' ability to impose changes in price strategy and drug availability on the consumers depends upon consumer sensitivity to risk and sale price.

Price-demand elasticity

Drug consumers adapt their consumption according to the full cost. The combination of the selling price of the drug, the time needed to procure it, and the anticipated cost of arrest, constitutes the full cost of the drug. If demand is not elastic, as in the left side of Figure 6.1, then even if law enforcement leads to a price increase, this increase does not lead to reduced consumption. That is why we assume in further discussion that the demand curve remains unaffected.

In Figure 6.1, the market is in equilibrium at the intersection of the demand (D) and supply (S) lines for a price P_0 and a quantity q_0. Repres-

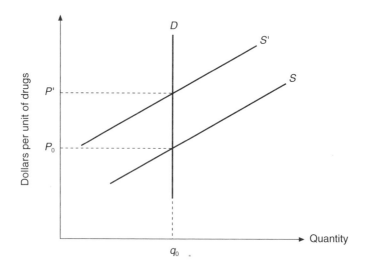

Figure 6.1 Inelastic demand

sion triggers a price increase from P_0 to P'; the quantity of drugs consumed, however, remains at q_0. If the demand curve is elastic to price as in
Figure 6.2, repression leads to a rise in prices but also a reduction in consumption from q_0 to q'.

Empirical results accumulated over a twenty-year period, and particularly the convergent nature of results emanating from the Beckerian
school and from the more heterodox group of the 'RAND Drug Policy
Research Center' indicate that drug demand is elastic to price. We call to
mind that according to Caulkins (1995a), price elasticity to demand for
heroin ranges from -1 to -1.5 (or -1.8 and -1.6 according to Chaloupka
and Saffer, 1995), while that of cocaine fluctuates between -0.72 and
-1.1, according to the latter two authors.

Effects of repression on profits

The elasticity or inelasticity of demand for drugs to price potentially
affects not only drug consumption, as we have seen, but also dealer profits.
Friedman (1991) and Choiseul-Praslin (1991) have amply criticized the
idea that prohibition could succeed in reducing consumption through the
action of price elasticity. They hold the view that in the event of rigid law
enforcement, traffickers are free to raise their prices. But the authors say
that since demand elasticity would be very weak, this policy would have no
effect. It would even boost the profits of dealers, who would be delighted
to be able to take advantage of the pretext of repression to increase their
prices. In this way, the drug economy would be stimulated by law enforcement. Police action would thus be discredited by the positive role it would
play in dealer profits.

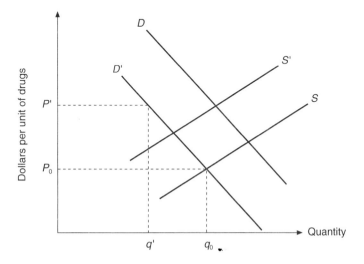

Figure 6.2 Elastic demand

This thesis can be illustrated by Figure 6.3, in which repression triggers an increase in drug prices. The price shifts from P_0 to P', bringing about a reduction in the external cost of drugs (surface area $aE'cE_0$ or $q'bdq_0$). Dealer income diminishes by the surface area $q'aE_0q_0$. These reductions are relatively small and moreover dealer income increases significantly by the surface area $P_0P'E'a$. Expenditure allocated to drugs is increased considerably. The consequences of the repressive action are therefore quite negative.

One has only to modify the demand elasticity hypothesis to reach the opposite conclusion. In Figure 6.4, repression triggers an increase in the price of drugs. The price shifts from P_0 to P' and the drug external cost reduction (surface area $aE'cE_0$ or $q'bdq_0$) and the production costs (surface area $q'aE_0q_0$) are significant, while increases in revenue ($P_0P'E'a$), of which a fraction is devoted to avoiding prohibition, are slight. Because demand is fairly elastic, total expenditure for drugs is reduced, creating a reduction of externalities linked to the quantity consumed.

The study by Wagstaff and Maynard (1988) focusing on the effectiveness of repressive public policy in Britain moves in this direction. The authors point out that the police seized between 1.3 per cent and 3.1 per cent of the heroin circulating in Britain in 1984. It would seem, incidentally, that the figure has risen substantially since then. At that time, the conditional probability that a dealer would be prosecuted or imprisoned was between 8 per cent and 11 per cent and between 15 per cent and 22 per cent, respectively. In the opinion of these authors doubling the rate of police seizure in the territory, that is, from 2.5 per cent to 5 per cent,

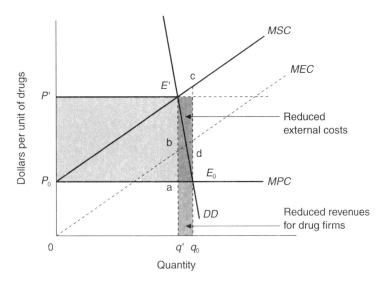

Figure 6.3 Enforcement effect with inelastic demand

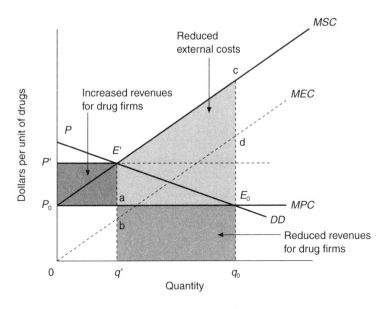

Figure 6.4 Enforcement effect with elastic demand

would bring about an increase in the price of heroin of between 1.4 per cent and 2.5 per cent. Wagstaff and Maynard conclude their study with an estimate of the effect of increasing the average prison term for heroin trafficking from five years to twenty years. Such a policy would lead to an increase in the overall price of heroin of between 9 per cent and 15 per cent and is likely to have an effect on the amount of heroin consumed. Using the higher estimate of 25 per cent and Caulkins (1995a) figure for the price elasticity of heroin of between −1 and −1.5, we find that a maximum increase of 25 per cent in the price of heroin would lead to a 37.5 per cent reduction in consumption.

Hence, the idea that repression could bring about a reduction in heroin consumption of almost 40 per cent simply by way of price interplay is no more than a crude illustration serving the loftiest assumptions. Leaving aside criticisms and debates about the empirical estimates of the parameters, we will apply ourselves to emphasizing a problem of reasoning.

Those favouring rigid repression base their stance on a hypothesis of strong demand elasticity, while liberalization proponents assume the opposite. But these two groups are in agreement in acknowledging that law enforcement actually provokes an increase in drug prices. Yet, this hypothesis appears highly debatable. It rests on two hypotheses: first, that drug traffickers are able to pass on to consumers the increases in risk that they incur following a wave of repression; and second, the assumption that all traffickers are equally exposed to the risk posed by law enforcement.

Enforcement without price increase

If a great deal of attention has been given to discussing the consequences for public policy of the hypotheses of elasticity and inelasticity of demand to prices, less attention has been paid to determining whether repression actually leads to an increase in the drug prices. However, this is a decisive question. If repression does not lead to an increase in drug prices, it is pointless to discuss its effects on consumption!

Retailers resell wholesale drugs to final consumers. The price of the drug sold at retail is high, as the margin coefficient of the resellers is all the higher as they are close to the final consumer. This means that they fix the selling price of the drug by multiplying the price at which they bought it by a large margin coefficient. In effect, the resellers at the end of the chain can only spread the risk over a small quantity of drug. The important difference between the price at which the final resellers buy the drug and that at which they resell it, does not correspond directly to profit. A part of the margin covers the risk. Numerous analysts 'forget' to treat the risk as a cost and thus over-evaluate the profit. This discussion took a decisive turn when many voices criticized the utility of repression policies. Liberal authors, such as Milton Friedman (1991) or radicals, such as Charles-Henri de Choiseul-Praslin (1991), both hostile to drug prohibition, consider that repression of traffickers would stimulate their profits, by virtue of the fact that the latter would use police repression to justify an increase in drug price. Some confusion reigns over this question. If repression has no real effect on traffickers, we do not understand why consumers do not react to price increase imposed upon them by resellers by decreasing their consumption, by the system of elasticity. Moreover, we are not certain that the sellers need the pretence of repression to increase prices. After all, if their control over the consumer is so strong, they can increase the price as they wish. If repression effectively threatens traffickers, the price increase which accompanies it does not engender a profit but legitimately covers the risk. Hasty assertions whereby the repression serves the traffickers by allowing them to increase prices and profit are based on an outdated hypothesis of total inelasticity of demand to price. It also neglects the threat of the entry of small dealers caused by the price increases (Reuter and Kleiman, 1986; Kleiman, 1989).

Our opinion clearly diverges from the two theses laid out above. For one thing, Wagstaff and Maynard do not take into consideration the fact that a substantial increase in the price of drugs would trigger the entry of new traffickers into the market. The argument does not hold up if the price increase only barely compensates for the increase in risk. In addition, we consider two phenomena that cause the arrival of new traffickers. First, before arriving on the market, a dealer does not know the exact risk to which he is exposing himself; he can thus confuse the calculated profit and the economic profit and enter the market, whereas according to the second variable his entry is not profitable. Second, seasoned criminals, coming from other sectors of activity (prostitution or bank robbery) can decide to enter the market and make a large economic profit as their acquired experience in criminality allows them to operate with a more advantageous cost function than the average trafficker already at work. To avoid giving rise to new traffickers and seeing their position of strength challenged, drug traffickers will reduce price rise and wait for the wave of repression to subside.

On the other hand, Friedman and Choiseul-Praslin refuse to accept the premise that police repression can be sufficiently effective to increase traffickers' probability of arrest and therefore their costs. Thus, if the traffickers moderately increase their prices in order not to induce the entry of new competitors, the price increase will not bring about an increase in profit.

Make them wait

Let us make a detailed examination of the case in which a temporary peak in enforcement is not accompanied by an increase in the price of drugs. Assume[1] that the market is in equilibrium for a price P_0 and a quantity q_0 at the intersection between the supply and demand curves S_0 and DD_0. Assume further that repression increases and displaces the supply curve to S_1 but that the dealers keep the price stable at P_0. This strategy can express the dealers' fear of seeing some of their customers driven from the market and opting for treatment programmes due to prices that are too high. If the dealers count on repression ending and things returning to normal, it is rational for them not to increase prices in order to preserve their future profits.

At a price P_0, the dealers must be content with offering a quantity q_1 for which consumers who remain in the market would still be prepared to pay P_1. Instead of raising the prices, the dealers will impose a rationing on the market by multiplying their precautions and withdrawing from their customary points of sale. The difference between P_1 and P_0 is squandered in the form of time lost by the consumers buying drugs under conditions that are more complicated than usual. The market slows down and the quantity sold declines to q_1. The value of the time lost is represented by the vertical rectangle (P_0cdP_1) and corresponds to the product $(P_1 - P_0)q_1$. This lost time is of no benefit to anyone; it only indicates the income that the dealers would have been able to claim if they had increased prices as the market allowed them to. We thus find that when dealers decide to keep prices low, they implicitly accept the dissipation of a portion of their potential income from the increase in suppression. Note that in this model, dealer adaptations affect the demand curve.

If, for medium-term strategic reasons, dealers maintain their policy of low prices, they will then try to recover this potential income (dissipated income) by reducing the quality of the product which is equivalent to raising the price. The curves corresponding to the new supply of a lesser quality drug and the new demand are represented by the lines S_2 and DD_2, and the equilibrium quantity by q_3. The quality of which the consumers are deprived was assessed by them at a price higher than what it cost the dealers to supply it; that is the reason it was initially offered. The drop in quantity consumed of q^* to q_3 reflects the fact that a poor quality drug does not attract as many consumers. The shift from q_3 to q_2 is explained by the fact that if the vendors still want to maintain the price at P_0, they can only put q_2 on the market at this price and must maintain a degree of rationing in the queue (see Figure 6.5).

When the market is in equilibrium, the quantity of drugs consumed q_2 is higher than that of q_1 which would prevail if the vendors had increased the price to P_1. A quantity q_2 sold at an apparent price of P_0 corresponds in fact to a price P_2 if one accounts for the additional alteration of the product. The final dissipation of the seller's income after the reduction in quality, represented by the rectangle in the dotted lines (P_2abP_0) combined in the 'triangle of welfare loss'[2] (abe) that is associated with it, is lower than the dissipation he would have faced without a reduction in quality.

In our model, the triangle measures the loss of welfare of drug consumers who leave the market because the price is too high in relation to the quality of the drugs. Their welfare decreases by a value represented by the triangle (abe) without producers being able to capture it because the

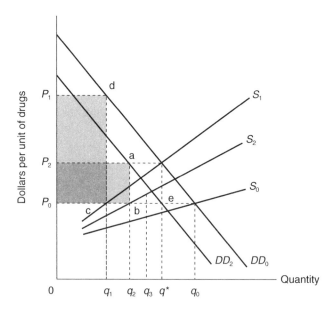

Figure 6.5 Rationing by queuing

consumers leave the market. On the other hand, the consumers who remain in the market, permitting the producers to increase their surplus accept the real price increase by the rectangle (P_2abP_0).

If the sellers are correct in thinking that repression will not last, their strategy of low prices is aimed at maintaining their potential for future clientele, and the reduction in quality limits the loss of potential income that would materialize if they completely adapted to the new market conditions.

What emerges from this model is the view that when public action attempts to reorient the operation of the markets by repression, if prices are stable, drug consumers will have to waste time restocking their supplies. Then, the dealers will lessen the drug quality to exploit the expression of the willingness to pay that the lost time represents, and a greater number of consumers will be served with a shorter wait.

Interpreting this scenario in terms of welfare is no simple matter. Should we celebrate the fact that in spite of the loss of economic welfare it represents, some consumers leave the market? The answer is a priori positive unless they turn to other products that are even more dangerous, or unless their suffering does not find palliative relief in the treatment system. How should we interpret the consequences of the reduction in the quality of drugs? The answer is ambiguous. If the adulteration is without serious consequences for health and if more dangerous modes of consumption do not emerge, the effect is positive; however, it is negative if these conditions are not observed. We will measure the complexity of the effects of repression on the operation of the drug market. If economic tools do not yet permit a complete view of all the consequences, we are certain that the simplified thesis that maintains without any reservation, that repression increases criminal profits is misleading.

Our reservations when faced with this thesis lie along the lines of earlier observations. Moore (1973, 1990) emphasizes the idea that the price paid by the consumer reflects the body of information relating to the cost absorbed by the consumer. One must also take into account the following cost elements: the degree of drug purity, the time spent looking for it, the risk of violence, the risk of arrest. For these reasons, Moore suggests not taking the 'observed price' into account but the 'effective price', which includes these factors and integrates the transaction costs. The consequences of this suggestion, where public policy is concerned, are very interesting. The 'old' and the 'new' drug consumers do not pay the same 'effective price'. The 'effective price' paid by the new consumers will be higher because they do not have a good supply network. Since their probability of being arrested is higher than that of the usual users, they do not dare to venture far in search of good contacts. The risk is too costly for them to expose themselves enough to be able to go through the more attractive distribution channels. Moreover, the demand of new consumers is more price sensitive than that of older consumers because they are not yet addicted. For these reasons, Moore advocates a policy that renders the 'effective price' of heroin higher for new consumers (in order to reduce their number) and lower for experienced addicts (to reduce their criminal pressure on society).

It thus emerges clearly from our observations that an increase in the price of drugs is not an inevitable result of repression. The sellers can, for strategic reasons, decide to maintain prices at their previous level; they can also increase the cost by reducing the quality while maintaining the same price. The thesis of a drug economy driven by repression therefore has neither theoretical nor empirical basis in our opinion.

Risk differentiation

Not only does repression not necessarily trigger a drug price rise; what is more, the effects of a price increase are not the same on all groups of drug dealers. Dealers make up a population that is very heterogeneous. From an economic point of view they differ one from the other according to their apprehension of risk incurred and their know-how. Their cost curve describes the sale price of the drug from which their cost is covered and it becomes profitable to enter the market. For a given drug price, some dealers must leave the market, because their cost is not covered; others make a profit of zero, and some others make a profit. Thus, and with the reservation that the price is uniform, meaning that each dealer cannot practise a particular price, the same repressive policy has different effects on different dealer groups

Being a dealer is also a job qualification

Let us assume, then, that repression can effectively trigger a certain price increase and examine its impact on the different types of drug dealers by using a necessarily schematic graphic representation. It should be understood that the prices paid by consumers for drugs do not reflect the 'real cost of risk' incurred by the dealers, because the most skilled dealers escape the risks and reap additional profits by making the consumer pay an exorbitantly high price. The experienced dealers and the novices do not face the same risks. The imperfection of the market (is every market with an upward sloping supply curve described as 'imperfect'?) permits everyone to charge the same price, so that some dealers benefit from a quasi-rent while others barely cover their costs. We distinguish[3] schematically two groups of dealers: the 'experienced ones' akin to organized crime members and the 'candidates for entry into the market', called 'entrants' for convenience. Each of these groups is characterized by a different supply function. The 'experienced' dealers benefit from sufficiently low costs that they make profits even when prices are low. The 'entrants' can only penetrate the market when the price P_1 exceeds the 'floor price' P_0

that balances out their costs. This difference between the cost functions is precisely what makes the 'barrier to entry' referred to above.

Profit and repression

In Figure 6.6, the price of drugs is P_0. At this price the demand line DD indicates that the quantity consumed is q_0. The experienced dealers supply this quantity. They do not supply the entire market because after the intersection of the price P_0 line and their supply curve SE, their price for the product becomes higher than the sales price. The supply curve of the experienced dealers rises because the more a group of traffickers grows, the more they become the target of suppression. The supply curve of the entrants merges with the line P_0, conveying the idea that as long as the drug is sold at this price, there will be a multitude of small vendors who will find the means to supply the market. Below that price, however, they must stop their activity as it ceases to be profitable. Let us assume that a sudden increase in repression is directed principally against the entrants. The price of drugs increases from P_0 to P_1. At this new price demand drops from q_0 to q_1. The entrants cease to offer quantity d. Moreover, at the new price, the experienced dealers can offer more of quantity b than that already placed on the market. The experienced dealers' share of the market rises at the expense of the entrants' share. In fact, since repression is directed against the entrants, the real risk threatening the experienced dealers does not increase with repression. The price increase, triggered by the entrants to cover their real increase in risk, favours the experienced dealers. The quasi-rent of the experienced dealers before repression – that is, the difference between the sales price of the drugs and the production cost – is represented in Figure 6.6 by the surface area designated 1 that becomes surface area 2 following the repression.

With the aid of Figure 6.7, we now transcribe the case in which repression is directed mainly against the best-organized groups of traffickers. Initially the market is in equilibrium for a price P_0 and a quantity q_0. The totality of drugs sold originates from the group of experienced dealers, because for P_0, the candidates becoming drug traffickers do not make enough money to enter into this activity. Repression leads to a price increase and a modification of the supply curve of the group of experienced dealers from SE to SE'. Shielded from any competition, the group of experienced dealers can transfer to the consumer the real risks incurred. Subject to a certain elasticity of demand to price, we observe a drop in consumption from q_0 to q_1. The quasi-rent of the experienced group represented before repression by the surface area 1 decreases (surface area 2).

Figure 6.8 also describes the case of repression directed against the group of experienced dealers. The market is in equilibrium for price P_0 and quantity q_0. The group of experienced dealers, who abandon quantity

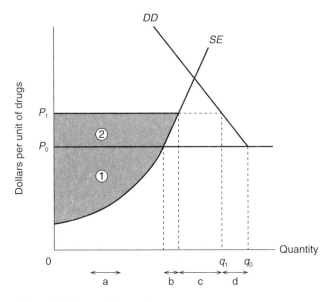

Figure 6.6 Repression against new entrants

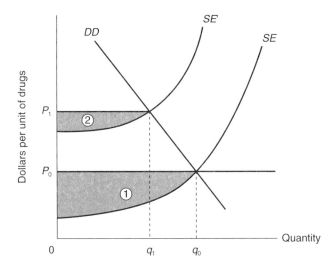

Figure 6.7 Repression aimed at a criminal organization monopoly

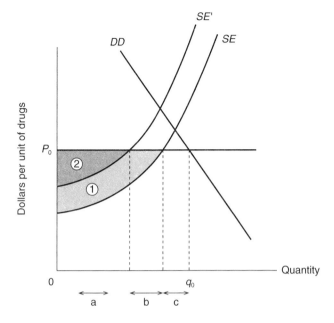

Figure 6.8 Repression aimed at a criminal organization in competition with
new entrants

c to entry-level dealers, supplies demand for a quantity a + b. Under these
conditions, the surface area 1 represents the quasi-rent of the experienced
group. Repression is launched against the group of experienced traffickers
whose supply curve is displaced from *SE* to *SE'*, but they cannot increase
the price because by doing so they would concede territory to the entry-
level dealers. The market finds a new equilibrium where prices and quantities are unchanged but where the market share has evolved. The
experienced group has reduced its share by a quantity b now supplied by
the entrants. In this case, the repression directed against the group of
experienced dealers increases the group's costs and reduces its quasi-rent
(surface area 2). In fact it is impossible for them to pass the increased costs
caused by repression onto their prices. Competition with the 'entrants'
forces the experienced dealers to moderate their prices. An increase
would attract even more 'new entrants' and would further reduce the
experienced dealers' share of the market.

Figure 6.9 describes the consequences of a prolonged war against the
group of experienced dealers. The market is initially in equilibrium for
a price P_0 and a quantity q_0. The group of experienced dealers has a
monopoly because at P_0 there is no motivation for candidates to enter
the market. In the face of repression, the group of experienced
dealers forms new alliances and consolidates its organization, or a new

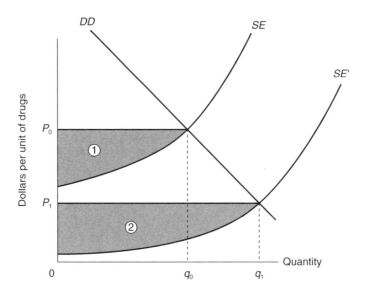

Figure 6.9 Repression aimed at a criminal organization and price war

organization comes along to replace the one that has sustained the blows of suppression.

The group of experienced dealers in the market reduces prices in order to avoid being 'removed' by another group. The price drops, the quantity of drugs consumed rises, and the guaranteed income of the experienced group rises (surface area 2 instead of surface area 1).

It appears clearly from Table 6.1 that the public policy-maker must clarify his objectives. Everything depends on the principal source of externalities linked to the drug. For example, if these are more linked to drug consumption than to the activity of organized crime, then it is necessary not to give priority to fighting one of the families of organized crime if other families are waiting for this chance to take over the market. On the other hand, if organized crime has a stable monopoly, an aggressive policy could be recommended. Inversely, if the fight against organized crime is a priority, then it is necessary to implement a treatment and prevention policy to counter the effects of an eventual drop in prices and rise in consumption.

Quality differentiation

The effectiveness of repression against dealers is also affected by the high variability of drug quality in the market. Economic theory since the Lemon's Theorem of Akerlof (1970) says that bad quality chases good in markets where the quality of products is not observable (adverse

Table 6.1 The effects of repression on dealers

	Repression directed against new entrants	Repression aimed at a criminal organization monopoly	Repression aimed at a criminal organization in competition with new entrants	Repression aimed at a criminal organization and price war
Entry and exit of the market	The less experienced dealers quit the market.	Entry of less experienced dealers on the market.	Entry of less experienced dealers on the market.	The experienced dealer reduces prices in order to avoid being 'removed' by another group.
Quantity supplied	At the new price, the experienced dealers can offer more of quantity.	Higher price and drop in consumption.	Competition with the 'entrants' forces experienced dealers to moderate their prices. Prices and quantities are unchanged.	Reduces prices in order to avoid being 'removed' by another group; the price drops, the quantity of drugs consumed rises.
Market share of the experienced dealers	The experienced dealers' share of the market rises at the expense of the entrants' share.	The share of the experienced dealers decreases.	The market share of experienced dealers is reduced	–
Risk	Repression is directed against the entrants; the real risk threatening the experienced dealers does not increase with repression.	The experienced dealers transfer the real risks incurred to the consumer.	The experienced dealers cannot transfer the real risks incurred to the consumer.	Increased risk.
Rent	The quasi-rent of the experienced dealers increased.	The quasi-rent of the experienced dealers diminishes.	Reduces its quasi-rent.	The quasi-rent of the experienced dealers increases.

selection). The drug market seems to correspond to this description, so we should then expect that among the tens of thousands of drug doses exchanged, daily doses of fairly pure drug disappear. The quality of the drug should be rather bad and the price/quality relationship of the drug sufficiently stable that an eventual change engendered by the repression would be perceptible by the consumer. This does not seem to be the case. Caulkins and Feinleib (1995) assume that an addict makes twice-daily purchases, or 600 in the course of a year. They assume further that, consistent with Riley (1997), the addict has fifteen suppliers. The buyer then makes an average of forty purchases annually from each vendor. With a simple Bernoulli model, even if each buyer and seller has a one-third probability of exiting the market during the course of the year (reflecting the cumulative effects of incarceration, ill health and violence from other participants), the probability that this dyad, after making a purchase, will transact again within a year is 0.98.[4] This high probability of a 'repeat performance' may be sufficient to induce cooperation.

In the classic repeated game model in which players cooperate, the interactions are of uniformly high quality. However, in this case cooperation does not always mean selling high quality drugs, because the vendor has imperfect knowledge, and, hence, imperfect control over quality. Sellers can decide to rip someone off, but they cannot simply decide to sell high quality drugs. They physically cannot sell drugs of greater purity than those they receive from their supplier, and they have at best imperfect knowledge of when that purity is sub-standard. Hence, even a cooperative seller furnishes a wide range of quality. Precisely because the buyer makes so many purchases from the same vendor, no single transaction is used to provide much information about the level of quality or cooperation. The vendor may aim to provide, over the ten transactions that occur in a quarter, a distribution of quality and price consistent with that generally in the market, but he will have only a very rough estimate of what that distribution is, both because there are no institutions to collect such data and because no buyer or seller can report purity and price per pure gram for a given transaction. On the other hand, the inevitability of dispersion in quality affords the seller the opportunity to cut the drugs a little more. So, some dispersion is unavoidable, and that dispersion creates incentives and opportunities for occasional further dilution as the drugs move from one stage to the next in the distribution chain.[5] Yet, excessive cutting or outright fraud are constrained by the repeat game character of the transactions. As dispersion of quality is a characteristic of the drug market, the effect of repression on the price is badly perceived by consumers. Dealers are free to adjust the risk increase incurred by a reduction in the average quality of the drug they distribute without the consumer noticing and adjusting his behaviour. The drop in consumption is therefore even more hypothetical, the more imperfect the market. Repressive policy aimed at dealers destined to operate a drop in consumption should not therefore be accompanied by an action which disorganizes the market and atomizes the transactions.

The different scenarios evoked cover only an outline of the possible consequences of supply side repression on the market. Hence, identical policies of repression can have very different effects on the society as a whole depending on the pre-existing structure of the market to which they are applied. We have concentrated on the impact of competition between large- and small-scale traffickers, and on the consequences of quality heterogeneity on the effects of public policy. This aspect is important, but it should be pointed out that the price level that prevails on the market before repression is launched also has a significant impact on the outcome of public policy.

Demand side enforcement

Repression can also be directed at the consumer. We have already amply discussed this question. By examining the effects of repression on the offer, we have already introduced the idea that the elastic or inelastic nature of the demand affects the result. Two complementary elements can, however, be introduced. First, depending on whether the initial price prevailing on the market is elevated or not, the repression will not have the same affect. Second, according to the degree of competition between the resellers, consumers will be more or less free to react to the price increase by changing supplier.

Is demand elastic or inelastic when prices are low?

Blair and Vogel (1973) consider that demand is elastic at low prices and inelastic when prices rise (Figure 6.10). Beginning from a situation in which the price of drugs on the market is rather low, P_0, repression causes the price to rise from P_0 to P_1, and the quantity consumed declines from q_0 to q_1. On the other hand, if the price is already somewhat high, P_0', repression triggers a rise in price that shifts to P_1', but the quantity consumed declines only moderately from Q_0' to Q_1'. This phenomenon depends on price demand elasticity decreasing in absolute value with the price, and the demand curve being convex. This graph would be useful, for example, in illustrating the situation of the heroin market in the Netherlands, where prices are relatively low. In that case, one finds consumers who are dependent, but also 'casual' consumers who can be discouraged by the price increase. In this way, beginning with a situation where the price of heroin is relatively low, the policy of suppressing supply could be effective, but it would then become useless as soon as the small group of occasional consumers were removed from the market.

In concrete terms, this shows that a small amount of police pressure on the Dutch market can have a positive effect precisely because the prices

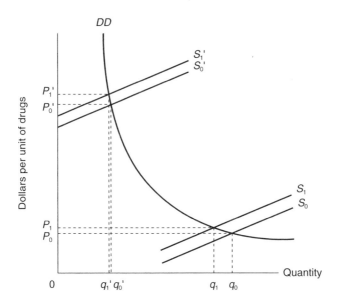

Figure 6.10 Convex demand

are low, whereas the same intervention in the Parisian market, where prices are high, could engender more disadvantages than advantages. The Parisian situation is described by the vertical asymptote of the demand line *b* represented in Figure 6.11. Increasing repression can be positive, however, not entailing exorbitant social costs on the condition *sine qua non* that the treatment system is wide open and offers an alternative to consumers sufficient to render insuperable the effort necessary to keep themselves in the market (Levine *et al.*, 1976). It appears that a certain drop in the price of Parisian heroin following the increase in supply of methadone and buprenorphine treatments can be interpreted as a market reaction to the type of chain of events where, thanks to substitute products, demand loses some of its urgency.

Blair and Vogel's analysis, however, has not met with unanimous agreement. White and Luksetich (1983) defend the exact opposite thesis (Figure 6.11). According to these authors, elasticity would be very weak when prices are low and strong when they are high (elasticity is rising and the demand curve is concave). Repression would therefore be very effective in a Parisian-type market (where prices are high). We do not subscribe to this approach, for it is based on the hypothesis of a non-convex configuration of consumer preferences already mentioned previously.

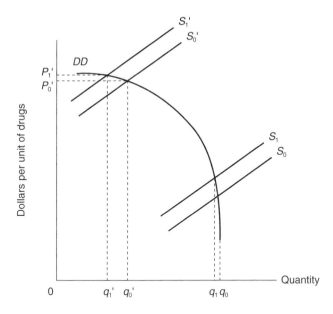

Figure 6.11 Concave demand

The roots of the controversy

The controversy between White and Luksetich, on the one hand, and Blair and Vogel, on the other, not only relates to the type of consumer preference but also to the type of competition prevailing between those offering the drugs. According to White and Luksetich's outline, if the market is slightly monopolistic and repression weak, the price of heroin is low, elasticity is weak, and repression policy thus tends to be relatively ineffective. On the other hand, if the market is strongly monopolistic and if the price at which an individual can procure heroin is not particularly dependent on the price charged by other vendors, then the dealers prefer to sell less but at a higher price. They therefore tend to increase prices to the point where elasticity would block an additional price increase. In this way, the repression policy would lead to a reduction in sales of heroin and in crimes connected with trafficking. White and Luksetich consider that the market is strongly monopolistic. Represented graphically, the situation is described by the upper portion of the demand curve in Figure 6.12, which no doubt correctly describes the market of the 1960s but is unrealistic for the present one. The barriers to market entry are weaker, and fearing the sudden emergence of new challengers observing a lower price policy, the sellers are careful not to charge exorbitant rates.

Repression of drug consumers does not necessarily provoke their eviction from the market. Nothing guarantees that repression causes a price

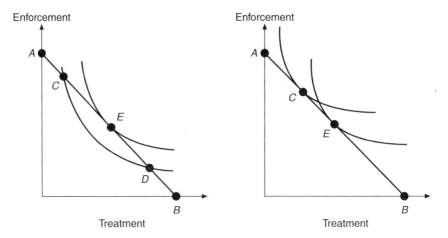

Figure 6.12 A locked sub-optimal policy

rise and even if this does intervene, the reduction in consumption depends on the elasticity of the consumer demand and the prevailing market price. Furthermore, an aggressive policy against consumers necessarily engenders negative effects (violence, unease), which are also vectors of social cost.

Policy mix

Repression is not the policy-maker's only course of action. He can also allocate part of his resources to treatment and prevention. The combination of these instruments must be optimal. The rule of efficiency of public policy tools is well known: public spending should be engaged only to the point (at the margin) where the benefit is superior to the cost. Thus, when the State uses two intervention instruments, the distribution of expenditure between the two forms of action is optimal when no dollar can be efficiently re-allocated from one instrument to another.

The sub-optimality of American public policy

Can we verify, even approximately, whether the US policy follows the two golden rules, the respect of which guarantees public policy efficiency? First, at the margin, the cost of public policy must be equal to the benefits it creates. Second, it must not be possible to re-allocate one dollar of the repression cost to health care or vice versa. Thus, not only the amount but the division of public spending is optimal.

We have a study that cannot be ignored illustrating that the allocation of public spending between care and repression in the United States is inefficient. Rydell and Everingham (1994) estimated the US could reduce cocaine consumption by 1 per cent by investing $34 million in additional treatment funds, a sum considerably lower than what it would take to achieve the same result with domestic law enforcement ($246 million), prohibition ($366 million) or source control ($783 million). A later study (Caulkins *et al.* 1997) estimated that $1 million spent on treatment could reduce US cocaine consumption by 105 kilogrammes, much more than if the same funds were spent on trying to lock up more dealers (13 kilogrammes). Of course these estimates are based on a fairly pessimistic estimate of treatment effectiveness.[6] In their analyses, treatment cost-effectiveness stems partly from temporary repression of consumption during treatment, but mainly from post-treatment reduction, even though they assume, based on prior studies, that only 13 per cent of those who enter treatment remain drug-free for fifteen years. A major social benefit comes from crime reduction generated by lower levels of drug use. The classic methadone study (Ball and Ross, 1991) indicates crime reductions of 70 per cent or more, due to treatment.

It therefore seems credible to put forward the thesis by which US drug policy is 'locked' in a sub-efficient equilibrium. Let us illustrate this situation representing US public expenditure with Figure 6.12, in which we put health costs in abscisses and the repression costs in ordinate. The position of *AB* indicates total amount of spending and its path is the relation between the two types of spending. An increase in public spending translates by a movement of *AB* towards the northeast of the chart and an increase in repression by a pivoting of the line towards the top around *B*. In the chart on the left, we observe a situation where the utility gained by the collectivity in *C* is inferior to that which it would be if the spending were rebalanced, a constant budget in favour of care. Effectively, point *E* is on a curve of superior utility.

However, nothing explains, in this configuration, why the equilibrium is established in *C* rather than in *D*, and above all, why the policy-maker does not accept the move towards *E*. It is clear that the idea according to which we could restore the equilibrium of expenditure in favour of one or the other facet (law enforcement or health care) by 'dipping into' the resources of one in order to favour the other appears somewhat utopian. Only by increasing the overall budget for drug expenditure can we make this readjustment. Actually, considering the portion of expenses for personnel and knowing that it is almost impossible to transfer civil servants from one administration to another, the room to manoeuvre which would allow the redistribution of a portion of expenses from one chapter of the diptych to another is tiny (Reuter, 1994). This resistance to re-allocation of resources is technical; we cannot turn policemen into nurses; but it is also political. This is illustrated by the right part of Figure 6.13 where point *C* describes the equilibrium which maximizes the objective function of the policy-maker and point *E* where it is the collectivity objective function

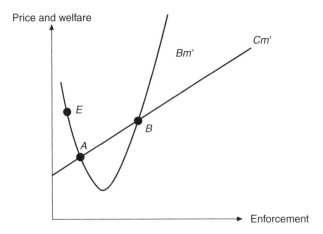

Figure 6.13 The zero tolerance configuration

that is maximized. We must simply take into account that the objective function of the collectivity might not coincide with that of the policy-maker. In our example, the public policy-maker has more marked preferences for repression.

The sub-optimality of the current policy is locked by the policy-maker's preferences. We can no doubt explain this by the perception they have of public expectations and their strategic consequences.[7] We touch here on the limits of the evaluation exercise; the public policy-maker is often animated by preoccupations which have nothing to do with the imaginary public policy-maker, dear to the hearts of normative economists. Consequently, economists will more often be ignored when a public decision is made or their methods criticized, often in the name of their excessive abstraction but more prosaically because their conclusions are often disturbing.

Repression and public policy

Let us go back now to the possibilities of changing policy. We have already mentioned that we exclude the idea that a solution could result from a utopian redistribution of resources between treatment and repression. It is, however, possible to unilaterally increase the drug budget in favour of care costs, which would improve well-being. Such an exit would of course come up against the scarcity of public funds and the imperative of controlling the budget deficit. Imagine that this constraint can be removed. It is not obvious that an increase in drug budget translates into a rebalancing in favour of care. It would suffice that the marginal cost curves of repressive public policy have the following forms to justify a unilateral increase of repression (see Figure 6.13).

Figure 6.13 illustrates a situation where the classic marginal cost of repressive policy grows, but it could be steady without modifying the conclusions. On the other hand, the marginal benefit of repressive policy decreases, and then increases. This implies that starting from point *E*, it is necessary to increase repressive expenditure, since at the margin it costs less than the price attributed to it by the members of the collectivity. From *A* it is no longer necessary to increase repressive spending because it is perceived as being more costly than beneficial.

Let us assume that the population considers that the reduction of crime associated with drugs, of, say, 25 per cent between *E* and *A* justifies the expense. On the other hand, reduced again, after *A*, criminality becomes too costly, unless a reduction of criminality between 80 and 90 per cent appears positive enough to fundamentally change the lifestyle. In this case, the individuals attribute an enormous value to the quasi-suppression of criminality and are ready to pay a lot for this. There is therefore a second point of equilibrium, in *B*. We are in the presence of a case of multiple equilibrium. The two equilibriums are stable, and the public policy-maker can choose between the two. Obviously, the greater the distance from the reference situation, from that aimed at equilibrium, the greater the time/cost of adjustment. The strategy of zero tolerance, remains undeniably based on a hypothesis of this type. The difficulty is, of course, to know if point *B* really exists and at what price it can be attained.

Furthermore, the consequences in terms of interpersonal and spatial equality are not examined in Figure 6.14. Is it possible to achieve a very low rate of criminality without a high degree of injustice? In effect, zero tolerance seems to translate into an increase in police errors, which more frequently affect ethnic minorities. If this tendency is not correctable, it will result in a trade-off between increasing the well-being of some and the risk of unjustified sanctions for others: a very unequal situation. Can this policy be put into effect over the whole territory or is the reduction in criminality explained by a crowding effect? Effectively, if criminal activity moves from downtown towards the suburbs while taxes are imposed uniformly, such a policy would once again be very unequal.

In any case what comes out of this brief discussion is that it is possible that the American public policy-maker remains blocked on a sub-optimal equilibrium if his preferences incline more towards repression than those of the well-being of the collectivity. It is also plausible that an increase in public spending in favour of repression without a rebalancing in favour of treatment is envisaged if the individuals have convex preferences in matters of security. The option of zero tolerance would then be efficient, in terms of individual representation of well-being. On the other hand, the consequences in terms of acuity still need to be examined, based on empirical studies which unfortunately do not exist yet.

Conclusion

Directing an effective public drug policy and one that encourages the support of the population is not simple. Strict repression policies of the offer generally have public favour as they appear to reconcile effectiveness with issues of social justice (interrupt the river of drugs at its source and justice will prevail) (save the addicts). In practice, the risk of favouring organized crime by intensifying repression of the offer is not inexistent when the wholesale market is divided between small and large dealers. Furthermore, the effectiveness of the repression of the offer crucially depends on the reaction of the consumers, and particularly on the elasticity of demand. More generally, the variables that affect the repressive policy are numerous and complex, representing a real difficulty in exactly predicting their effect. The case of the purity of drugs is fairly emblematic; it is counter-intuitive but true that the great disparity in the quality of the drug on the market is an obstacle to public repressive policy. Effectively, this situation confuses the signals sent by the policy-maker to the market, via the prices.

The introduction of multiple equilibrium further complicates the policy-maker's task. This is not a free theoretical sophistication but the transcription of the fact that the policy-maker could be aiming at several different objectives, each assuring certain equilibrium to his policy. Once blocked in a sub-optimal equilibrium, there are perhaps reasons to see the policy-maker change his strategy, even if economists assure him of the existence of another equilibrium, superior for the collective well-being. But should we believe the economists?

7 Fighting money laundering and organized crime

Introduction

The fight against organized crime and money laundering constitutes a special form of repressive policy against drug trafficking that has been the subject of impassioned debates for decades. Numerous excellent police films have popularized the idea that it is not in the interest of organized crime to bring on a visible explosion of criminality that could provoke a wave of police repression. Thus, the image of organized crime networks assuming the role of policemen within the criminal world has often informed public debates on organized crime. The movies have also popularized the idea that laundering is the Achilles' heel of drug trafficking. Therefore, to concentrate repression on this link of drug trafficking would seem to be an effective means of dissuading traffickers. Since these questions return us directly to the notion of public policy efficiency, economists have actively besieged them. A quick review of their theories gives a contrasting impression. No doubt economic theory has amply advanced discussion, in enriching terms, of effectiveness in the fight against laundering. It is in this area that the results are most pronounced: while it seems clear that the resulting policies have encountered several obstacles, we can say that, without it being a real consolation, the theories put forward really have made some contributions to our thinking on the issue. In matters of organized crime, we remain more sceptical about the range of the analysis undertaken. Using hypotheses we consider to be unrealistic, various authors have illustrated that the presence of organized crime is not necessarily more harmful to collective well-being than its absence. But this is on the condition, however, that we consider that organized crime's only effect on society occurs via the quantity of criminal goods and services offered to the public. By not taking into account the fact that organized crime engenders important externalities that erode the very base of our societies, economic analysis follows a short cut that is too striking. The challenge presented to economic analysis by organized crime reminds us of the squaring of the circle. Either we exclude the intrinsically harmful character of organized crime from the hypotheses and we miss its particularity, or we include it, which means taking as a hypothesis that which we are trying to illustrate.

Money laundering strategies

The laundering of money earned is the last link in the strategic chain of drug trafficking. Drug trafficking generates significant amounts of income, at least for some players. In order to benefit from the criminal proceeds of trafficking, the traffickers must launder these sums to conceal their criminal origin.

An overly sensitive subject

In 1997, the ONDCP (Office of National Drug Control Policy) held that drug trafficking yielded $350–450 billion annually. In 1989, the FATF (Financial Action Task Force on Money Laundering) proposed a lower estimate of $125 billion and deduced that $85 billion of that was laundered annually. IMF President Camdessus, for his part, stated during an address delivered in 1989, without identifying his sources, that around 5–10 per cent of international GDP was laundered, or between $590 and $1,500 billion. The press, moreover, sometimes cites a figure said to come from the United Nations, according to which $200 billion is laundered each year.

Calculations of the demand for money laundering, when they claim a scientific basis, rely on estimations of profits drawn from criminal activities, profits that are themselves calculated on the basis of an estimate of the sales turnover of criminal enterprises. Generally, the only criminal income taken into account is that generated by drug trafficking. This almost exclusive attention to drug trafficking results from the fact that FATF operations were designed to combat criminal money laundering arising from drug trafficking. It was therefore logical to concentrate on the latter. The fact that data already existed on the prevalence of drug consumption in the United States facilitated the calculation. Similarly, observations on the ground or by satellite provided an approximation of the extent of cultivation. From a technical standpoint, drug production appeared to be easier to assess than racketeering or smuggling. Politically, the accent was placed on drugs, so it was normal for the assessment to focus on money laundering resulting from drugs.

This focus on drug money is not without a certain basis, since drug trafficking remains the activity par excellence that brings in large revenues and requires international movements of capital. Since burglars, pimps, and other petty criminals launder their proceeds by simple methods, the enforcement system seemed rather complete. It is the sudden emergence of drug money that has pointed out the existence of a 'vacuum' into which criminal organizations have rushed.

Not only did the drug profits seem unfathomable, but the techniques of money laundering also attributed to international traffickers seemed to utilize mysteries of the international banking and financial system on a scale never before seen. The essence of the technical literature devoted to money laundering thus focused on the most complex methods of laundering, notably those using the most sophisticated instruments offered by the international banking and finance system.

Little or no attention was accorded to the more rudimentary methods of money laundering. Yet the simple fact of consuming the product of a criminal activity constitutes the most elementary and most common form of laundering. Similarly, a large portion of criminal proceeds is simply stored in safes, deposited in one or several accounts or used for real estate purchases.

It is in this way that a striking oversimplification has been carried out. On the one hand, an extremely high estimate of criminal money, tied to drugs and subject to being laundered, has begun to circulate persistently among the different international agencies. On the other hand, most attention is focused on the most sophisticated modes of money laundering. These circumstances have given rise to the illusion that this was actually the sum that the international banking and finance system was contributing to money laundering. Last but not least, a dramatic touch was added to this picture: behind this gigantic sum of money was discovered the hand of 'organized crime'. The circle was complete. Since one must combat the most sophisticated forms of money laundering, those that use the most modern channels of the banking and finance system and that are the exclusive prerogative of large criminal organizations, it was necessary that the numbers fit this image.

Over-estimated data

There are few precedents in scientific literature for the recent situation of drug data, in which figures so manifestly erroneous circulated for ten years without the FATF at any time being eager to correct them publicly.[1] We will quickly show that the quantitative studies of the magnitude of money laundering have systematically led to absurd results through the use of totally inappropriate techniques.

The over-estimation of drug trafficking sales turnover

The FATF (1990) estimated, in 1990, that the turnover of drugs sold retail during the 1980s was $108 billion in the United States and $16.3 billion in Europe: that is, a total of $124.3 billion (see Table 7.1). This estimate of annual drug sales turnover is rather questionable and no doubt somewhat overestimated for the 1980s, because several uncertainties[2] hang over the details of the calculation.

Table 7.1 Estimate by the FATF of turnover of retail drug sales (Europe and
United States) (billions of dollars)

Type of drug	United States	Europe	Total
Cannabis	67.2	7.5	74.7
Heroin	–	–	12
Cocaine	–	–	28.8
Total	106	16.3	122.3

Source: FATF (1990).

Even if the turnover were $125 billion, however, international drug
trade does not exceed $20–$25 billion. This is the case because one can
consider that the retail price of drugs is roughly six times higher than the
wholesale price.

From turnover to profits

Now it is necessary to shift from retail drug sales turnover to the share of
profits destined to be laundered. Proceeding from international drug trafficking turnover misguidedly confused with retail drug sales turnover, and
thus very much overestimated, the FATF assesses the amount of money
coming from drug trafficking and subject to being laundered each year at
between $61 billion and $85 billion. Yet, it appears once again that the calculation allowing the transition from sales turnover to amounts for laundering is open to criticism.

For example, in the case of cocaine in the United States, we saw in
Table 7.1 that the turnover by retail dealers was estimated at $28.8 billion.
The calculation of the profits consists of subtracting from this turnover the
cost of purchases, or $5.1 billion, yielding $23.7 billion. The dealers' net
profit is obtained by subtracting the famous 10 per cent that is supposed to
correspond to customs seizures. That leaves $21.33 billion. The net profit
of the wholesalers, for their part, is estimated at $4.88 billion. The total
net profit of cocaine trafficking (dealers + wholesalers) thus amounts to
$26.21 billion.

The report then causes some uncertainty to persist as to the meaning of
this figure. A serious ambiguity arises in allowing this result to be interpreted as the amount of cocaine trafficking money that is ready to be laundered. Such an interpretation is obviously incorrect, since it amounts to
considering that small-scale dealers and wholesalers launder all of their
profits. The FATF thus considers that 50–70 per cent of the drug sales
turnover is available for laundering. With a turnover in the order of $122
billion for the United States and Europe, between $61 billion and $85
billion would thus be available for laundering.

It is not logical to treat the profits of small dealers and of wholesalers the same way. By definition, the entire profit is used, therefore laundered, more or less effectively in the event of monitoring. A sum of $122 billion is thus 'laundered' as long as its holders have no worries, on the other hand, that they will be the object of the somewhat elaborate banking and finance manipulations aimed at muddying the waters for only a fraction of the wholesalers' profits and for those alone.

From profit to money laundering

By way of a very rough approximation, one can consider that a portion of the $20–25 billion of wholesale international trafficking is subjected to sophisticated laundering. The amount of money constituting a more or less centralized resource in a position to corrupt the world economy thus does not exceed $20 billion.

Note that this figure must be clearly understood. We do not suggest reassessing at $20 billion the amount of money that may be in line for laundering but ask to make a distinction between the sums that may be in the hands of criminal organizations and those that pass through the hands of small dealers and are dispersed into the legal economy, notably through bank deposits.

This idea of dispersal of the proceeds can be clarified by a 'rule of thumb' calculation. The 5 million regular US consumers of cocaine require about 500,000 dealers (1 dealer for every 10 consumers), yielding a turnover of $40,000 per dealer. Deducting the purchasing costs leaves roughly $20,000 (Reuter and Kleiman, 1986). It is still necessary to deduct consumption of drugs and staples, leading to the realization that, at this stage of drug distribution, sophisticated laundering does not exist. It is all played out among the several thousand cocaine wholesalers who, according to the FATF, share among themselves a profit of $5 billion and will launder a portion of it by setting up rather complex banking logistics.

Money laundering constitutes a constant preoccupation of criminal organizations, in particular those implicated in drug trafficking. We will show that contrary to images that often circulate, laundering based on the use of the most sophisticated channels of the banking and finance system turns out to be such a costly operation that criminals, including criminal organizations, often prefer rather primitive forms of laundering.

Different laundering techniques

Traditionally, a money laundering operation is considered as having three successive stages. During the 'placement', the money is introduced into the financial system. Next, the 'layering' phase consists of accumulating a number of transactions to reduce the traceability of the funds, which renders possible their final 'integration' in the form of investments in various sectors.

We propose to review the different techniques used (Blum *et al.*, 1998) at any given stage, listing them in order of increasing complexity. The governing idea here is to take a look at the techniques of piling up layers of transactions that allow the criminal proceeds to be separated from their origins, and those that permit an explanation of the origin of the enrichment. All these different procedures are classified in order of increasing cost, in particular transaction cost, that is, the cost of implementing the strategy.

Laundering on the territory of the crime

The simplest techniques take advantage of gambling laws. Casinos permit the laundering of small sums by disguising them as winnings, and the winning lottery and race tickets are repurchased with a bonus to their holders. The stock exchange can also be used by buying a call and a placement simultaneously. Only the profitable transaction is registered and the broker is reimbursed. The money to be laundered appears as a capital gain. Purchases and sales of property are another possibility. A piece of property is purchased at a lower-than-market price and a portion is paid under the table. The property is resold at the market price and the added value justifies the origin of the money.

Laundering outside the territory of the crime

*   *Using the informal banking system.* The principle is that of multiple transfers.[3] Two banking systems of two countries are used and one intermediary, a veritable banker of the informal sector, ensures the simultaneous action and the successful conclusion of the transactions on both sides. This can function even better in the case of ethnic groups with far-reaching diasporas in several countries. Smuggling traffic or immigrant wages, especially of illegals, also offer cover for the transfer of criminal funds.
*   *Using the banking system.* The use of numbered accounts permits the launderer to take advantage of banking secrecy. The use of an 'offshore' company and a numbered account adds commercial secrecy to banking secrecy. The inclusion of lawyers on the board of the company offers a third layer of protection: judicial secrecy. This mechanism can be infinitely complicated by taking advantage of fictional addresses and front men. Let us point out that the more complicated the mechanism, the more costly it is to control and the greater the risks of betrayal. The funds can be repatriated by debiting a credit card issued abroad. The bills can be settled directly by a foreign bank.
*   *Using commercial transactions.* Debts in the source countries are paid by an offshore company. Fees can be paid by the offshore company to fictitious consultants in the source country. The criminal sells the real estate that he has in his possession to an offshore company at an ele-

vated price and the money is deposited to the account of the real estate agency. A similar transaction can take place for raw materials or stocks. The capital can also be repatriated in the form of loans granted by the offshore company (this is becoming a major trend).

The different techniques listed above do not require equal levels of competence or the same networks. They are not used for the same amounts of money and do not have the same cost.

The cost of money laundering

This question of the cost of money laundering turns out to be decisive to understanding what procedure the trafficker will choose. Whatever technique he uses, the total cost of laundering[4] for the criminal is composed of two elements: the margin paid to intermediaries, which is often in the order of 10–15 per cent, and the costs that must be covered for the laundering operation to take place, that is, the transaction costs (see Figure 7.1).

In concrete terms, a trafficker must not only pay a margin to intermediaries, but he must also take care of various costs such as payment of lawyers, transfer fees, various legal fees, fixed costs, rights of entry into the criminal milieu, etc. Using a complex financial network carries a certain risk that also represents an expected cost for the criminal. The transaction costs linked to a money laundering operation can be grouped into two categories: the cost of implementing the strategy and the cost of the risk:

- *Margins deducted by intermediaries*. It is legitimate to consider that the money laundering market functions in a sufficiently competitive manner so that the margins paid are more or less identical from one intermediary to another. While we unfortunately do not have data on the amount of the margin, it is generally considered to be between 10 per cent and 15 per cent of the amount laundered. The indices, however, tend to show that the requirements of intermediaries have increased with the intensification of anti-laundering actions. It is reasonable to imagine, nonetheless, that the search for the lowest margin does not play a strong incentive role in the choice of laundering technique.

TOTAL COST OF MONEY LAUNDERING

=

MARGINS DEDUCTED BY INTERMEDIARIES

+

TRANSACTION COSTS
cost of implementing the strategy

+

cost generated by risk

Figure 7.1 The cost of money laundering

- *The cost of implementing the strategy.* This consists of the expenses of operating inherent to the chosen laundering strategy. Laundering money by buying back winning lottery tickets or mounting an offshore enterprise does not generate the same type of information gathering cost, transfer, legal counsel, and other fixed operating costs. The amount and frequency of the sums to be laundered must justify recourse to sophisticated schemes. The criminal organization only implements a complex money-laundering scheme if it is in a position to predict the flow of its revenues and if it considers that the paths that allow the plan to be set up are stable. An individual criminal does not have a well-enough established strategy to adhere to a costly laundering scheme.
- *Costs engendered by risk.* The risk is of two types: risk that enforcement poses to the money to be laundered and the risk of internal defections. The risk tied to enforcement lies not only in the fact that laundering is an activity that is monitored but also in that a criminal may be under surveillance for other reasons and lead the police to the money-laundering channels. The risk of betrayal results from the fact that the criminal complicity necessary to put the laundering pipeline into place may be tempted to betray the organization. By widening its base, the criminal organization increases its costs of coordination in illegality and increases the risks of opportunism.

The logical economic behaviour of criminals, or of a criminal organization, is to try to use the least costly money laundering technique. It must therefore take into account the three preceding components of cost. An optimal money laundering strategy thus requires that the expected profit from laundering will at least cover its costs, consisting of the sum of the margin taken by intermediaries, the cost of access to the market, and the cost of risk.

We have represented the link between the laundering techniques and the total cost of laundering in Figure 7.2. The left part of Figure 7.2 describes the different techniques used to conceal the criminal origin of a sum (layering). The different layers of protection that can be used are located horizontally, and the total cost generated by the operation (integration) is represented vertically.

The right part of Figure 7.2 shows the different possibilities for using the money, again classified as a function of transaction costs. This part of the figure describes the techniques of 'integration': that is, the implementation of measures that permit a justification of the origin of the laundered funds. On the abscissa are located the different layers of secrets that can be used; on the ordinate is the transaction costs of the operation.

Figure 7.2 sheds light on the total cost generated by the chosen combination between a technique of layering and a method of integration. It appears clear that the total cost of implementing money-laundering

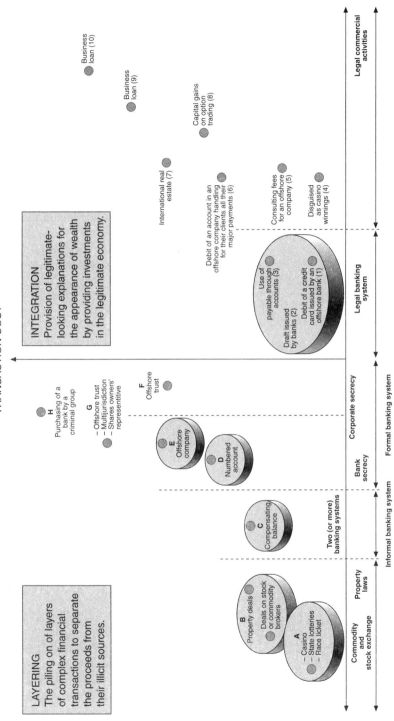

TRANSACTION COST

LAYERING
The piling on of layers of complex financial transactions to separate the proceeds from their illicit sources.

INTEGRATION
Provision of legitimate-looking explanations for the appearance of wealth by providing investments in the legitimate economy.

Business loan (10)

Business loan (9)

Capital gains on option trading (8)

International real estate (7)

Debit of an account in an offshore company handling for their clients all their major payments (6)

Consulting fees for an offshore company (5)

Disguised as casino winnings (4)

Use of payable through accounts (3)

Draft issued by banks (2)

Debit of a credit card issued by an offshore bank (1)

H
Purchasing of a bank by a criminal group

G
– Offshore trust
– Multijurisdiction
– Shares owners' representitive

F
Offshore trust

E
Offshore company

D
Numbered account

C
Compensating balance

B
Property deals

Deals on stock or commodity brokers

A
– Casino
– State lotteries
– Race ticket

Commodity and stock exchange

Property laws

Two (or more) banking systems

Bank secrecy

Corporate secrecy

Legal banking system

Legal commercial activities

Informal banking system

Formal banking system

Figure 7.2 The total cost of money laundering

strategy can become exorbitant. Considerations of cost can thus conflict with the use of sophisticated laundering techniques.

To the extent that consistency obliges concealing the origin of the funds (left section) and using laundered money (right section) according to the methods located at almost the same level on the graph, that is, that generate a similar level of transaction costs, the total cost of laundering can increase quite rapidly.

Criminal strategic management

Recourse by a criminal organization to rather simple laundering techniques can often be explained by the cost of setting up a complex money-laundering system and the risks that it poses to the one who sets it up.

Having recourse to sophisticated money laundering techniques by mobilizing the international banking system can only be done by criminal organizations that carry substantial weight, whether because of the number of countries that they cover or because they belong to a well-established Mafia family.

Optimization of money laundering techniques

When a criminal organization belongs to a solid core of organized criminality (Chinese triads, Colombian cartels, Camorra, etc.), it will use the international banking system to launder its proceeds. Such a practice presupposes that the hierarchical positions in the organization are sufficiently stable that access to the laundered sums will not constitute a source of subsequent discord. Such stability of relations is rarely achieved. Consequently, money laundering does not serve the purpose of putting significant sums that belong to the organization as such out of sight of the justice system on a long-term basis. Indeed, the concept of a 'sum belonging to the organization' is too unstable to be operational. In general, criminal organizations will choose to use the international banking system to cut the money off from its origin and reinvest it in the legal economy. Front men will carry the title to the property and a portion of the income from the transactions conducted this way will be legally paid to members of the organization. Such a system is sufficiently flexible. When a member of the organization dies, sometimes in a manner that is anticipated, it suffices to change the consignee of the payment. The front men are not able to sell their share, since they cannot do so without alerting the other shareholders. They prefer thus to collect a bonus rather than to expose themselves to risk. Such a laundering technique subscribes to fundamental rules of preservation of inherited property peculiar to criminal organizations. The way the property is kept must therefore discourage potential betrayals and be flexible enough to change with modifications of the balance of power within the organization.

It seems to us equally important to distinguish money-laundering practices put in place by the members of organizations on an individual basis from strategies implemented collectively for the organization and for its leading elite. When the members of a criminal organization, if it is very large, launder their proceeds, they use strategies that are rather primitive and common to the criminal group as a whole (purchase of real estate, use of front men, cash deposits and foreign accounts).

Recourse to a complex laundering scheme only makes economic sense in certain very limited cases. When a criminal organization is old enough and the evolution of the positions of the members in the internal hierarchy is relatively well regulated, the organization can have a view that is sufficiently long term to envisage a money-laundering strategy in the service of the group. This is the case, most notably, when the combined pressure of police and tax authorities on the known leaders of the criminal organizations is such that they can no longer enjoy their benefits without being immediately charged with tax fraud. This was the case, for example, of the Italian-American Mafia chiefs on the East Coast of the United States in the late 1960s. It was then essential that they put in place a rather sophisticated money-laundering scheme.

Criminal organizations also follow a sort of 'life cycle' that can lead them to try to implement strategies of redeployment into the legal economy. De facto, this is not a matter of dislodging and recycling the entire organization toward legal activities, but of permitting the leaders, accompanied by a limited number of indispensable close associates, to buy participation in legal activities. This particular form of 'gentrification' is also aimed at furthering the transfer of fortunes to the families of members of the organization. From the time the concern to organize the future emerges, when the horizon of economic rationality goes beyond the person of the criminal alone and embraces a family group whose future becomes a subject of anxiety, setting up complex money laundering schemes becomes indispensable. Such an observation explains why a criminal organization where the family plays a strong symbolic role (Italian-American family on the East Coast of the United States) will set up techniques that are more complex to perpetuate inheritance than will a motorcycle gang.

Use of the sophisticated mechanisms of the international banking and finance system to launder the money is not accomplished in the same way by all criminal organizations. A current trend consists of mixing up the transfer of funds and the laundering strategy. Colombian traffickers in the 1980s essentially repatriated their proceeds to Colombia and reinvested them without any particular precautions. The majority of the funds were repatriated in cash, by transfers, or by means of exchange establishments, and they covered the need for dollars tied to exchange monitoring. The need for sophisticated techniques arises only when the country where the funds must be used conducts an active policy of combating drug trafficking or when fiscal officers have considerable authority at their disposal. Thus, Pakistani heroin traffickers do not use a complex money-laundering strategy. In view of the situation in the country, their problem does not exceed that of the logistics necessary to transport the funds and divide them up. Laundering has not yet emerged as a problem in itself, so that recourse to the banking and finance system is limited and confined, essentially, to transfer operations.

Laundering a sum of money assumes that the ownership of the sum in question is clearly established. As long as a sum of money is retained in cash, its distribution can be held in abeyance. The rules of confidence governing a common stockpile of cash shared by a group of associated criminals are not very complex. Alarms quickly go off if one of the associates tries to seize the sum alone. From the time the money is laundered in a foreign account, and even if several associates have authorization, the risk of betrayal becomes even greater in that the bank's mission is precisely never to contact its foreign clients.

The act of laundering a sum of money thus assumes that the distribution rules are clearly set among the associates, and therefore multiplies the risk of betrayal by distancing the holder of the sum from them. The absence of authorization over the accounts makes the holder take the risk of not having access to it in case of incarceration. Accounts with multiple holders carry a risk of betrayal. The act of initiating a money-laundering procedure generates a certain irreversibility in the allocation of funds that often delays the decision to have recourse to it.

Setting up complex money laundering strategies thus requires that prior relations of confidence and clear rules of dividing up the proceeds be established among associates. As long as property rights are not clearly defined and relations of opportunism prevail among the criminals, there will be a strong reluctance to turn to money laundering.

Money laundering and intergenerational altruism

Laundering money serves the purpose of depositing savings and thus assumes that the criminal entrepreneur or criminal organization is planning for the future. But the economic choices of criminals are often characterized by a very low actualization rate. By sharply devaluing the future, criminals are not very tempted to agree to incur expenses today for the uncertain chance of profits tomorrow from inheritance thus constituted. This law of psychology seems to us plausible and is probably accompanied by a second behaviour specific to the criminal: a low degree of intergenerational altruism. Assuming that criminals are less disposed than the rest of the population to make an effort to deposit a portion of their proceeds in the form of savings to be available for their descendants, they have one reason less to launder their money. To be sure, the inheritance behaviour of criminals has not been the subject of specific studies. A number of anecdotes, however, in particular relating to the Medellin trafficking group, leads us to believe that the majority of them are not concerned with the fate of their descendants. Only a close circle, among the most powerful, will try to shelter their families, in a broad sense. These strategies generally have something of the nature of a symbolic demonstration of power. By leaving the poverty of the extended family, the criminal demonstrates his power and facilitates his insertion into 'good' society by cutting ties with an often destitute origin. Consequently, the inheritance strategy of criminals consists most often of purchasing real estate in the name of those close to them, using the latter, moreover, as fronts. This type of strategy is limited both by the number of criminals who have recourse to it and by the amount of sums required. Such money-laundering strategies mobilize quite primitive laundering techniques such as investment in real estate. The only major risk incurred is generally of a fiscal nature. How, indeed, can relatives of traffickers justify their enrichment? But the tax authorities are often more easily corruptible than the judicial authorities, and consequently shut their eyes.

These few observations underscore the importance of curbs that limit recourse to the most sophisticated money-laundering techniques.[5] Criminal organizations are anxious to use only those money-laundering techniques that are adapted to their organizational configuration. Their spontaneous hostility to excessively complicated techniques that exceed the ingenuity of their members conveys precisely the existence of transaction costs that can turn out to be exorbitant. Only a few organizations will use the most complex techniques. The bulk of the money laundering will continue to make use of simplified channels.

Common errors

From an analytical point of view, the simple fact of taking an interest in the overall cost of money laundering, and not just in the margin deducted by intermediaries, leads to a radical re-evaluation of the cost of laundering, which explains why the great majority of criminals avoid it. As a rule, only criminal organizations know how to profit from and have an interest in using the resources of a financial system to disguise the criminal origin of their income.

The more sophisticated the money-laundering operation, the more it requires time and expertise. The greater the number of persons associated with the operation, the greater the risk of betrayal. The more frequently it is repeated in an identical way, the greater is its risk of being exposed. Because criminal organizations are well informed about these dangers, they calculate carefully whether it is in their interest to undertake a complex money-laundering operation.

The tendency to over-estimate the degree of coordination of criminal organizations constitutes one explanation of the difficulty in restoring to the phenomenon of sophisticated money laundering its true dimension. Criminal organizations, with a few exceptions, are loosely centralized; their hierarchy is unstable, and the relationships of internal forces are fluid. In such circumstances, laundering assumes separating the money from members of the group who aspire to use it and who believe that they own it in common without the rules of distribution necessarily being clear. Now, it is precisely because the logic of individuals takes precedence over that of the organization that these individuals will generally be hostile to seeing their gains grow distant and enter a financial circuit over which they have little control.

Criminals and criminal organizations will therefore generally try to avoid turning to sophisticated money laundering methods because they are aware of the costs and risks of destabilization inherent in using complex schemes in the context of rather crude management.

It is interesting to note that our various observations on both criminal organizations and money laundering strategy share a certain scepticism as to the all-powerful nature of organized crime. Criminal organizations are subject to constraints analogous to those of legal businesses: their survival depends on their efficiency and even their mode of grouping together hinders their capacity to adapt. The systematic introduction of the importance of transaction costs constitutes the key that allows us to explain the difficulties and the weaknesses of criminal organizations. The difference from previous approaches that neglected to focus their attention on the black box that the enterprise constitutes – even if it is criminal – lies in the fact that from the time that one no longer likens the enterprise to a simple production function, one is in a position to understand the internal dynamics better.

Money laundering incentives and sanctions

In 1931, in Chicago, Al Capone was condemned to seven years in prison. For what crime? Racketeering, manslaughter? No. Al Capone 'tumbled' for tax evasion. His case illustrates that in the struggle against organized crime, indirect action based on repression of crime and violations induced by criminal activity may appear to be more efficient than direct action! Rather than attacking infractions which contribute to the constitution of criminal revenue head on, it can thus be preferable, because it is less costly and more effective, to latch on to limiting the possibilities for criminals to enjoy their revenue. This involves intensifying the fight against laundering. Developed countries seem to be orienting criminal policies in this direction since the middle of the 1990s by reinforcing penalties for money laundering.

There are two aspects involved in the implementation of an effective policy as far as money laundering is concerned: one is repressive and the other preventative. The first concerns the mechanisms to detect and sanction those persons or companies who transgress the law. This most often concerns criminals, and, more rarely, banks created by a criminal organization that attempt to whitewash criminal revenue so it can be spent without threat of discovery. The public policy-maker assigns a budget to those public agents who are most likely to arrest criminals of a certain level and then varies the severity of the sanction in order to obtain effective repression. In the case of laundering, the fact that infractions can be committed with the complicity of bank personnel who hide behind a 'professional breach of confidence' makes a second aspect necessary in order to complete criminal policy: prevention. This aspect involves implementing a system of banking and financial sector 'moralization' that aims to encourage the banks to increase their vigilance, and in particular, to give them the possibility of detecting dubious clients and denouncing them to the competent authorities.

Countries that fight criminal laundering have in common policies intending to dissuade individuals likely to participate in laundering criminal revenue. They alter the parameters of the economic calculation by modifying the severity of the sanctions and increasing the probability of arrest. This direct repression of the perpetrators of laundering comes up against numerous difficulties, most notably the fact that the repressive authority is incapable of untangling the financial transactions are entwined under shelter of the banks' 'breach of confidence' clause.

The preventive aspect is characterized by a marked opposition between the American model, which is designed around a system of regulatory authority based on the bank's criminal liability, and the continental model, in which banks' behaviour is shared by voluntary adhesion to a standard. The American model is intended to force the bank to efficiently monitor its personnel and clients by extensively invoking its legal liability. Thus the banks can be condemned for infractions committed by their employees or their clients, even if they themselves do not benefit, providing it is ascertained that they did not implement an adequate private monitoring system. On the other hand, continental criminal policy, e.g. France's, accords only limited importance to the bank's legal responsibility. This can only be engaged if the representatives of the banking establishments commit infractions in the name, and in the interest of, the company. Also if the bank does not respect the FATF standards, it only runs the risk of administrative sanctions (and these have never yet been applied) and not penal sanctions.

The points discussed in this chapter are to examine, still from the point of view of economic efficiency, the form taken by criminal policy when it tries to prevent money laundering. In order to provide a contextual presentation we use microeconomic models to illustrate the different aspects of public policy. Discussions debating the efficiency of laundering are generally very confused. From an empirical point of view, statistics are rare and we never know whether the data reflect the efficiency of the policy or repressive activity of agencies, especially when we do not know the total amount of money laundered in a given country. In short, beginning with the facts does not seem to be the easiest path forward to forging an opinion about the effectiveness of anti-laundering measures. We will therefore use our usual method of reasoning from simple theoretical models, highlighting the ways in which they contribute to our knowledge.

Drug dealers: to launder or not to launder?

Repression of the laundering of criminal revenue resulting from drug trafficking was presented at the beginning of the 1990s as a new and particularly effective technique, of stopping the traffic by targeting the personal assets of dealers. The idea put forward was simple: the stronger the repression, the less the dealers could enjoy their gain. Thus they would be discouraged from continuing their criminal activities. However, this innovation in repressive technique runs up against several obstacles. We notice that on the one hand, the dealers re-bill the increase in risk to the consumer, while also arranging their insolvency. It is thus unlikely that repression seriously places their personal assets in jeopardy. Consequently, we remain fairly dubious about the effectiveness of repression when it is presented as a decisive weapon in the fight against drug traffic. In practice, it is fairly rare that dealers are charged with laundering without also being charged for trafficking. From our rapid examination it appears that the fight against laundering more closely resembles a method of dealing out heavier sentences to traffickers who are arrested for trafficking than a system for arresting more of those who would otherwise slip through the holes in the net.

Evaluation of the efficiency of policies geared towards the repression of laundering involves a clear understanding of the behavioural hypothesis on which this action is based. The confusion characterizing the economist's examination of criminal laundering policy is due to the fact that laundering infractions cover a continuum of situations which run from tax evasion to organized crime. If economic literature has some difficulty realizing the stakes involved in creating laundering repression policies, it is no doubt because most authors have reduced laundering to a particular kind of tax evasion. For example, Usher (1986), Kaplow (1990), Cowell (1990), Cramer and Gahvari (1994) use the structure of the canonical model of Allingham and Sandmo (1972) and content themselves with adding a cost that describes the dissimulating activity of the criminal origin of sums involved in tax evasion. These authors only consider the fiscal infraction and reduce laundering to a strategy that permits reduction of the probability of the fraud being discovered. But the defrauder does not commit one but two infractions: the first by defrauding and the second by using illegal means to conceal the fraud. The move to implicitly treating laundering as a specific infraction is attributed to Yaniv (1999). In his model, the defrauder decides on the amount of revenue he wishes to declare, then the amount he will attempt to launder, knowing that each of these infractions engenders a cost. On their side, public authorities allocate distinct sums, a part for direct repression of tax evasion and a part for laundering repression. Following the example of Slemrod and Ytzhaki (1987), Yaniv concludes that the public policy-maker must stop increasing the amount of repressive spending when the marginal benefit becomes less than the marginal cost of its implementation. But the originality of his contribution is that he illustrates that the return on investment from the fight against laundering is often greater than that of the fight against tax evasion. In any case, the strategy of individuals who wish to launder legally earned sums in order to escape taxes differs from that aimed at dissimulating revenue of purely criminal origin. We can reasonably represent the choice of a doctor deciding whether or not to evade tax, as the result of the comparison between the hoped for benefit per laundered dollar and the cost of the sanction involved. On the other hand, the criminal is confronted with a very different choice: there is no way he can declare his criminal revenue to the tax authorities. He must therefore either conserve the money issuing from his criminal activity in cash or try to launder it.[6]

Let us examine the average case of an individual trying to launder his criminal revenue by following Yaniv's (1999) indications. Once the activity that produces revenue is illegal, it is impossible for the holder to declare it to the tax authorities. A criminal may then choose to keep his illegal revenue Y^c in cash, in which case the usefulness of the sum is minimized by a factor β (with $0 < \beta < 1$) reflecting the fact that cash cannot be used for all of the transactions that the criminal would like to make: for example, the purchase of an apartment or business.[7] The criminal may also decide to launder his revenue. In order to do this, he must pay intermediaries. The cost of laundering Z is assumed to be proportional to the sum to be laundered, $Z = z.Y^c$. If the laundering is detected, with a probability σ, the criminal risks a sentence of which the monetary cost is worth f. The levels of utility attained by the criminal in the different possible situations are:[8]

$U(Y^l) = Y^c - \beta Y^c$ if he does not launder his revenue,
$U(Y^s) = Y^c - z Y^c$ if he launders his revenue and is not arrested,
$U(Y^e) = Y^c - z Y^c - f$ if he launders his revenue and is arrested.[9]

The expected utility of laundering is thus written:

$$E[U(Y)] = (1 - \sigma)U(Y^s) + \sigma U(Y^e)$$

Supposing that the criminal knows the probability σ with which he will be arrested and the cost he must pay to launder z; he will only attempt a laundering strategy if the benefit b of this strategy is superior to its cost, or $b = Y^c(\beta - z) > \sigma f$. This schema can be adapted to cover more complex cases in which the author of the laundering is not a person but a business or an accomplice of another criminal, without greatly altering the reasoning. Now that the reasons for which a dealer wants to launder his illegal revenue have been elucidated, let us examine society's reaction.

Optimal sanction

Let us suppose that the laundering inflicts harm on the collectivity h (without harm, there is no problem of public policy). The public policy-maker must then calibrate the level of the legal sanction in such a way as to effectively dissuade potential criminals. This problem of public policy then obviously belongs to that treated by Becker (1968) and more generally by crime economics. From this point of view, laundering constitutes a crime like the others.

By following the path opened by Becker, we can consider that the distribution of individuals, the level of profit expected being responsible for their decision whether or not to break the law, is given by the function of density $l(b,h)$ of the distribution function $L(b,h)$. The benefit to the criminal is situated in an interval of $[0,B]$ and the social cost h in $[0,H]$. The policy-maker chooses a level of monetary sanction f and a level of public spending on repression c which permits crime detection with a probability σ, with $\sigma_c > 0$ and $\sigma_{cc} < 0$ in such a way that the collective well-being W is maximized:

$$W = \int_0^H \int_{\sigma(c)f}^B (b - h)l(b, h)\mathrm{d}b\mathrm{d}h - c \qquad (7.1)$$

A monetary sanction $f^* = \dfrac{h}{\sigma}$ thus effectively dissuades potential criminals

without necessarily completely eradicating laundering, as the policy-maker must stop allocating money to repress laundering when the marginal cost of the repression is greater than the reduction in social cost of laundering which it permits him to attain (Polinsky and Shavell, 2000). This analytical framework, which serves to measure the dissuasive effect of sanctions against individuals (authors or accomplices of infractions), can be extended to the rarer case, in which a whole banking establishment is created in order to carry out a criminal activity (as in the affair BCCI). This is why, following the example for individuals, criminal law includes a regime of reinforced sanctions for businesses that commit infractions of laundering laws.

This dissuasive scheme, common to different criminal policies, still comes up against numerous problems. First, because laundering infractions primarily involve the recycling of money gained from drug trafficking, racketeering and organized crime, in many cases criminals are able to re-bill the final consumer for the cost expected from a tightening up of criminal policy. For example, in the case of drug traffic, the commission demanded by intermediaries in laundering does not exceed 2 per cent of the price of cocaine sold on the street, according to the estimate made by Caulkins and Reuter (1998). Even if, in reaction to criminal policy, the intermediaries who help the traffickers launder doubled their demands, the price of cocaine sold in the street would only increase by 2 per cent. As the consumers of cocaine are practically insensitive to such a small price increase, the drug traffickers could re-bill the increase demanded by the intermediaries to the consumers without fear of seeing consumption decrease. The increase in intermediary margins caused by the repression does not therefore penalize dealer profits, and so we cannot expect a marked effect on the quantity of laundering (Kopp, 1995).

Second, it is common for criminals who launder money to have organized their insolvency, meaning they cannot pay the fine they receive. We should then substitute prison sentences for fines, based on the fact that criminals will consider in their financial calculation the inutility of incarceration time and the opprobrium that accompanies it. In any case, the effectiveness of incarceration is very relative as its duration is short and its cost (negatively) affects collective well-being

Third, we come up against a serious problem of marginal dissuasion. When the sentences are not accumulative, and those incurred for drug trafficking are usually more severe than those linked to infractions of laundering laws, it is probable that they will have no dissuasive effect when individuals combine the two activities. It seems, therefore, for the reasons already mentioned, that the ability of a repressive policy to slow down laundering, and, above all, the crimes which permit the offshore constitution of criminal revenue should not be overestimated.

Fourth, we note that the compared costs of police inquiries in the strictly criminal area and in the domain of laundering infractions do not necessarily make the struggle against this a simple and less costly method of condemning criminals. In France, to our knowledge, there is no case where a drug dealer has been condemned for laundering without having first been condemned for trafficking. Thus, the information necessary to interrogate the agents of laundering proves costly to obtain, as the State cannot directly observe financial and banking transactions, these being protected by banking confidentiality.

It is this last observation that justifies the present interest in bank criminal liability. Recently introduced into the French penal code (1996) and those of some other EU countries but timidly used since, this disposition is, however, often mobilized on the other side of the Atlantic in order to force the banks to monitor their personnel, and even their sub-contractors, as the State considers they are in a better position to do so than it is. Thus we will now study the financial operation of the preventive mechanism implemented in America.

Self-regulation of the banking system: the US model of corporate liability

The American model is based upon the idea that banks are in a better position to monitor financial transactions than the State is. Since the State cannot observe the behaviour of bank employees, it delegates this monitoring mission to the banks, which choose either to directly observe their employees' behaviour, or to implement a private control mechanism. If the banks are considered guilty of negligence under their legal responsibility, they risk sanctions, the amount of which must permit the perfect internalization of the social cost of the laundering they could not prevent.

From an economic efficiency point of view, as the banks can dissuade their personnel from committing infractions at less cost than the State can, the State's delegation of monitoring to the banks finds its justification in the application of the principle of minimization of dissuasion cost: 'least cost-enforcer'. If such a mechanism is beneficial for the collectivity, it consists of transferring the weight of monitoring from the collectivity as a whole (public financing) to only the banks. It is then up to the banks to exploit the possibilities offered by specific methods of payment of their personnel to try to prevent them from committing infractions, even ones that might be profitable to them, in order to reduce the frequency of condemnation for the establishment and the amount of fines paid.

The basis for the interest of American economists in legal responsibility stems from the possibilities offered by the specific remuneration system for bank managers. This consists of a fixed salary and a variable (bonus) which depends upon the valorization of the establishment. This special form of remuneration should permit banks, according to economists, to control their personnel by making their compensation dependent upon the effort they make to reduce the number of infractions they commit or facilitate. The State thus aligns the banks' objective function with its objective of minimizing social cost for anti-laundering, with the implication of the banks' legal responsibility. The banks obtain adapted personnel behaviour by implementing an incentive for remuneration that induces a level of effort on personnel involved in maximizing bank profits, once the amount of fines they would have to pay for infractions they could not prevent is taken into account.

From this observation, it was of course tempting to apply the principal–agent model to forge an opinion of the efficiency of the technique used in the United States to improve the banking system. The wealth of theoretical developments that follow must not make us lose sight of the fact that a non-negligible part of the bank complicity that criminals benefit from does not necessarily stem from managers who are sufficiently highly placed to benefit from bonuses. The dissuasive range of the mechanism then depends crucially on the degree of generalization of incentive bonuses.

A principal–agent model

The American mechanism for preventing laundering infractions may be treated with the help of an agency model where the government is the principal, the bank the supervisor, and the bank managers the agents. The State is in a situation of moral risk, it cannot observe the behaviour inside the bank: it therefore delegates the mission of personnel control (role of supervision) to the bank.

In the analysis that follows, we use the original corporate liability analysis (Arlen, 1994) and its model (Arlen and Kraakman, 1997), as well as the first consideration of the question in terms of the principal–agent model proposed by Garoupa (2000) and partially inspired by Gans (2000).

The model considers that the social value of a bank depends on two types of activity: one being its normal activity m and another criminal activity n, which it shelters, voluntarily or not – for example, laundering – imposes a social cost h on the collectivity. The value of the portion of bank capital held by the managers is given by $\alpha G(m,n)$ where α represents the part of capital held by the managers and $G(.)$ the value expected of the bank's capital. The value of capital is determined thus: it is worth 1 with a probability $m+n$ and 0 with a probability $1-m-n$. So the bank's expected value is $G(m,n) = m + n$. The private value expected of the criminal behaviour of management is given by $E(n)$, with $E'(n) > 0$ and $E''(n) < 0$. The fixed component of the managers' salary is w. The managers' effort is described by the cost $C(n,m)$ with $C_n', C_m' > 0$ and $C_n'', C_m'' < 0$. Thus, n indicates the influence of managers' criminal behaviour on the bank's value, u is a random variable of which the distribution function is $F(.)$, and n and u are considered to have additive effects. Crimes then appear only if $n + u > 0$. If crimes are committed by the managers, the State can detect them following a probability σ, and the guilty then suffer a sanction S_a and the bank S_p. We will thus examine these cases in perfect and imperfect information.

Perfect information

Suppose that contrary to the State (principal), the bank (agent) can observe the efforts made by the managers for legal activity m and illegal activity n. Under these conditions of perfect information, the optimal contract content tying the managers to the bank is given by the resolution of a procedure maximizing the bank's expected profit under the restriction of the participation of management n where k designates the value of the utility of reserve of the agent.

The remuneration expected from management[10] is:

$$U = \omega + \alpha(m + n) + E(n) - C(n, m) - P(n)\sigma S_a \qquad (7.2)$$

The profit expected from the bank is written:

$$V = (1-\alpha)(m+n) - \omega - P(n)\sigma S_p \qquad (7.3)$$

The bank's problem is to find the levels of legal activity m and illegal activity n, solutions to the programme:

$$\left| \begin{array}{l} \max_{m,n} V \\ sc\ U \geq k \end{array} \right.$$

The values of optimal equilibrium of m and n are given by the solution of the conditions of the first order of the problem:

$$V_n = 1 + E_n - C_n - P_n\sigma(S_a + S_p) = 0 \qquad (7.4)$$

$$V_m = 1 - C_m = 0 \qquad (7.5)$$

When the second order conditions are satisfied, we deduce the optimal contract $(\hat{m}, \hat{n})$. We then easily show that laundering activity decreases with σ, S_a, S_p and productive effort increases following the same values as $C_{mn} > 0$. We define the function of collective well-being of the State as the sum of the bank's benefit and that of the managers, minus the social cost of the criminal activity:

$$W = m + n + E(n) - C(m, n) - k - P(n)h \qquad (7.6)$$

In the absence of sanctions, the difference between the State's objective function (to maximize collective well-being) and the bank's (to maximize profit) corresponds exactly to the social cost expected from the criminal activity σh. By arranging the level of sanction in such a way that the sum of sanctions imposed on managers and bank is equal to the social cost divided by the probability of being arrested or $S_a + S_p = \dfrac{h}{\sigma}$, the State can bring the objective function of the bank closer its own. The bank then behaves as the State would if it possessed the necessary information. It matters little who, the managers or the bank, is effectively punished: whether $S_a = \dfrac{h}{\sigma}$ and $S_p = 0$ or the contrary is of no consequence to the State. The State leaves the problem of negotiating between them the distribution of the sanctions to the bank and its managers.

This mechanism, however, is limited by the managers' solvency: they cannot pay more than they possess. It is possible to remove this constraint by substituting prison sentences for fines. But, as incarceration is costly, it is preferable for the State to introduce some form of legal responsibility for businesses conforming to the logic of 'deep pocket', which consists of making businesses pay the fines rather than the managers. As the constraint of managers' wealth is given by $\bar{\omega}$, it is sufficient to distribute the amount of the optimal sanction in such a way that $S_a = \bar{\omega}$ to obtain effective dissuasion.

Thus, in sound theory, when the bank can observe the managers' behaviour, the introduction of corporate liability is necessary to compensate for management insolvency and improve the social well-being of the collectivity by substituting effective private spending for inoperative repressive public spending. This mechanism, however, constitutes a supplementary burden for the banks.

Imperfect information

In fact it is more realistic to assume that the bank cannot observe 100 per cent of the criminal behaviour of its managers. In a situation of symmetrical information, the bank can only observe the legal activity m and illegal activity n of the managers. Managers choosing the level of effort $(\hat{m}, \hat{n})$ maximize their expected remuneration (situation of moral risk). The State, for its part, institutes bank criminal liability in order to compensate for the problem of manager insolvency and sets the sanction at optimal level

$S_p = \dfrac{h}{\sigma} - \bar{\omega}$, which allows total internalization of the cost of laundering.

With this method, the State forces the bank to behave as it would under the same conditions. The idea is then to analyse the behaviour induced by this situation that is optimal for the bank to adopt. The bank must then resolve the problem of the following programme in order to find the coefficient of the remuneration variable α that constitutes the optimal contract to maximize the bank's profit under the constraint of the managers' participation ($U \geq k$) and the constraint of compatibility of incentives ($\hat{m}, \hat{n}$).

$$\begin{cases} \max_{\alpha} V \\ sc: \\ \max_{m,n} U \\ U \geq k \end{cases}$$

Thus, even when the bank cannot monitor its personnel 100 per cent, it remains theoretically efficient, from the State's point of view, to delegate the monitoring of bank personnel to the banks by installing the banks' criminal liability. To compensate for the effects of criminal liability, the bank offers an incentive contract to its managers and maximizes its profit by bringing the number of infractions to their optimal level. This situation is expensive, however, as it continues to be condemned for the residual infractions that are still committed by its executives and which are sometimes discovered by the State.

The US reflex for private monitoring

In this environment of imperfect information (moral risk), when the banks are liable for management behaviour, they are encouraged to introduce a private personnel monitoring mechanism in order to decrease infractions and to try to obtain greater profits than in the preceding case (without private monitoring).

Corporate profit and monitoring

This idea, introduced in 1994 by Arlen, considers that when the managers are the subject of monitoring, their criminal activity is detected following probability ρ by the bank and will always be reported to the State. If the bank does not detect the managers' criminal behaviour, it can still be detected by the State following probability σ. The sanction on the manager's risk is S_a. The sanction imposed by the bank is S_q if the bank discovers the fraud and S_p if it is the State that discovers it.

As the bank (supervisor) cannot observe the effort that the managers invest in legal activity m and illegal activity n, it is they who choose the level of effort $(\hat{m}, \hat{n})$, which allows them to maximize expected revenue. The bank must then maximize its profit V using $(\hat{m}, \hat{n})$ as given data.

To maximize collective well-being, the State must determine the sanction level in such a way as to align the objective function of the bank with its own by using legal responsibility. It suffices to establish the sanction expected equal to the social cost of laundering, for the objective function of the bank to become identical to its own, at a cost approaching that of the private monitoring mechanism. Using legal sanctions, the State aligns the objective function of the bank with its own. To maximize profit, the bank must then propose an optimal contract to the managers, establishing, on the one hand, the descriptive parameter of the managers' remuneration variable a, and on the other, the effort of private monitoring ρ, under the constraint of management participation $U \geq k$ and the constraint of accounting of incentives $(\hat{m}, \hat{n})$, or the solution to the following programme:

$$
\left\{
\begin{array}{l}
\max_{\alpha,\rho} V \\
sc: \\
\max_{m,n} U \\
U \geq k
\end{array}
\right.
$$

The perverse effect of private monitoring

The introduction of a private monitoring system creates perverse effects identified by Arlen (1994) and elaborated by Arlen and Kraakman (1997). The more effort the banks make to monitor their personnel, the more they detect infractions that they must report, thus increasing their exposure to legal sanctions. If the bank implements an efficient monitoring system, on the one hand, the number of management infractions committed decreases, but on the other, each of those remaining involves a sanction against the firm. In the presence of the 'Arlen effect' it is not in the bank's interest to implement just any private control in order to avoid being condemned for the infractions it discovers. In all other cases, the bank will implement what is a sub-optimal level of monitoring from the State's point of view. That which is referred to as the 'Arlen effect' may be interpreted as a bias in the alignment of the objective function of the State (principal) and the bank (supervisor).

In order to compensate for this problem, American law explores a possibility that does not exist in continental law: measuring the sanctions pro rata in relation to the monitoring effort effectively engaged in by the banks. The difference between S_a and S_p thus corresponds to a new form of responsibility, 'mitigation liability', which should encourage the banks to adopt a monitoring mechanism for surveilling their employees. This bias is due to the ambiguous effects of the private employee monitoring mechanism, and it can shift the bank's behaviour away from that which the State prescribes in areas of private personnel monitoring; the limited responsibility is then a means of reducing this bias, and forcing the banks to adopt an optimal level of private employee monitoring.

To conclude this rapid examination of the American model, observe that the criminal policy is based on the extensive use of the criminal qualification, as much in matters of personnel monitoring as in those of client activity. This approach is reputed to permit compensation for the asymmetry of the State's information, while it is precisely because of information problems that the main criticisms of this system emerge. We can thus question whether or not the informational advantage that was the basis for granting the State's monitoring role to the banks was not greatly overestimated.

First, what is the operational range of such a mechanism? Only the low percentage of bank personnel who effectively benefit from incentive bonuses is effectively sensitive to the combined variations of their two sources of income. The optimal incentive contract that constitutes the lever of extensive application of legal responsibility to businesses can then be extended to only a small minority, which limits the banks' capacity to modify personnel behaviour. Second, when the banks must monitor their personnel, they have the choice of whether or not to implement a private monitoring system. In certain cases, this can negatively influence their profit. They are therefore forced to not systematically exploit a strategic advantage that would permit them, with the help of a private monitoring mechanism, to be more active than State-assured monitoring. The imperative of profit maximization can then drive them to voluntarily maintain a type of rational ignorance of their internal operations.

Third, judicial inquiries in cases of criminal liability become particularly lengthy and costly, and contribute considerably to encumbering the judicial system in a domain where the burden of proof of the incriminated bank's negligence is particularly complex. The State must then assume the weight of an unexpected cost when it has precisely transferred its monitoring role onto the banks to limit spending. Of course, each of these objections has a solution: extension of bonus remuneration, implementation of proportional responsibility, simplification of procedures. In any case, the risk exists, as in any regulatory system based on the introduction of a standard using legal dissuasion and monitoring delegation, of seeing savings in informational costs obtained by delegation counterbalanced by an increase of cost in applying the law. The probability of bringing bank behaviour in line by using incentives, along with that of using a system of business legal responsibility, thus seems fairly low due to the complexities of implementation faced by the state. Without the unlikely event of a virtuous modification in agent behaviour, we risk seeing the banks being forced to take the responsibility for internalizing the social cost of laundering, and trying to slow down this process by paralyzing the legal machinery when their legal responsibility is implicated.

Self-regulation: the continental system

In contrast to the United States, the majority of continental European countries do not wish to use the threat of criminal law to create the desired transformation in the morality of the banking system. For example, French law has introduced the obligation of cooperation with public authorities throughout the whole banking sector,[11] but it does not sanction an eventual violation of this obligation, except by disciplinary sanctions that are only slightly restrictive.[12] The continental mechanism counts on a flexible self-regulation of the banking system based on progressive and voluntary adhesion to a standard of behaviour. This schema does not require a great deal on the part of the regulator, but its major inconvenience is that it offers an easy way out to the banking establishments who continue to participate in laundering activities by allowing their 'negligence' to be used as an alibi.

From an analytical viewpoint, this form of banking self-regulation does not directly adhere to cases involving the spontaneous emergence of a private standard, a type of resurgence of the old *lex mercatoria* that recently gave rise to an abundance of literature.[13] The classical schema of *lex mercatoria* is that of the emergence of professional practices which are spontaneously imposed on members of a corporation, and are generally codified much later. This codification intervenes when the cost of information necessary for self-regulation becomes exorbitant due to the size of the system. The obligation to minimize the costs operates in favour of externalization of regulation towards the judicial system.

In the case of laundering, neither the banks, nor the financial system were practitioners of particularly virtuous behaviour, any more than they took the initiative in favour of the law to which, on the contrary, they were initially vigorously opposed. We are therefore confronted with a particular case where the standard of behaviour is proposed to the actors in the sector without including very restrictive sanctions. It seems, however, that this step could be crowned with success by bringing into effect a noticeable change in the behaviour of actors in the banking and financial sectors. For example, in France, after the adoption of the 1990 law on laundering, French banks found themselves faced with a dilemma: collectively, the 'self-regulation' of the system was in their interest, but individually, their best interest was to perpetuate their old practices, as no sanction was foreseen. Instructed to adopt a standard that belonged to a collective property, the banks were subject to the pernicious action of the prisoners' dilemma.

The logic of collective action

The fear of damaging their reputation and modest State intervention could be at the origin of a favourable solution to this problem. It is possible to adapt to our specific case Granovetter's (1978) initially advanced proposition, which was retained by Cooter (1995b) for illustrating the existence of conditions that permitted, in certain cases, an escape from the prisoners' dilemma. In this type of model (called 'de seuil') developed around the case of collective demonstrations such as strikes, the cost of entry into collective action decreases with the number of participants while each individual is characterized by a different cost threshold at which he decides to participate in collective action. We then observe a type of chain reaction where the increase in number of participants in the collective action reduces the cost of adhesion and activates more rallying.

In the case of banks, each time a bank adopts the new standard, it contributes to lowering the cost of future adhesion for those who have not yet done so. In effect, the fewer the number of banks who continue to participate in criminal laundering, the easier it is for them to use the argument with their clients that it becomes impossible to continue being the Lone Ranger. Let us illustrate with Figure 7.3 by tracing the curve $C(E)$ that describes the bank's cost to implement the law in the number of establishments who adopt this new attitude. This curve is waning: the more banks who respect the law, the less costly it is to respect it, as renouncing laundering becomes the dominant attitude. The curve $E(C)$

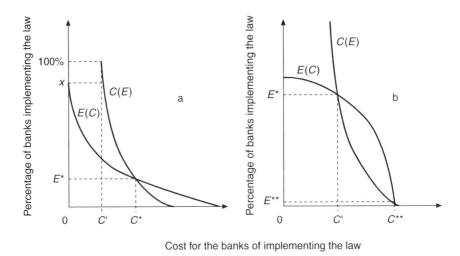

Figure 7.3 Conditions for generalization of the standard of good conduct

describes the distribution of the percentage of banks that are ready to adopt the law in function of the cost of its implementation.

By following the position of $E(C)$, we observe that the number of banks adopting the new law increases while the cost of implementation is less than their inclination to pay for changing their behaviour. If the two curves are convex (Figure 7.3a), the position of x on the ordered axis indicates that there are no more banking establishments for whom the cost of implementation of the law is less than their willingness to pay to be up to standard, and the percentage of banks who adopt the standard cannot be greater than percentage x. Once x per cent of banks adopt the new standard, the minimal cost of this implementation never falls below C'. The equilibrium intervenes for a percentage E^* of establishments when there are no more establishments whose willingness to pay is higher than the corresponding cost C^*. If the public policy-maker considers that this level of self-regulation of the banking system is insufficient, he can intervene to accentuate the cost for the banks to not play the game of standardization, thus decreasing their adaptation cost and forcing the move toward another more favourable equilibrium.

Multiple equilibrium

To move towards an equilibrium is more complex when the curve $E(C)$ is concave (Figure 7.3b), which describes a fairly realistic situation in which the cost of adaptation for the banks decreases more slowly when few banks follow the movement, then, more rapidly, when the standard becomes generalized.[14] The banking system finds itself in a situation characterized by multiple equilibrium. The majority of banks adopt the standard when the cost of respecting the law is less than their willingness to pay for this change. Once the curve $E(C)$ is situated above $E(C)$, the number of banks respecting the law ceases to increase. Once the curves cross each other again in C^{**}, the cost of respecting the law becomes superior to the banks' willingness to pay, while the number of banks respecting the law moves towards zero. The two balances are unstable. As long as the system has not found its equilibrium, the public policy-maker hopes of course to see the system converge towards optimal balance (C^*,E^*) but must be aware of the risk of seeing a local improvement lead to a suboptimal equilibrium (C^{**},E^{**}).

The public policy-maker may influence the localization of the equilibrium. It suffices that he manifest a renewed desire to see the standard of self-regulation adhered to for the cost, in terms of reputation, of the non-respect of the standard to increase. Inversely, as the cost of creating conformity decreases, the number of banks whose willingness to pay is higher than the cost increases. The policy-maker can thus drive the banking and financial systems towards a virtuous equilibrium by playing on the threat of lost reputation that moves the various banks' threshold of participation in the collective action.

The continental system is attractive, as it does not require complex intervention by the State, which needs only a little information in order to play its role. Absent is the risk of seeing more and more complex rules on liability pile up, as well as counter-measures intended to compensate for perverse effects, circumstances that typify the US system. On the other hand, the system is fairly lax, as it does not foresee real sanctions for the establishments who do not conform to the desires expressed by the policy-maker. This mechanism is also fairly easy to manipulate, as the handling of the threat of ruining the reputation of a banking establishment is highly political. The filing of a legal procedure and its follow-up provide all sorts of opportunities for ruining an establishment's reputation that can easily be shaped by politics. Finally, this type of regulation is devoid of exemplarity of legal application and contributes to maintaining a certain opacity about the operation of banking establishments which could be damaging with respect to the law, in general, and to the overall reputation of the system. The opposition between the US system centred on bank criminal liability and the continental model of regulation based on adhesion to a standard of behaviour is thus stimulating. It permits a better understanding of why the USA has a fairly large number of legal proceedings involving the legal responsibility of banks (for example, in the resounding case of the charges against the Bank of New York), while in Europe procedures are rarely filed directly against financial establishments in matters of laundering, and only very rarely against their directors. The American

184 Drugs, crime and the law

system, in order to regulate its financial and banking systems, depends on the legal treatment of laundering and the dissuasive effect of the sentences imposed. The continental system relies on the self-discipline of the establishments, and considers that the costs of legal treatment would be more than the benefits expressed in terms of dissuasion.

Is the law enforced?

Examination of the effectiveness of criminal policy in the struggle against laundering provides an opportunity to observe a special case of articulation between, on one side, the choice of rules of law and, on the other, the methods of attribution (public or private) of the job of implementing the law. It appears from the study of the situation in countries under American law that in the absence of a very special type of responsibility (proportional to the monitoring effort) we cannot affirm the effectiveness of delegating the mission of monitoring personnel to the private sector. From its side of the Atlantic, the continental system of placing the task of monitoring in the hands of the private sector rests on the hope of a progressive adoption of the new standard. This hope is certainly well founded, but the problem of mobilizing personnel around this objective when the revenue is not indexed on the reputation of the bank remains.

Thus, the possibility for the private sector to exploit an informational advantage that would justify its responsibility for the monitoring function remains largely hypothetical. The need for this direct intervention of the public regulator in the area of monitoring is thus reinforced by this brief examination of the present systems. Our report, based on inspiration rather than theory, confirms the observation of concrete difficulties in the struggle against laundering. We note, in fact, that both models run up against common difficulties. In the US, as in Europe, the preventive strategy rests on the idea that the banks can identify undesirable clients and turn them away. It is more than probable that the criminals would quickly learn how to hide their company name from their partners in the banking system. This is why the 'declaration of suspicion' will soon be out of date in the panoply of the struggle against laundering. The public authority will then need to find new regulations and implement an ad hoc mechanism. The multiplication of direct regulations (declarations of transfer, ban on cash payments over a certain amount, etc.) is the prelude to this probably inevitable tendency towards re-regulation. In any case, when the law progresses in the countries of the FATF zone, other States can seize the opportunity thus created to make themselves a place offshore, the reabsorption of which is a burning theme underlining the limits of purely national criminal policies. Here again, delegation of monitoring is not a substitute for direct international intervention directed at banning (which constitutes a form of regulation) the utilization of fiscal paradises, which make possible the execution of anonymous transactions. Finally, the struggle against laundering requires, as in the majority of cases of financial and economic delinquency, the strong international cooperation of the repressive agencies. These still come up against the disparity in the laws and procedures in the different countries concerned. The growth in the number of countries conforming to the rules promoted by the FATF certainly represents a positive step, but this must not obscure the often insurmountable difficulties of coordination of inquiries, including those in the heart of the European Union. Here again, the public policy-maker should intervene and devote resources to the satisfactory execution of transnational inquiries. Finally, the implementation of an effective mechanism to fight financial crime in general, and laundering in particular, will require the development of original forms of coordination between public and private bodies. No doubt this theme will mobilize law economists.

The virtues of organized crime

The fight against organized crime naturally constitutes the second major area of study on drug repressive policies. In effect, wholesale drug trafficking is often the main activity pursued by a criminal organization, a situation we have already discussed. As in the debates on laundering, the economic discussion about the fight against organized crime concerns the respective places of public and private action. The Chicago School of economists has in fact defended the idea that public spending in crime fighting could be reduced, while at the same time increasing collective well-being. When organized crime dominated the crime market, part of its activity, via private spending, was in fact devoted to protecting its monopoly. By racketeering petty delinquents and blocking access to certain criminal professions, organized crime would reduce, at a lower expense for the State, the quantity of criminal goods and services circulating. It is therefore, as in the case of laundering, the distribution of roles between public and private (in this case the Mafia) that lies at the heart of the discussion.

Organized crime versus competition among the criminals

The thesis defended by the supporters of Chicago economics (Buchanan, 1973; Posner 1998) considers that competition amongst criminals is less efficient than a monopoly, since optimal criminal production is greater in competition than in monopoly. Let us assume that the demand (D) describes the demand for 'bad', i.e. vice, sin or illegal drugs and (S), the supply. In Figure 7.4, we can observe that the intersection of demand (D) and the marginal revenue curve (MC) (which is the same as the supply curve (S)), determines the price (P_c) and the output (Q_c) under competitive conditions. The intersection of the marginal revenue curve (MR) and the marginal cost curve (MC) determines the monopoly level of

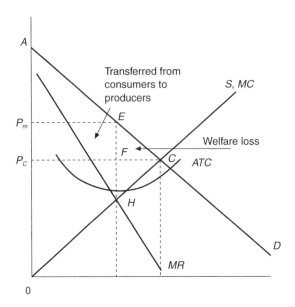

Figure 7.4 Monopoly versus competition

production (Q_m). The monopoly price is (P_m). Thus, one of the obvious distinctions between competition and monopoly is that the price of criminal 'bads' will tend to be higher and output lower under monopoly conditions than under competitive conditions. Another important distinction can be found in the impact on consumer and producer surplus. Under competitive conditions, the consumer surplus is equal to the area of triangle P_cAC. Under monopoly conditions in a market of criminal goods, consumer surplus is equal to the area P_mAE. Consumer surplus is, therefore, lower under monopoly conditions.

The critical question is: what has happened to the portion of consumer surplus that is no longer enjoyed by the consumers? First, the monopolist (the Mafia) captures a portion of it in the form of producer surplus. In other words, under competitive conditions, the producer surplus is equal to the area P_cCG. With a monopoly, this is expanded to P_mGHE. Part of this new expanded producer surplus, area P_mP_cEF, was originally part of consumer surplus and has now been transferred to producers. Another portion of what was consumer surplus, the area EFC, is not captured by the monopolist. This is called the welfare loss. Consequently, the presence of a criminal organization reduces the quantity of criminal merchandise, increases the price which limits the access, and transfers a portion of consumer surplus to the producer, which is the price to be paid so that the 'honest' population is kept as far as possible from the criminal merchandise. We can of course object that this analysis does not take into account the negative externalities created by the presence of a criminal organization in that it does not question the existence of those linked to consumption of illegal goods such as drugs. A complete treatment of the question involves verifying if the social cost engendered by the presence of a criminal organization is superior to the reduction of the social cost linked to the consumption of drugs due to monopolization of the market by organized crime. A partial treatment of this question leads to a potentially dangerous analysis that gives the impression to public policy-makers that economists are recommending a type of 'soft method' in the struggle against organized crime.

Among Chicago economists, Grosman (1995) developed certain ideas from Buchanan's model, but in a slightly different manner. He, in any case, also underlines some positive effects of crime monopoly. The Mafia is analysed as an alternative to the State in the production of collective goods. His model illustrates that as long as taxation permits it, the competition between the Mafia and the State increases the offer of collective goods and the producer's net profit. This is why the honest producer must accommodate the Mafia. The Mafia is thus considered to be a sort of producer of collective goods destined for the private sector: an alternative to the State. The effectiveness of its competitive offer depends upon compared advantages of pairs composed of the quantity of collective goods and the level of taxes respectively proposed by the two suppliers, State and Mafia. According to Grossman, the presence of the Mafia can be beneficial when it leads to moderation of government cleptocratics.

The thesis inspired by Chicago economics therefore generally tends to upgrade the Mafia's role as a regulator of the bureaucratic tendencies of the State or as an informal regulator of the criminal world. We observe fairly rapidly that the solidarity of these approaches is dependent upon the crucial manner of hypothesis made as to the absence of externalities necessary to the existence of a criminal organization. If we do not understand the Mafia's economic role other than through its production of criminal goods and services, it is then probable that it is preferable to an unbridled criminality. The conclusions change when we introduce the idea that criminal organization engenders negative externalities: in other words, that it constitutes an evil per se.

Organized crime and petty criminals: a vertical integration model

We have seen that the economic analysis of the Chicago School examined comparisons of social well-being according to whether or not criminal production is monopolized by organized crime. Garoupa (2000), while writing in an analogous analytical perspective, explores a new path by investigating a vertical integration configuration in which the dominant firm (the Mafia) extracts a surplus from small criminals. Such a criminal organization possesses a vertically integrated structure where the agents are individual criminal firms. Expressed in terms of the principal–agent model, the Mafia is the principal and will discipline the small criminals by introducing a constraint incentive. This constraint is more or less credible in function of the threat the principal applies on the agents. Garoupa finishes with a conclusion similar to that of Buchanan: public policies must not necessarily be centred on the fight against organized crime.

To demonstrate, Garoupa uses literature devoted to 'Corporate crime', mentioned previously in the discussion of money laundering and particularly in our consideration of Shavell's (1997) contribution. Shavell defends the idea that the mechanism of law implementation (enforcement design) must be such that the principal behaves in an optimal manner in controlling its agents. Yet, the precise distribution of sanctions between the principal and the agent, according to Shavell, is not very important, as the principal and the agent(s) can reallocate the sanctions between them, via their internal contracts. The post-contractual sanction is thus independent from the pre-contractual division of sanctions. This rule, however, only applies when one of the parties is incapable of paying the fine (for example, when the Mafia escapes from certain sanctions as its employees have limited wealth) or when the principal cannot force the agent to behave in an optimal manner (for example, if the threat of Mafia reprisal is not credible). In these circumstances Shavell considers that the sanctions of imprisonment and implementation of personal criminal responsibility of Mafia agents is necessary to compensate for the inoperable effects of the constraint of agent solvency.

Pure competition

Let us rapidly examine how Garoupa's model functions. The individuals are neutral to risk and decide to commit criminal acts, which procures a benefit b for them and inflicts a damage h on the collectivity. We propose that $h > 1$ implies that crimes have a social cost. The public policy-maker does not know the benefit b of the criminals, but he knows the distribution of individuals by type that is given by a distribution function which is uniform over the interval $[0,1]$ and a cumulative distribution b. The policy-maker chooses a sanction f and a probability of detection p. The public spending necessary to reach a probability p is given by cp where c is a positive cost parameter. The objective function that must be maximized by the policy-maker is the sum of the individual benefits less the damage caused by the crime and the cost of repression. The maximum sanction is F that describes the constraint of wealth of the individuals. The sanction has no application cost.

An individual who is neutral to risk commits a crime when $b \geq pf$. Collective well-being is thus given by:

$$W = \int_{pf}^{1} (b - h)db - cp \tag{7.7}$$

The public policy-maker maximizes this function in f (severity of sentence) and p (probability of being punished) under the condition that $0 \leq f \leq F$. At the end of the calculation, we find Becker's classic result: 'the optimal fine is the maximum fine'. The optimal probability of detection and punishment satisfied $p * F = h - c/F$, indicates that some degree of sub-detection is necessary.[15] The number of criminals present on the market is thus given by cutting the expression of this condition to 100 per cent of the population, or to the value 1, or: $1 - (h - c/F)$ We represent this equilibrium of pure competition in Figure 7.5, point C.

Cournot and Stackelberg equilibrium

Individuals are supposed to be neutral to risk and choose to commit an infraction knowing that they will have to pay y to a monopolizing Mafia in order to enjoy the benefits from their criminal activity, b. We consider thus

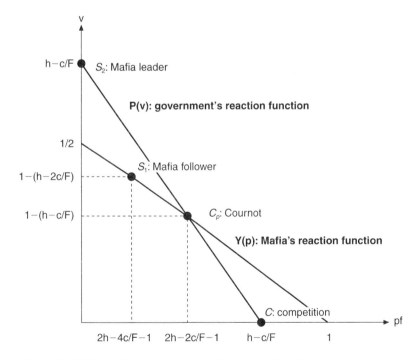

Figure 7.5 Mafia and individual criminals: a case of vertical integration

that the criminals must buy a licence from the Mafia. To simplify, we consider that the Mafia maximizes its profit and that the government cannot punish it. Public action is exercised then against criminals and not against the Mafia. The individuals commit misdemeanours when $b \geq pf + y$.[16] The Mafia's profit π depends then on the number of individuals who commit crimes:

$$\pi = \int_{pf+y}^{1} y\,db, \tag{7.8}$$

The Mafia maximizes its profit under the usual first-order condition:[17]

$$\frac{\partial \pi}{\partial y} = 0 \Rightarrow 1 - pf - 2y = 0 \tag{7.9}$$

The pair pf,y that satisfies this condition are solutions. We can then calculate the reactive function of the Mafia to the public policy, meaning the set of prices of criminal licences, y^{RF}, in function of the levels of sanction expected, pf. We must successively examine the two classical equilibrium configurations: that of Nash–Cournot, in which the government and Mafia decisions are simultaneously made, and that of Stackelberg, in which one of the actors is leader and the second follower. Let us first examine Cournot's equilibrium. The government and the Mafia[18] make their decisions simultaneously.

The objective function of the policy-maker is:

$$W = \int_{pf+y}^{1} (b - h)\,db - cp \tag{7.10}$$

We calculate the reaction functions.[19] The function of the government's reaction is written:

$$p^{RF}F = 2\left(h - \frac{c}{F}\right) - 1 \tag{7.11}$$

The function of Mafia reaction is written:

$$y^{NC} = 1 - \left(h - \frac{c}{F}\right) \tag{7.12}$$

The equilibrium intervenes at the intersection of the two right angles. We then proceed with the same type of calculation in the two cases of

Stackelberg's equilibrium: the first when the government is the leader and the Mafia the follower, and the second when the government is the follower and the Mafia the leader.

More about equilibrium

Figure 7.5 allows us to situate all of the equilibrium in relation to one another. In absciss, we represent the sanction hope (pf); in ordinate, we represent the price of criminal licences delivered by the Mafia (y). The curve $p(y)$ describes the reactive function of government and the curve $y(p)$ the reactive function of the Mafia. The reaction functions are read as follows, if we take Cournot's example. From a given level of pf, we find the optimal value of y, then for this y, the optimal value of pf, and so on. We arrive at an equilibrium Nash–Cournot for the pair (pF^*, y^*) situated at the intersection of the two reaction functions. We notice that the number of criminals is the same in pure occurrence and under a Cournot equilibrium, or $1 - (h - c/F)$. We thus find Buchanan's (1973) conclusion in demanding a criminal payment: in passing from C to $C_n n$, or the equilibrium of competition of Cournot's equilibrium, the Mafia decreases the cost effectiveness of small criminal activity, the dissuasion increases, and public repressive spending can then decrease.

The values taken by the probabilities of detection of crimes and by the price of criminal licences can thus be classed:[20]

$$0 < p^{St2} < p^{St1} < p^{cn} < p^*$$
$$0 < y^* < y^{cn} < y^{St1} < y^{St2}$$

So, when the price y of criminal licences is low, misdemeanours become attractive for delinquents, and the cost of entry into the criminal market decreases. There are then more criminals present on the market. The government must thus increase the probability of detection and sanction. Well-being increases as for a constant number of crimes, and public spending decreases. By the extortion of an entry fee imposed by the Mafia on all criminals, the Mafia makes infractions less attractive, and the probability of detection decreases. Finally, the Stackelberg game in which the Mafia is leader is an extreme case in which the presence of the Mafia permits the policy-maker to reduce his public spending to zero. The public sector (the State) delegates the totality of its function to the private sector: the Mafia. The Mafia's role is then that of a regulator who makes the spending go down, increasing the cost of entry onto the criminal market. Mafia presence permits an increase in well-being.

Is organized crime really a good thing?

It seems shocking to see economists converge on the idea that the Mafia is, in the final analysis, a positive crime regulation factor. Some consider that the fear of seeing an argument on organized crime in favour of public intervention explains this attitude. Somehow the defence of economic liberalism arrives at a revalorization of private regulation, even if it is Mafia regulation. It seems that over and above quarrels about doctrines, the range of the Chicago models is limited by restrictive hypotheses. It is then a too hasty vulgarization of the conclusions of these models that should be the object of criticism rather than the theories themselves.

The Mafia is an evil per se

Several remarks justify a certain scepticism regarding theses outlining the benefits of Mafia presence. First, it is possible that criminals can re-bill the 'honest' population for the increase in the cost of Mafia extortion, either by increasing their criminal activity, or by making it more efficient. Everything would then depend on the elasticity of the supply of crime and the offer of public policies. If the consequence of Mafia presence is that criminals must be more efficient, and public policy reacts more slowly to the citizens' demand for security than the criminals do to Mafia pressure, social well-being will be undermined. Second, the Mafia imposes an intrinsic social cost on the collectivity that is not taken into account by the different models we have examined. Even if, H, this cost, corresponds to the fact that the Mafia only carries out reprehensible acts against criminals, its simple existence constitutes a real unpleasantness for the collectivity.

We can then rewrite the function of social well-being, supposing that H is a type of fixed cost, independent of the volume of Mafia activity:

$$W = \int_{pf}^{1} (b - h)\mathrm{d}b - H - cp \qquad (7.13)$$

During the different maximizations that permit the calculation of the different equilibrium, this value H will not intervene, as it disappears with the derivations.[21] The optimal fine F does not change, nor do the optimal possibilities of detection. What changes are the conclusions on the eventual well-being engendered by the Mafia? In Garoupa's article, the comparison between the levels of well-being in competition (note W^*) and in Cournot situation (W^{CN}) is trivial. If we integrate the function of collective well-being on the same number of criminals, only the probability and thus the cost in spending on security vary:

$$W^* = \int_{p^*F}^{1} (b-h)db - cp^* = \int_{h-\frac{c}{F}}^{1} (b-h)db - cp^*$$

$$W^{NC} = \int_{y^{NC} + p^{NC}F}^{1} (b-h)db - cp^{NC} = \int_{h-\frac{c}{F}}^{1} (b-h)db - cp^{NC}$$

or, as:

$$p^* \geq p^{NC} \Rightarrow W^{NC} \geq W^*$$

If we integrate the intrinsic damage due to the presence of the H, we must write W^{NC} in the following manner:

$$W^{NC} = \int_{h-\frac{c}{F}}^{1} (b-h)db - cp^{NC} - H \tag{7.14}$$

Then:

$$W^{NC} - W^* = c(p^* - p^{NC}) - H$$

It is then no longer evident that W^{NC} is superior to W^*: it depends on the relation between H and $c(p^* - p^{NC})$. If H is sufficiently weak $(H < c(p^* - p^{NC}))$, we could continue to consider that a situation with Mafia (in Cournot equilibrium) is preferable to a situation without Mafia, as $W^{NC} > W^*$, keeping in mind that this is a situation with non costly extraction, without violence or political corruption. If H is high, $H > c(p^* - p^{NC})$, the situation with Mafia will be less favourable than that which reigns without Mafia even without violence or corruption. The favourable conclusions to the presence of the Mafia are then seriously placed into question by the introduction of an intrinsic cost linked to Mafia activity. We find here an example of the difficulties, recurrent in economic modelization, of generalizing the conclusions dependent on restrictive hypotheses.

Competition among criminals is not very efficient

It is understood that organized crime is fed by exploitation of illegal markets (drugs, prostitution). It is then tempting to consider that the legalization of certain 'vices' would deprive organized crime of resources. Depenalization of victimless crimes, such as prostitution and bookmaking, should reduce the demand for organized criminal-supplied input and lead to increased self-supply among individual criminal enterprises. But, disorganized and organized crime do not have the same incentive to internalize external costs associated with crime, such as violence, and will tend to over-supply 'social nuisances' (such as prostitution and gambling). Dick (1995) recalls the example cited by Schelling (1967) of an individual criminal who might be tempted to kill a witness. The Mafia firm might be more reluctant because it will consider the likelihood that its action would increase future cost of doing business by prompting general public outrage and heightened police scrutiny. While an individual criminal's action could prompt the same outrage and scrutiny, these effects would be spread over the entire criminal population and therefore would not be internalized to the same degree by the actual perpetrator. Because of these differing incentives for the internalization of violence, decriminalization of victimless trade might inadvertently increase the total amount of violence and 'social evils' by substituting supply away from organized and towards disorganized crime. On the other hand, because disorganized criminals will usually be less well positioned to exploit economics of scale and scope in undertaking crimes, the pervasiveness and range of victimless crimes might decrease when the involvement of organized crime is reduced. The loss of an organized crime firm's superior enforcement services, compared to disorganized criminals, could also tend to reduce the aggregate level of crime. As Dick (1995) wisely concludes, whether, in the balance, decriminalization would increase or decrease criminal activity, is an empirical question. More often, transactional cost theory highlights how policies designed to increase business costs within criminal firms may simply alter crime's organizational structure while having an ambiguous impact on its net supply.

Conclusion

Resorting to the use of economic analysis to fight organized crime certainly proves to be fascinating intellectually, but may be somewhat disappointing from an operational point of view. In contrast, in the area of the fight against laundering, intellectual stimulation and help in decision-making go hand-in-hand. However, the question is the same: how to define the respective roles of public and private intervention in the fight against a particular form of criminality. This immediately raises another question: why the private contribution to the fight against organized crime has been reduced to Mafia action, when, in fact, such action does not even constitute a very private form, in any classical sense. It is therefore probable that future economic discussions will be oriented around the efficiency of methods of private action, and notably the role of codes of good conduct or self-regulation of professions at risk by the intermediaries themselves.

8 Conclusion

Drugs constitute a major problem, seldom explored by economic analysis. What, in fact, can economic analysis contribute to the study of the social impact of drugs? What can the reader expect to learn, aside from the fact that the tools of economic analysis also apply to drugs, which, we admit, only constitute satisfaction in the eyes of an audience already convinced of the value of this discipline? Illegal drugs raise a fairly general problem. How should society regulate merchandise whose private value is superior to its social value? This definition includes not only drugs, but also other merchandise usually referred to as vice: gaming, alcohol, prostitution, etc.

It is obvious that the first remark consists in observing that important aspects of the problems posed by drugs arise more from their prohibition than their psycho-pharmacological particularities or even the consequences of their consumption on an individual. To conclude that total liberalization of drugs constitutes an obvious solution is short-sighted. Moreover, claiming that part of the drug problem is due to repressive laws does not eliminate the need to take other sources of negative consequences into account, the aggregate effects of which would be multiplied with the increase in consumption resulting from liberalization.

This is why the policy-maker is faced with a difficult choice: ban drugs knowing that a certain level of consumption will subsist, or legalize them and thus favour an increased level of consumption? This book defends the point of view that it is impossible to know what the best solution is. The indicator of social cost which must constitute the compass of a good drug policy cannot be calculated – and never has been – in a hypothetical liberalization situation: the speculations remain! For some, legalization would mean an increase in consumption and concomitant negative consequences that would not be compensated by the derived benefits. They argue that legalization would cost more than it would return. For others, it is the reverse. The commonly retained solution, prohibition, leads therefore to having the collectivity assume the social cost of drugs in order to limit growth in consumption. The reason for such a choice, if unanimously shared by the different nations, comes not only from the self-reinforcing character of the different international treaties that limit the field of social experimentation, but also from the wish to limit the number of psycho-active substances freely accessible, and, more generally, from an ideo-logical hostility to mind-altering substances. The question posed by drugs is not so much to know whether in a purely abstract world, it would not be preferable to invert the status of cannabis and alcohol in view of their respective danger. It is more suitable to place ourselves within a realistic world where institutional trajectories are modified with difficulty. From there, good public policy consists in making certain choices that may seem insignificant, but which can often result in thousands of deaths avoided: for instance, when it means discussing – or not discussing – the implementa-tion of a programme for exchanging syringes. It is from this perspective that economic analysis makes sense. As a matter of fact, the scope of its message appears clear: making the minimization of social cost the criterion for the selection of policies seems to us salutary in an area where ideology and religious convictions pointlessly burden the discussion. Ensuring that public intervention does not have merely so-called moral aims but actually contributes to reducing damage caused by drugs is the first step towards a rationalization of public action; clearly emphasizing the role required of each of the groups of actors further advances the process ot a point worthy of satisfaction.

Aside from the good report we award to the economic approach for the global manner in which it addresses the drug question, it also permits the unravelling of several specific questions, the obscurity of which converge with the difficulties that prevent satisfactory public policies from being formulated.

The economist's toolbox contains instruments which give coherent explanations for several recent tendencies of the drug market. For example, the reduction of cocaine consumption in the United States, while the price has dropped considerably, seems, to say the least, counter-intu-itive. Yet, once we take the complete cost of drug consumption and not only the street price of the product into account, including the effect of the growing stigmatization of drug consumers and the increased probability of long-term incarceration, we can better understand why the number of con-sumers and the frequency of their consumption can decline. This observa-tion does not, however, constitute a cause for celebration, for the objective of public policy should be to decrease the social cost, not consumption, and these do not necessarily go hand-in-hand.

Moreover, the study of market dynamics allows us to specify the con-ditions under which a repressive policy can be effective. From an eco-nomic point of view, the terms and conditions of repression make up a series of signals which modify the cost of the practice of consuming drugs. Not only does price elasticity change with the price level, which implies that the same level of repression does not have the same effects on con-sumption according to the level of price pre-existing on the market, but above all, the same reduction in consumption does not create the same variation of social cost. This forms, as we have seen, the rule by which the efficiency of drug policy should be measured.

Let us consider the question of drug consumer behaviour. The critics will smile at the ostentatiousness of the main authors in considering drug consumers to be intertemporal optimizers adjusting to perfection their consumption in relation to their environment. It is not very charitable of us to observe that the other sciences have not succeeded any better than economic analysis in offering a convincing framework for interpreting the basis of consumer behaviour.

Economic analysis at least has the merit of participating in the theoretical movement towards granting to the subject, in these circumstances the drug consumer, true decision-making autonomy, and this in an intellectual environment where the user has often been described as possessed by his deviance. Modelling the reaction of consumers to price and to events affecting their life is part of a conceptual movement which restores drug consumption to its status as behaviour: damaging certainly, but normal, and in any case justifying an examination allotting to the individual a real autonomy of decision. No science escapes from a form of utilitarianism in which the function assigned to the comprehension of consumer behaviour stems, above all, from a concern with improving the internal coherence of the tool of analysis. Economic analysis is not immune to this. What interests economists about drug consumption is less its individual roots than the impact that public policy, once reduced to only the cost dimension, has on consumers and their level of consumption. The hypothesis of rationality of choice is essential to this study, but even when it accompanies choices that generate regrets, as is the tendency in the latest theoretical developments, it reduces, de facto, the individual decisions to choices perfectly optimum, leaving little room for justification of public intervention.

On the supply side, interpretation difficulties must not prevent us from making the advances in knowledge facilitated by economic analysis. For example, when we commonly represent the organizations of drug traffickers as perfectly centralized authentic multinationals, the consideration of transaction costs inherent to criminal activity has seriously modified the picture. This issue is important, for when the idea of a crime monopoly prevails, it seems natural that this is better than competition, which would create a higher crime level. On the contrary, taking into account the presence of transaction costs leads us to represent the criminal sector as an oligopoly with fringe members, whose core is constrained by the risk of defection and whose periphery is desirous of acquiring the criminal organization's protection when the asset it needs to operate is not so specific that organized crime benefits from economies of scale by its supply. Once again, behind the economic rhetoric we foresee implications for public policy. Organized crime loses its theoretical attraction, and the design of repressive policies should be reconsidered in such a manner as to make the supply of services less attractive for organized crime.

Money laundering is another excellent example. If our approach is convincing, it should lead to a new understanding about the role of drug money laundering in the global flow of dirty money: not negligible, but infinitely weaker than that perceived by specialized agencies. Our re-evaluation of the gravity of money laundering is not based exclusively on a critical discussion of calculation techniques, but employs a strong theoretical framework. We feel the criminal organizations that launder drug money choose organizational schemas which minimize transaction costs, which is why laundering most often remains primitively organized, recourse to the complexities of the financial system being the exception. It is obvious that there is no need – in the case of drug money – for the thousands of fiscal paradises inventoried. The consequence of this for public policy is disappointing: the repression of international financial delinquency should use more imagination, and cease to make drug money the principal target in the struggle against laundering, an idea that makes the operators concerned smile from the Virgin Islands to the Bahamas.

Once again, the objective that should be pursued by public policy is not a drop in consumption but a reduction in social cost, which do not necessarily go hand-in-hand. The major difficulty that economic analysis still comes up against resides in the difficulty of employing the usual tools in the service of such an optimal public policy. The classical approach in economics in the presence of an externality stumbles over the fact that there is no univocal connection between consumption level and social cost. From that point on, calibrating the level of repression like a Pigovian tax and arriving at an optimum level of consumption makes no sense. Similarly, a policy badly inspired by Becker's work, which would recommend reaching the so-called optimal level of crime by choosing the appropriate extent of enforcement, cannot pretend to guarantee the minimal level of social cost. And this for the same reason: the same level of consumption can be accompanied by very different levels of criminality. The whole problem, as far as drugs are concerned, is the fact that the externalities are not proportional to the level of consumption. As opposed to pollution, which grows globally with the level of industrial production, here the institutional context, the design of the laws and the rules of their implementation, are at least as important as the level of activity.

There is nothing exalting about concluding this way. Failing a miraculous theoretical recipe, we still have to sift each public policy through its effects on collective welfare. This can most effectively be done with an informed knowledge of the ways in which the markets interpret the level of repression and the offer of treatment, and then convert them into decisions on consumption, rules of use, and types of traffic organization. The damage inflicted by drugs on society depends upon the outcome of these interactions. The aim of this book was to indicate the ways to favourably orient with public policy the results of those decisions made by actors in the drug market.

Notes

1 Drug supply and criminal organizations

1 Formerly Burma.
2 Contrary to the affirmations of UNDCP (1997) the 'trade flow' of drugs is not 'larger than the international trade in Iron and Steel, and motor vehicles, and about the same size as the international trade in textiles' but in the same range as many agricultural products, such as coffee and tea. Drugs are a moderate contributor to total world trade.
3 In the case of cocaine, if we make E, the global demand for wholesale cocaine, P the export price of cocaine and W_p the retail price, F a mark-up parameter, c the elasticity price of the demand, and C a coefficient, we obtain:

$$W_p = P + F$$
$$E = C(W_p)^c.$$

4 We adopt a definition of organized crime close to that of P. Reuter: 'organized crime consists of organizations that have durability, hierarchy, and involvement in a multiplicity of criminal activities'. A criminal organization can thus also just as easily be: a grouping of criminals whose objective, one assumes, is to be in a position to conduct larger-scale operations than an isolated petty criminal can attempt, as a fictitious protection agency against the real threat that it poses; a producer of 'intermediary criminal goods', i.e. a supplier of inputs used by the petty criminals (outside the organization) to produce the final output 'crime' (it supplies arms to hold-up men, cameras to paedophiles ...); a food distribution enterprise (which supplies bars and restaurants) at excessive prices; or even a drug distribution cartel, a street gang, etc.
5 In France an analogous study directed by Schiray et al. (1994b) underlines that if the consumption of hashish is largely trivialized, that of heroin remains even more marginal. For example, in the district of Val d'Argent in Argenteuil (28,000 inhabitants, 22 per cent between 18 and 24 years of age, 17 per cent of the population foreign, unemployment rate higher than average), the study evaluates that 80 per cent of boys between 15 and 30 years of age regularly consume hashish, and 50 per cent of girls. The regular consumer population of heroin amounts to around 50 people. The traffic of hashish is due to users–resellers who gain only low net revenues from their activity. Heroin traffic occupies around five resellers, of which one is susceptible to benefit from a lasting enrichment. If we carry over the strict cost of spending for annual consumption of drugs (3 million francs), (excluding all forms of social cost) from the benefits of traffic, it appears clearly that the district is largely unprofitable. Also the limited number of persons receiving revenue from drugs invalidates the idea of an underground economy, the size of which might compete with the

legal economy. Among these 150,000 persons living in the area of Aulnay, 47 per cent are under 20 years of age. The rate of unemployment is 21 per cent. Around 80 per cent of youth use hashish regularly, and the number of heroin users amounts to around 130. The traffic is run by less than five dealers of a certain size (traffic per kilo carrying over to other communities) and by numerous users–resellers making little profit. The study underlines once again that the few financial successes linked with trafficking remain exceptional and that, on the whole, the cost of the drug exceeds greatly the benefits for the neighbourhood.

6 Often at their expense, but sometimes at their initiative, criminals have to turn to the services of the judiciary, whose presence is a part of the institutional environment surrounding the existence of the criminal markets. Its cost is socialized. Only the legal fees are directly charged to the parties.

7 Let us not lose sight of the general nature of the reasoning. Whether it is a question of complicity or of smuggling channels, the same reasoning can be applied.

8 An input is said to be specific when it can be used only by a single firm. For example, the mould of a piece of a car is of value only to the firm that produces the car. A skilled worker is thus strongly specific; computers, on the other hand, are weakly specific.

9 To use game theory terminology, opportunism is a 'dominant strategy'. Let us consider the case of the independent criminal. If the organization adopts loyal behaviour, the independent criminal records a gain of 5 if he himself is loyal and a gain of 7 if he is not. He thus has an interest in being opportunistic. In the case where the organization opts for opportunistic behaviour, he would gain 2 for being loyal and 4 for not. In this case, he also has an interest in being an opportunist. Since the matrix of gains is symmetrical, the same reasoning is applied to the organization. In this way, whatever the behaviour of the other, each has an interest in preferring opportunism to loyalty; in all cases, opportunistic strategy wins out over a strategy of loyalty.

10 This is also a question of a classical result of game theory. When a game of the prisoner's dilemma is repeated a number of times indefinitely, mutual opportunism is no longer the sole solution for equilibrium. The agents can rationally choose loyalty.

11 These are criminal activities per se, activity whose criminal nature lies in circumventing a law, activity whose criminal nature results from the forced monopolization of the market, and activity whose criminal nature lies in the obstacle that it poses to the implementation of the law.

12 This positive effect must, however, be balanced by the negative effect that breaking legal rules, even badly formed ones, always engenders.

2 Addictive consumption

1 That a behaviour that is rational with regard to time means that the agent envisages the future consequences (up to the point of death) of his present decisions. When it is technically possible to represent his preferences over this period by an intertemporal utility function, the agent will try to maximize this function of intertemporal utility. We write that $U^x = \sum_{x}^{T} \alpha_t u_t(C_t)$ where the individual has an existence of T periods, C_t represents his consumption during the period t, and u_t is the instantaneous utility at the period t of the consumer. The individual depreciates future consumption and has a preference for present

consumption, indicated by the coefficient α_t, which shows, for each age, the rate of depreciation of the future. The fact that the rate of depreciation of the future depends only on the age t and not on its distance from the present $(t - x)$ expresses the stability of the system of preference and guarantees the consistency of intertemporal choices. In other words, the rate of depreciation of the future that the individual will have at age 80 is the same as that which he integrates into his economic calculation starting now, for example, when he decides to buy a supplementary pension. If at age 20 such a purchase makes him happy and he regrets it at age 80, then he is temporally inconsistent, since his depreciation of the future has changed. He is therefore not in a position of having an optimal life strategy.

2 It also assumes the existence of an institutional system that gives Ulysses the power to command.

3 Note that the *kd* in the above formula was represented by the sign σ in the discussion of the Becker and Murphy theory in the previous section.

4 We observe that unlike Becker and Murphy, for whom all drug consumers are dependent, Orphanides and Zervos would define addiction as the manifestation of negative externalities for the drug consumer. Under this definition, consumption that has no consequences for health is judged to be non-addictive.

3 Economics of prohibition

1 In practice we consider that the price paid by the consumer for a drug purchase compensates its utility. The private cost assumed by the consumer is therefore equal to their private benefit: in other words, the utility. Private cost and benefit being equal, it suffices then to fix the objective of the public policy to mimimize the negative effects of drugs on the consumer and the rest of society. We will return to these problems of measure in Chapter 6.

2 This amounts to adopting the Hicks-Kaldor criterion or Posner's maximization of wealth. These two criteria permit one to indicate, between two situations, the one that is socially preferable. Basically, according to Hicks-Kaldor the transition from one situation to another is positive when those gaining from the change can compensate the losers: that is to say, when the net wealth is at its maximum or the social cost is minimized.

3 A computable general equilibrium approach is impracticable for lack of data.

4 Elasticity of demand price indicates in what measure an increase in the drug price creates a drop in consumption.

5 Microeconomies generally makes the hypothesis that consumer preferences are convexes; in other words, they like diversification. Concretely, between two baskets of goods *A* and *B* supplying the same satisfaction for the consumer, he will prefer all intermediary baskets to these two, or the baskets composed with a weighted average of the two baskets. When the hypothesis of convexity is not respected, the preferences are concave. This time the consumer prefers systematically extreme baskets. If the consumer prefers to hold a large quantity of one of the two goods to a combination of the two, he is monomaniac.

6 The fact of injecting drugs fosters the spread of certain diseases. This is not inevitable any more than smoking near a gasoline container necessarily starts a fire. In the two cases, there exists a probability not equal to zero of causing injury.

7 This theorem can be viewed as saying that an initial assignment of rights that is allocatively inefficient – that is, assigned to the party who does not attribute the greatest value to the right – will be corrected by the market.

8 All exchanges have a cost. These costs are called transaction costs. It is important to note that a transaction cost is not the price of an item or a right. Instead, it

is the cost of the transaction itself. These costs include search costs, information costs, the costs of meeting, negotiation and any other costs incurred to make the primary exchange occur.

4 Optimal public intervention

1 This equivalence will be proven in Chapter 4, p. 114.
2 The hypotheses on the shape of the curves can of course be modified without altering the conclusions radically. One can, for example, consider that the marginal benefits of the traffickers increase with the frequency rapidly at first, then decrease suddenly. Similarly, one can consider that a weak level of infraction of the drug laws engenders a social cost of zero, or even a positive one.
3 Let us adapt the example given by Friedman (2000) to drug trafficking. Assume that the latter engenders damages of $900 each time it is committed. Imagine that the sanction is in the form of a fine. In fact, the perpetrator of the trafficking is not assured of being sentenced to this sanction; he is threatened by a combination of probability and sanction. This combination permits a calculation of the expected fine, or $E(p) = p_1 f$, with p_1 the probability of being sentenced and f the monetary value of the sanction for the trafficker. Let us suppose that the expected sanction has a value of $900. If the public policy-maker decides to increase the anticipated fine from $900 to $901 and if the traffickers are rational, then they will avoid an additional offence. Unfortunately, society will have to spend $50 to arrest and punish the criminal. Does such a public policy make sense? The answer depends on the social benefit that one ascribes to the fact of avoiding an additional offence. Preventing an additional offence will permit society to save $1,000. From the traffickers' point of view, it would not be tempting to commit crimes if it did not bring them any gain. To calculate the benefit for society, it is necessary to subtract the benefit that the criminal is giving up. How is this gain to be measured? Obviously, it is impossible to question the trafficker on this point, the more so because no one has arrested him precisely because he has in fact given up committing the crime! It is enough to consider that if the crime had brought him less than $900, he would have already given up committing it long ago. If he renounces it only when the anticipated fine has reached a value of 901 E and not 900 E, it is because the value of his crime lies between $900 and $901. Therefore, from the point of view of society, to dissuade this crime brings in $1,000 but reduces the welfare of the criminal by about $900 and costs $50 allotted to implementing the suppressive policy. The gain is $50, and so the new policy of suppression brings in more than it costs, and is therefore positive.
4 One finds that the optimal fine is equal to the harm caused by the criminals minus the cost of suppression not covered by the fine divided by the probability of being arrested: that is to say, multiplied by the probability of not being arrested. In fact, for the sanction to be a disincentive, it is necessary that it take into account the fact that in the majority of cases criminals commit crimes and are not arrested.
5 p is lower than one, and therefore the fine is greater than the harm.
6 A dollar has less value for a wealthy person than for a poor one.
7 There is general agreement that a magistrate has more to lose in occasionally consuming drugs than does an engineer.

5 A new design for drug policy

1 The demonstration is taken from Miceli (1977).
2 One way to resolve this problem of incomparability is to specify a social welfare function. Such a function possesses the arguments of the levels of utility of all members of society. Thus, in our example with two persons, the function is written $W = (U_A, U_B)$. The function of collective well being attributes a weight to individuals in order to be able to classify two allocations, which are not Pareto-comparable. If the form of W is known, then the optimal point (maximizing social well being) on the utility possibility frontier can be localized by finding the highest curve of indifference of W tangent to the *UPF*. In practice, it is impossible to know the form of W so this approach is not productive.
3 On the one hand, this criterion of choice is sometimes limited by its circularity. The change of D towards E can be efficient in the sense of Hicks-Kaldor, but the change of E towards D can also thus be an indeterminate result. On the other hand, victims of change must not be indemnified, as this would create new distortions due to the alteration of the marginal rate of substitution between the items But without an indemnization, such a change is difficult to put into practice.
4 Incidentally, we notice that in a world of two individuals, when the utility of the two individuals reaches its maximum level, or 1, the total utility is equal to 2. The same result may be achieved with a distribution that procures a utility of 2 to the first individual and zero to the second. Economic efficiency is maximal in the two cases but the degree of social justice differs.
5 It is possible to measure the consumer surplus without estimating the demand function if the price elasticity at the market equilibrium is known.

6 Drug law enforcement

1 We adapt here Yoram Barzel's model from *Economic Analysis of Property Rights*, 1989.
2 The triangle of welfare loss generally measures the loss of welfare in the existence of a monopoly that imposes a surcharge on society as a whole. The fact that the monopoly charges a higher price than that of the competition increases the surplus of the producer at the expense of that of the consumer. But some consumers are driven from the market by the elevated price, and their welfare decreases without the monopoly being able to capture it since they no longer buy its product. Geometrically, the loss-of-welfare triangle measures at the abscissa the number of individuals who give up the product and at the ordinate the price that the individual would have been ready to pay to procure it, a price that proves to be too low.
3 Following an idea of Mark Kleiman (1992) in *Against Excess: Drug Policy for Results*.
4 $(0.98)^{40} = 4/9 = (2/3)*(2/3)$.
5 It is easy to tell stories about why one party or another's degree of preference for immediate reward rather than delayed gratification may vary, e.g., because the customer is in withdrawal or one party owes money to someone who is about to employ violence as a collection tactic.
6 A controversy was opened by the National Academy of Science Committee (Manski *et al.*, 1999), which argued that given the limitations of existing data, the Rydell and Everingham conclusions were speculative; alternative modelling assumptions can support conclusions either more or less favourable.
7 We will return to this point in the Conclusion.

7 Fighting money laundering and organized crime

1 FATF decided to convene a commission that concluded the impossibility of quickly assessing the amount laundered (2001).
2 Regarding the calculations on heroin, Van Duyne (1992) rightly pointed out that it is impossible to know what street sales price figure is used to arrive at the $12 billion figure. For cocaine, the result of $28.8 billion is obtained by using the highest amounts in the bracket (price: $80–$190 and quantity: 100–150 tons).
3 The basic framework is the following. Suppose that individual A, located in country 1, owes a sum $X to individual B located in country 2, and that B owes $X to C located in country 1. A sends $X to B and B sends $X to C. That makes two international transfers and four operations of withdrawal and deposit. To settle different debts, everything functions as if A in country 1 settles the debt of B to C in country 1. There are only two bank transactions between A and B and no international transfer.
4 The total cost of money laundering corresponds to the margin paid to intermediaries added to the transaction costs (i.e. the cost of implementing the strategy and the cost of risk).
5 The thesis that organized criminals do not massively have recourse to the most sophisticated money-laundering techniques seems to be supported on a number of empirical grounds. Some studies (rare, it is true) give indications that point in this direction. All the qualitative studies (Reuter, 1983; Zaitch, 1998) show that setting up complex money-laundering strategies only arises in a limited number of instances of drug trafficking of some importance in the market. It is worth underscoring the curbs on such strategies. Zaitch (1998) notes the systematic exaggeration of figures relating to drug production. For the latter, the exaggeration is not solely quantitative, but also pertains to methods attributed to traffickers. To be sure, some operations can be very complex and well planned. It seems, however, according to Zaitch, who conducted an ethno-sociological study of Colombian traffickers in Amsterdam, that the number of these cases is considerably exaggerated by the media and by certain official reports. The majority of Colombian traffickers he was able to observe were content to send their profits to Colombia through the bank or exchange bureaus. Zaitch confides being constantly on the lookout for a real money-laundering professional in Amsterdam in the milieu of Colombian cocaine traffickers. In questioning the contacts on the simplistic nature of their method of money laundering, he always heard the same response given: 'These methods are enough if one does not make stupid mistakes.' For this author, it is thus clear that briefcases full of cash and bank transfers remain by far the methods adopted by the great majority of traffickers. The image of ultra-sophisticated money-laundering techniques relates to the fantasy of very centralized cartels organized like multinationals. Zaitch notes that his interlocutors recall with humour how this milieu is inclined to transform the isolated purchase of a quantity of drugs from organization X into a membership in said organization. In the same way, simple conveyers of funds present themselves as 'money managers' without having any specific expertise. Even B. Margens, who has often been presented as an intermediary between the 'Colombian cartels' and the 'Italian Mafia', whose role was brought to light on the occasion of operation 'green ice', and who played nearly every role in cocaine trafficking, did not, as far as money laundering was concerned, go beyond escorting valises of cash in the direction of Gibraltar. For Zaitch, the case of F. Jurado demonstrates that, even in this dossier, where the money-laundering techniques used were very sophisticated

and corresponded to the archetypical case of money laundering directly put in place by a large criminal organization (the Cali cartel), some of the Colombians arrested held more than 100 bank accounts in over fifteen countries. This proves that the sophisticated methods are always coupled with more primitive techniques.

6 We can, in passing, ask ourselves about the exact field of application of the models issuing from tax evasion repression in the case of laundering. Effectively, the anti-laundering laws, following different recommendations from the FATF, generally apply only to serious infractions linked to drug trafficking, terrorism, or organized crime. The problematic of the defrauding doctor is not covered, according to most of the actual legislation, by anti-laundering laws but by tax evasion laws.

7 Most countries place a ceiling on the payments that can be made in cash.

8 In order to simplify, we consider that the criminal launders his illegal revenue and that when he is arrested his assets are not confiscated.

9 The sanction f describes both the sentences related to laundering and those for trafficking, in the case where the charge for laundering leads to a second charge for trafficking.

10 We suppose that the managers are neutral to risk.

11 The law of July 12, 1990 introduced the obligation of monitoring clients and reporting suspicion to the TRACFIN agency, attached to the Ministry of Finance. TRACFIN can decide to transmit information to the Public Prosecutor if the conditions of Article 5 of the Anti-laundering Law are met, or if the information received brings to light proof of a crime or a misdemeanour linked notably to organized delinquency.

12 The banking commission may decide upon administrative sanctions, and these arise from warnings of withdrawal of approval to obligatory resignation of directors. These sanctions have not yet been imposed.

13 This *lex mercatoria* or 'merchant law' defined a number of obligations which the members of corporations and guilds had to satisfy (Greif *et al.*, 1994).

14 In Figure 7.3b, at the point of abscissa C^*, a slight decrease in the cost of respecting the law engenders a slight increase of the number of virtuous banks, and is thus very inelastic to the cost of respecting the law. At the point corresponding to C^{**} a slight reduction in cost of respecting the law creates a strong movement for adoption of the law; the number of honest banks is thus very elastic to the cost of respecting the law.

15 The policy-maker's programme is:

$$\begin{cases} \max W = \int\limits_{pf}^{1} (b-h)db - cp \\ sc.\ 0 \le f \le F \end{cases}$$

We write the Lagrangian:

$$L_{\lambda,f,p} = W + \lambda(F-f)$$

$$= \int\limits_{pf}^{1} (b-h)db - cp + \lambda(F-f)$$

$$= \left[\frac{b^2}{2} - bh \right]_{pf}^{1} - cp + \lambda(F-f)$$

We derive the Lagrangian in relation to f and p:

$$\frac{\partial L}{\partial f} = -p^2 f + ph - \lambda = p(h-pf) - \lambda = 0 \qquad \frac{\partial L}{\partial p} = -pf^2 + hf - c = f(-pf) - c = 0$$

Suppose that the optimal fine is not the maximum fine. With the first derivative, we obtain $h = p^* f^*$. In any case, with the second we know that this is impossible. So the optimal solution must be $f^* = F$ with $\lambda^* > 0$.

The second derivative indicates the interior solution:

$$p^* F = h - \frac{c}{F} \Rightarrow p^* F < h$$

16 The benefit b is distributed between 0 and 1, but we only consider the case where: $b \geq pf + y \Rightarrow b \in [pf + y, 1]$ as we are only interested in the criminal population.
17 We carry out the following calculations:

$$\text{Max } \pi = \text{Max} \int_{pf+y}^{1} y db$$

$$= \text{Max} \, [yb] \Big|_{pf+y}^{1}$$

$$= \text{Max} \, y - (pfy + y^2)$$

$$= \text{Max} \, y - pfy - y^2$$

18 And not the criminals who observe the probability of being punished and the level of Mafia extortion before making their decision.
19 The public policy-maker maximizes the collective well being by choosing f and p under the condition $0 \leq f \leq F$. We define the Lagrangian:

$$L_{f,p,\lambda} = W + \lambda(F-f).$$

The first-order conditions of maximization of collective well being are:

$$\frac{\partial L}{\partial f} = p(h - pf - y) - \lambda = 0$$

$$\frac{\partial L}{\partial p} = f(h - pf - y) - c = 0$$

We know that the equilibrium $\lambda(F-f) = 0$ with $\lambda \neq 0$ thus $f^* = F$. We rewrite then the second condition replacing f by F:

$$F(h - pf - y) - c = 0$$
$$Fh - pF^2 - yF - c = 0$$
$$h - pF - y - \frac{c}{F} = 0$$

We then obtain the reactive function of government p^{RF} to the Mafia reaction:

$$p^{RF}F = h - y - \frac{c}{F}$$

Then we calculate the reactive function of the Mafia. We replace in the second condition y by

$$\frac{1 - pf}{2} \text{ and } f \text{ by } F.$$

We obtain:

$$pF = 2\left(h - \frac{c}{p}\right) - 1$$

We replace the second condition pf by $2\left(h - \frac{c}{p}\right) - 1$, and obtain the Mafia's reactive function to the public action in a Nash–Cournot game:

$$y^{NC} = 1 - \left(h - \frac{c}{F}\right).$$

20 The exponents $St2,St1,CN,*$ refer respectively to the following equilibriums: Stackelberg or the Mafia is leader; Stackelberg or the Mafia is follower; Cournot, competition.
21 The derivative of a constant is equal to zero.

Bibliography

Abelson, H. and Miller, J.D. (1985) *A Decade of Trends in Cocaine Use in the Household Population*, Rockville, MD: NIDA.

Ainslie, G. (1999) 'Addiction and discounting', *Journal of Health Economics*, 18, 393–407.

Akerlof, G. and Yellen, J. (1994) 'Gang Behavior, Law Enforcement, and Community Values', in A. Henry, T. Mann and T. Taylor (eds) *Values and Public Policy*, Washington, DC: Brookings Institution, pp. 173–209.

Akerlof, G.A. (1970) 'The Market for "Lemons": Quality Uncertainty and the Market Mechanism', *Quarterly Journal of Economics*, 84, 488–500.

Alley, P. (1984a) 'Drug Use Among Young Adults: The Impact of Role Status and Social Environment', *Journal of Personality and Social Psychology*, March, 47, 629–645.

Allingham, M.G. and Sandmo, A. (1972) 'Income Tax Evasion: A Theoretical Analysis', *Journal of Public Economics*, 1, 323–338.

Andreano, R. and Seigfried, J.J. (eds) (1980) *The Economics of Crime*, Cambridge, MA: Schenkman.

Arlen, J. (1994) 'The Potential Perverse Effects of Corporate Criminal Liability', *Journal of Legal Studies*, 23, 830–860.

Arlen, J. and Kraakman, R. (1997) 'Controlling Corporate Misconduct: A Comparative Analysis of Alternative Corporate Incentive Regimes', *New York University Law Review*, 72, 687–779.

Bachman, G., Johnston, L. and O'Malley, P. (1984) *Illicit Drug Use, Smoking and Drinking by America's High School Students, College Students, and Young Adults*, Washington, DC: US Department of Health and Human Services.

Bachman, G., Johnston, L., O'Mallingham, M.G. and Sandmo, A. (1972) 'Income Tax Evasion: A Theoretical Analysis', *Journal of Public Economics*, 1, 323–338.

Bachman, G., O'Malley, P. and Humphrey, R.H. (1988) 'Explaining the Recent Decline in Marijuana Use: Differentiating the Effect of Perceived Risks, Disapproval and General Lifestyle Factors', *Journal of Health Society Behaviour*, 29, 92–112.

Bachman, G., O'Malley, P. and Johnston, L. (1990) 'Explaining the Recent Decline in Cocaine Use Among Young Adults: Further Evidence that Perceived Risk and Disapproval Lead to Reduced Drug Use', *Journal of Health and Social Behavior*, 31, 173–184.

Bachman, J. and Witte, A. (1980) 'The Effectiveness of Legal Sanctions on

Individuals Addicted to Alcohol or Drugs', in I. Leveson (ed.) *Quantitative Exploration in Drug Abuse Policy,* New York: Spectrum Publication, pp. 111–127.

Backer, G. (1992) 'Incentive Contracts and Performance measurement', *Journal of Political Economy,* 76, 598–614.

Ball, J.C. and Ross, A. (1991) *Effectiveness of Methadone Maintenance Treatment: Patients, Programmes, Services and Outcome,* New York: Springer Verlag.

Barré, M.D. (1994) *Toxicomanie et délinquance: Du bon usage de l'usager de produit illicite,* series 'Études et données pénales', 70, CESDIP.

Barzel, Y. (1989) *Economic Analysis of Property Rights,* Cambridge: Cambridge University Press.

Becker, G. (1968) 'Crime and Punishment: An Economic Approach', *Journal of Political Economy,* 76, 2, 169–217.

Becker, G., Grossman, M. and Murphy, K. (1990) *An Empirical Analysis of Cigarette Addiction,* Working Paper, No. 3322, Cambridge, MA: NBER.

Becker, G., Grossman, M. and Murphy, K. (1991) 'Rational Addiction and the Effect of Price Consumption', *American Economic Review,* 81, 2, 237–241.

Becker, G. and Murphy, K. (1988) 'A Theory of Rational Addiction', *Journal of Political Economy,* August, 96, 675–700.

Becker, G.S. and Mulligan, C.B. (1997) 'The Endogenous Determination of Time Preference', *Quarterly Journal of Economics,* 112, 3, 729–758.

Benson, B., Lljoong, K. and Rasmussen, D. (1994) 'Estimating Deterrence Effects: A Public Choice Perspective on the Economics of Crime Literature', *Southern Economic Journal,* 61, 1, July, 161–168.

Benson, B., Lljoong, K., Rasmussen, D. and Sollars, D. (1995) 'Police Bureaucracies, their Incentives, and the War on Drugs', *Public Choice,* 83, 1–2, April, 21–45.

Benson, B., Lljoong, K., Rasmussen, D. and Zuehlke, T. (1992) 'Is Property Crime Caused by Drug Use or by Drug Enforcement Policy?', *Applied Economics,* 24, 679–692.

Benson, B. and Rasmussen, D. (1991) 'Relationship Between Illicit Drug Enforcement Policy and Property Crimes', *Contemporary Policy Issues,* 9, 4, 106–115.

Bettancourt, D. (1991) 'Los cincos focos de la mafia colombiana: elementos de historia, 1968–1985', *Revisita Folio Universidad Pedagogica Nacional,* 2, 35–54.

Blair, R. and Vogel, R. (1973) 'Heroin Addiction and Urban Crime', *Public Finance Quarterly,* 1, 14, 457–467.

Blum, J., Naylor, T., Levi, M. and Williams, P. (1998) *Financial Havens, Banking Secrecy and Money Laundering,* Vienna: UNDCP.

Blumenstein, A. and Graddy, E. (1981–1982) 'Prevalence and Recidivism in Index Arrests: A Feedback Model', *Law and Society Review,* 16, 2, 68–79

Boekhout Van Solinge, T. (1996) *L'héroïne, la cocaïne et le crack en France: Trafic, usage et politique,* Amsterdam: Centre de recherches sur la Drogue (CEDRO).

Bouhnik, P. (1995) 'Le monde social des usagers de drogues dures en milieu urbain défavorisé', PhD thesis, Paris VIII.

Bourgois, P. (1996) 'In Search of Masculinity: Violence, Respect and Sexuality among Puerto Rican Crack Dealers in East Harlem', *British Journal of Criminology,* 36, 412–428.

Boyum, D. (1992) 'Reflections on Economic Theory and Drug Enforcement', PhD thesis, Cambridge, MA: Harvard University.

Boyum, D. and Rocheleau, M.A. (1994) '*Measuring Heroin Availability in Three Cities*', Washington, DC: Office of National Drug Control Policy.

Braga, A. and Clear, T. (1995) 'Community Corrections', in J.Q. Wilson and J. Petersilia (eds) *Crime*, San Francisco, CA: Institute for Contemporary Studies, pp. 421–444.

Bretteville-Jensen, A.L. and Sutton, M. (1996) *Under the Influence of the Market: an Applied Study of Illicit Selling and Consuming Heroin*, York: University of York, Centre for Health Economics.

Brown, G. and Silverman, L. (1974) 'The Retail Price of Heroin: Estimation and Applications', *Journal of American Statistical Association*, September, 69, 347, 595–606.

Brown, G. and Silverman, L. (1975) *The Retail Price of Heroin*, Arlington, VA: Public Research Institute, Center for Naval Analysis.

Buchanan, J. (1973) 'A Defense of Organised Crime', in U.M.I, American Enterprise Institute for Public Policy Research (eds) *Economics of Crime and Punishment*, Washington, DC: UMI.

Bui-Trong, L. (1993) 'L'insécurité des quartiers sensibles: une échelle d'évaluation', *Cahiers de la sécurité intérieure*, 14, August–October, 235.

Bui-Trong, L. (1995) 'Drogue et violence: le reflux du trafic de drogue vers certaines banlieths', *Revue d'Etudes et d'Informations de la Gendarmerie*, 179, 22.

Caballero, F. (1989) *Droit de la drogue*, Paris: Précis Dalloz.

Calabresi, G. (1970) *The Cost of Accidents: A Legal and Economic Analysis*, New Haven, CT: Yale University Press.

Calabresi, G. and Melamed, D.A. (1972) 'Property Rules, Liability Rules and Inalienability: One View of the Cathedral', *Harvard Law Review*, 85, 1089–1128.

Cameron, S. (1988) 'The Economics of Crime and Deterrence: A Survey of Theory and Evidence', *Kyklos*, 41–2, 301–323.

Cartier-Bresson, J. (1994) 'Rente, pouvoir discrétionnaire et corruption', *Le Débat*, 77, October, 24–32.

Caulkins, J. (1990) 'The Distribution and Consumption of Illicit Drugs: Mathematical Models and their Policy Implications', PhD, Massachusetts Institute of Technology.

Caulkins, J. (1994) *Developing Price Series for Cocaine*, MR-317-DPRC, Santa Monica, CA: The Rand Corporation.

Caulkins, J. (1995a) *Estimating the Elasticities and Cross Elasticities of Demand for Cocaine and Heroin*', Pittsburgh, PA: Carnegie Mellon University.

Caulkins, J. (1995b) 'Domestic Geographic Variation in Illicit Drug Prices', *Journal of Urban Economics*, 37, 38–56.

Caulkins, J. and Reuter, P. (1998) 'What Price Data Tells Us about Drug Markets', *Journal of Drug Issues*, 28, 3, 593–613.

Caulkins, J.P. and Feinleib, J. (1995) 'Modeling and Forecasting 1990–1995: "Dealing with the Country's Drug Problem"', *OR/MS Today*, February, 32–40.

Chaiken, J. and Chaiken, M. (1990) 'Drug and Predatory Crime', in M. Tonry and J.Q. Wilson (eds) *Drug and Crime*, vol. 13, Chicago, IL: University of Chicago Press, pp. 203–239.

Chaloupka, F. (1991) 'Rational Addictive Behavior and Cigarette Smoking', *Journal of Political Economics*, 99, 4, 722–742.

Chaloupka, F., Grossman, M., Brown, C. (1996) *The Demand for Cocaine by Young Adults: A Rational Addiction Approach*, Working Paper No. 5713, Cambridge, MA: NBER

Chaloupka, F. and Saffer, H. (1995) *The Demand for Illicit Drugs*, Working Paper No. 5238, Cambridge, MA: NBER.

Chaloupka, F.J., Grossman, M. and Tauras, J.A. (1998) *The Demand for Cocaine and Marijuana by Youth*, Cambridge, MA: NBER.

Choiseul-Praslin, C.H. de (1991) *La drogue, une économie dynamisée par la répression*, Paris: Presse du C.N.R.S.

Clague, C. (1973) 'Legal Strategies for Dealing with Heroin Addiction', *American Economic Review*, May 63, 2, 263–269.

Clayton, R. and Voss, H. (1985) *Young Men and Drugs in Manhattan: A Causal Analysis*, Research Monograph 39, Rockville, MD: National Institute of Drug Abuse (NIDA).

Coase, R.H. (1937) 'The Nature of the Firm', *Economica*, 4, 386–405.

Collins, D. and Laspley, H.M. (1996) *The Social Costs of Drug Abuse in Australia in 1988*, Canberra: Australian Government Printing Services.

Cook, P.J. and Tauchen, G. (1982) 'The Effect of Liquor Taxes on Heavy Drinking', *Bell Journal of Economics*, 13, 379–390.

Cooter, R. (1995a) *Decentralized Law for a Complex Economy: The Structural Approach to Adjudicating the New Law Merchant*, Working Paper No. 95–2, Berkeley, CA: University of California, School of Law.

Cooter, R. (1995b) *The Theory of Market Modernization of Law*, Working Paper No. 95–3, Berkeley, CA: University of California, School of Law.

Cooter, R. and Ulen, T. (1996) *Law and Economics*, Reading, MA: Addison-Wesley.

Corman, H. and Mocan, N. (1996) *A Time Series Analysis of Crime and Drug Use in New York City*, Working Paper No. 5463, Cambridge, MA: NBER

Cornwell, C. and Trumbull, W. (1994) 'Estimating the Economic Model of Crime with Panel Data', *Review of Economics and Statistics*, 76, 360–366.

Cover, J.P. and Thistle, P. (1988) 'Times Series, Homicide and the Deterrent Effect of Capital Punishment', *Southern Journal of Economics*, January, 54, 615–622.

Cowell, F.A. (1990) 'Tax-Sheltering and the Cost of Evasion', *Oxford Economics Papers*, 42, 221–243.

Cramer, H. and Gahvari, F. (1994) 'Tax Evasion, Concealment and the Optimal Linear Income Tax', *Scandinavian Journal of Economics*, 96, 219–239.

Crétin, T. (1998) *Finances criminelles*, Paris: PUF.

Davies, T. and Groom, C. (1998) 'Developing a Methodology for Measuring Illegal Activity from the UK National Accounts', *Economic Trends*, 536, 56–74.

DCRG (1995) *Violence, drogue et repli identitaire dans les quartiers sensibles*, Paris: DCRG.

Dick, A. (1995) 'When Does Organized Crime Pay? A Transaction Cost Analysis', *International Review of Law and Economics*, 15, 25–45.

Dieu, F. (1999) *Politiques publiques de sécurité*, Paris: L'Harmattan.

Dilnot, A. and Morris C.N. (1981) 'What Do We Know about the Black Economy?', *Fiscal Studies*, 2, 1, 58–73.

Dilulio, J. (1996) 'Help Wanted: Economists, Crime and Public Policy', *The Journal of Economic Perspectives*, 10, 1, 3–24.

Dilulio, J. and Piehl, A. (1991) 'Does Prison Pay?', *Brookings Review*, 4, 29–35.

Ditton, J. and Sperits, K. (1982) *The Rapid Increase of Heroin Addiction in Glasgow during 1981*, Glasgow: University of Glasgow.

Donzelot, J. (1991) 'Le déplacement de la question sociale', in J. Donzelot (ed.) *Face à l'exclusion: Le modèle français*, Paris: Editions Esprit.

Dorn, N. and South, N. (1990) 'Drug Market and Law Enforcement', *British Journal of Criminology*, 30, 2, 81–92.

Dorn, N., South, N. and Lewis, R. (1992) *Traffickers: Drug Markets and Law Enforcement*, London: Routledge.

Duprez, D. (1997) 'Jeunesse délinquante: des représentations aux réponses institutionnelles', *Cahiers de la sécurité intérieure*, 29, 5–26.

Eatherly, B. (1974) 'Drug-Law Enforcement: Should We Arrest Pushers or Users?', *Journal of Political Economy*, 82–1, 210–214.

Ehrlich, I. (1975) 'The Deterrent Effect of Capital Punishment: A Question of Life and Death', *American Economic Review*, 65, 397–417.

Ehrlich, I. (1981) 'On the Usefulness of Controlling Individuals: An Economic Analysis of Rehabilitation, Incapacitation and Deterrence', *American Economic Review*, 71, 307–332.

Ehrlich, I. (1996) 'Crime, Punishment, and the Market of Offense', *Journal of Economic Perspectives*, 10, 1, 43–67.

Elster, J. (1979) *Ulysses and the Sirens: Studies in Rationality and Irrationality*, Cambridge: Cambridge University Press.

Etile, F. (1999) *Economie de la consommation de drogue: une revue de litterature*, Paris: Université de Panthéon-Sorbonne.

Fajnzylber, P., Lederman, D., Loayza, N. and Ayres, R.L. (1999) 'La rationalité économique de la criminalité', *Problèmes économiques*, 2609, 1–5.

FATF Working Group on Statistics and Methods (1990a) *Narcotics Money Laundering: Assessment of Scale of the Problem, 1989*, Financial Action Task Force on Money Laundering report, Paris: FATF.

FATF (1990b) *La Lutte contre le blanchiment des capitaux*', Paris: La Documentation française.

Fazey, C. and Stevenson, R. (1990) *The Social and Economic Costs of Drug Abuse in the UK and the Netherlands*, London: Commission of the European Communities.

Fiege, E.L. (1981) 'The UK's Unobserved Economy: A Preliminary Assessment', *Economic Affairs*, 1, 4, 205–212.

Fonseca, G. (1992) 'Economie de la drogue: taille caractéristiques, et impact économique', *Revue Tiers Monde*, July–September, 33, 131, 489–516.

Frank, B. (1995) '*Ökonomische Ansätze zur Erklärung des Suchtverhaltens*', in *Mit dem Markt gegen Drogen!*', Stuttgart: Mathias Erlei, pp. 93–121.

Frey, B. and Weck, A. (1984) 'The Hidden Economy as an Unobservable Variable', *European Economic Review*, 26, 1–2, 33–53.

Friedman, D. (2000) *Law's Order*, Princeton, NJ: Princeton University Press.

Friedman, M. (1991) 'The War We are Losing', in M.B. Krauss and E.P. Lazear (eds) *Searching for Alternatives: Drug Control Policy in the United States*, Stanford, CA: Hoover Institution Press, pp. 53–67.

Gambetta, D. (1992) *La mafia siciliana: un industria dealla protezione privata*, Turin: Einaudi.

Gans, J. (2000) *Incentive Contracts, Optimal Penalties and Enforcement*, Melbourne: MBS.

Garoupa, N. (2000) 'Corporate Criminal Law and Organization Incentives: A Managerial Perspective', *Managerial and Decision Economics*, 21, 243–252.

Gérard-Varet, L. (1992) *Réflexions autour de développements récents de la théorie de la décision en incertitude*, Marseilles: CREQE.

GERI (2000) *Criminalité et délinquance apparentes: une approche territoriale*, Paris: La Documentation française.

Godefroy, T. and Laffargue, B. (1984) 'Crise économique et criminalité – Criminologie de la misère ou misère de la criminologie', *Déviance et société*, 8, 1, 73–100.

Goldberger, M.F., Choffel, P. and Le Toqueux, J.L. (1998) 'Les zones urbaines sensibles', *Insee Première*, April, 573.

Goldstein, P. (1985) 'The Drug/Violence Nexus: A Tripartite Conceptual Framework', *Journal of Drug Issues*, 15, 493–506.

Goldstein, P., Brownstein, H. and Ryan, P. (1992) 'Drug-Related Homicide in New-York: 1984–1988', *Crime and Delinquency*, 38, 4, 459–476.

Granovetter, M. (1978) 'Threshold Models of Collective Behavior', *American Journal of Sociology*, 83, 6, 1420–1443.

Greene, W.H. (2000) *Econometric Analysis*, Englewood Cliffs, NJ: Prentice-Hall.

Greif, A., Milgrom, P. and Weingast, B.R. (1994) 'Coordination, Commitment, and Enforcement: The Case of the Merchant Guild', *Journal of Political Economy*, 102, 3, 745–776.

Grogger, J. (1991) 'Certainty vs Severity of Punishment', *Economic Inquiry*, 29, 297–309.

Grossman, H.I. (1995) 'Rival Kleptocrats: The Mafia Versus the State', in G. Fiorentini and S. Peltzman (eds) *The Economics of Organised Crime*, Cambridge: Cambridge University Press.

Grossman, M. and Chaloupka, F.J. (1998) 'The Demand for Cocaine by Young Adults: A Rational Addiction Approach', *Journal of Health Economics*, 17, 4, 427–474.

Gujarati, D.N. (1995) *Basic Econometrics*, New York: McGraw-Hill.

Hadreas, J. and Roumasset, J. (1977) 'Addicts, Fences, and the Market for Stolen Goods', *Public Finance Quarterly*, April, 247–272.

Hammond, P.J. (1976a) 'Changing Tastes and Coherent Dynamic Choice', *Review of Economic Studies*, 43, 159–173.

Hammond, P.J. (1976b) 'Endogenous Tastes and Stable Long-Run Choice', *Journal of Economic Theory*, 13, 329–340.

Harrison, J. (2000) *Law and Economics*, St Paul, MN: West Group.

Harrison, L. (1992) 'The Drug Crime Nexus in the USA', *Contemporary Drug Problems*, 19, 2, 203–246.

Hartnoll, R. and Lewis, R. (1984) *The Illicit Market of Heroin in Britain: Towards a Preliminary Estimate of National Demand*, London: University College Hospital.

Ingold, F.R. (1984) 'La dépendance économique chez les héroïnomanes', *Revue Internationale de Criminologie et de Police Technique*, 3.

Ingold, F.R. (1992) '*Approche ethnographique de la consommation de cocaïne à Paris*', Paris: IREP.

Institut Suisse de Prophylaxie de l'Alcoolisme (1990) *Le Problème de la drogue, en particulier en Suisse, consideré sous son aspect social et préventif*, Lausanne: Office Fédéral de la Santé Publique.

Isachen, A. and Strom, S. (1980) 'The Hidden Economy, the Labor Market and Tax Evasion', *Scandinavian Journal of Economics*, 82, 304–311.

Isachen, A. and Strom, S. (1985) 'The Size and Growth of the Hidden Economy in Norway', *Review of Income and Wealth*, 31, 1, 21–38.

Janod, V. (2003) 'La theorie de l'addiction nationelle selon G.S. Becker et K.M. Murphy', *Cahier de la MSE*, Serie verte, Paris, 33 pp.

Jeanrenaud, C., Vitale, S. and Priez, F. (1998) *Le Coût social de la consommation de tabac en Suisse*, Neuchâtel: Institut de Recherches Economiques et Régionales, Université de Neuchâtel.

Kalmanovitz, S. (1993) '*Documento de discussion*', Bogota, Colombia: CIDE.

Kaplow, L. (1990) 'Optimal Taxation with Costly Enforcement and Evasion', *Journal of Public Economics*, 43, 221–236.

Kaufman, D. and Kaliberda, A. (1996) *Integrating the Unofficial Economy into the Dynamics of Post Socialist Economies: A Framework of Analyses and Evidence*, World Bank Policy Research Working Paper No. 1691, Washington, DC: World Bank.

Kennedy, M., Riley, K. and Reuter, P. (1993) 'A Simple Economic Model of Cocaine Production', *Mathematical and Computer Modelling*, 17, 2, 19–36.

Kensey, A. and Jean, J.-P. (1993) 'Usage licite de chiffres stupéfiants', *Pénombre*, 2, 5–9.

Klaus, P. (1994) *The Cost of Crime to Justice*, Crime Data Brief, Washington, DC: US Department of Justice.

Kleiman, M. (1989) *Marijuana: Cost of Abuse, Cost of Control*, Connecticut: Greenwood Press.

Kleiman, M. (1992) '*Against Excess: Drug Policy for Results*', New York, NY: Basic Books.

Koch, J. and Grupp, S. (1971) 'The Economics of Drug Control Policies', *International Journal of Addictions*, 6, 571–584.

Koch, J. and Grupp, S. (1973) 'Police and Illicit Drugs Markets: Some Economic Considerations', *British Journal of Addiction*, 68, 351–362.

Kopp, P. (1992a) 'Les analyses formelles des marchés de la drogue', *Tiers-Monde*, 131, July–September 33, 565–581.

Kopp, P. (1992b) 'La structuration de l'offre de drogue en réseaux', *Tiers-Monde*, 131, July–September 33, 517–537.

Kopp, P. (1994a) 'L'efficacité des politiques de contrôle des drogues illégales', *Revue Futuribles*, 185, March, 83–101.

Kopp, P. (1994b) 'Consommation de drogues et efficacité des politiques publiques', *Revue Economique*, 5, November, 1333–1355.

Kopp, P. (1995) *Le blanchiment de l'argent de la drogue – Analyse économique*, Paris: Cahier Ethique Finance de l'Association d'Economie financière, Paris: CDC editeur.

Kopp, P. (1996a) 'Politiques publiques: La répression du trafic de drogue est-elle efficace?', *Economie Appliquée*, 49, 2, 107–132.

Kopp, P. (1996b) 'L'analyse économique des organisations criminelles', *Communications*, 62, 155–167.

Kopp, P. (2001) *Les délinquances économiques et financières transnationales*, Paris: IHESI Etudes et Recherches.

Kopp, P., Fenoglio, P. and Parel, V. (2003) 'The Social Cost of Alcohol, Tobacco and Illicit Drugs in France, 1997', *European Addiction Research*, 9, 1, 1–52.

Kozel, N. and Lambert, E. (1994) *Monitoring the Future: A Continuing Study of the Lifestyle and Values of Youth*, quoted in 'L'abus de drogue aux Etats-Unis', *Futuribles*, 185, March, 57–73.

Krauthausen, C. and Sarmiento, L.F. (1991) *Cocaïna & Co, 'Un mercado ilégal por dentro,'* Tercer Mundo (eds), Bogota: 239 pp.

Labrousse, A. (1991) *La drogue, l'argent, les armes*, Paris: Fayard.

Labrousse, A. (1994) 'Géopolitique de la drogue: Les contradictions des politiques de guerre à la drogue', *Futuribles*, 185, March, 9–23.

Lacko, M. (1996) *Hidden Economy in East European Countries in International Comparison*, Working Paper, Luxemburg: International Institute for Applied Systems Analysis (IIASA).

Lagrange, H. (1998) 'Du diagnostic à l'action: l'échelle pertinente du territoire', *Cahiers de la sécurité intérieure*, 33, IHESI, Paris, 120–133.

Lagree, J.C. and Lew Fai, P. (1988) 'Chômage, délinquance, environnement urbain – France', in *Chômage des jeunes, délinquance et environnement urbain – Recherche bibliographique*, Strasbourg: Commission des communautés européennes, pp. 86–229.

Lancaster, K. (1966) 'A New Approach to Consumer Theory', *Journal of Political Economy*, 74, 132–157.

Layson, S. (1985) 'Homicide and Deterrence: A Reexamination of the United States – Time Series Evidence', *Southern Economics Journal*, 52, 1, 68–89.

Lemennicier, B. (1992) 'Prohibition de la drogue: diagnostic et solutions', *Journal des Economistes et des Etudes humaines*, December, 493–523.

Levine, D., Stoloff, P. and Spruill, N. (1976) 'Public Drug Treatment and Addict Crime', *The Journal of Legal Studies*, 5–2, 435–462.

Levitt, S. (1995) 'The Effect of Prison Population Size on Crime Rates: Evidence from Prison Overcrowding Litigation', *Quarterly Journal of Economics*, 111, May, 319–352.

Levitt, S.D. and Venkatesh, S.A. (2000) 'An Economic Analysis of a Drug-Selling Gang's Finances', *Quarterly Journal of Economics*, 115, 3.

Lewis, R. (1985) 'Serious Business: The Global Heroin Economy', in A. Henman, R. Lewis and T. Malton (eds) *Big Deal: The Politics of the Illicit Drug Business*, London: Pluto.

Lewit, E. and Coate, D. (1982) 'The Potential for Using Excise Taxes to Reduce Smoking', *Journal of Health Economics*, August, 1, 217–230.

Little, A. (1967) *Drug Abuse and Law Enforcement: A Report to the President's Commission on Law Enforcement and Administration of Justice*, Washington, DC.

Liu, J.T., Liu, J.L. and Chou, S.Y. (1996) '*The Demand for Opium in the Japanese Colony of Taiwan, 1914–1942*', Taipei, Taiwan: Institute of Economics.

Lucas, B. (1996) 'Politique française en matière de drogue', *Psychotropes*, 2, 2, 75–97.

MacAffee, K. (1980) 'A Glimpse of the Hidden Economy in the National Accounts', *Economic Trends*, 316, 81–87.

MacBride, D. (1981) 'Drugs and Violence', in J. Inciardi (ed.) *The Drugs Crime Connection*, Beverly Hills, CA: Sage, pp. 105–124.

MacCoun, R.J. and Reuter, P. (2001) *Drug War Heresies*, Cambridge: Cambridge University Press.

MacCoun, R.J., Reuter, P. and Schelling, T. (1996) 'Assessing Alternative Drug Control Regimes', *Journal of Policy Analysis and Management*, 15, 1–23.

MacCoy, A. (1972) *The Politics of Heroin in Southeast Asia*, New York: Harper and Row.

MacDonnell, R. and Maynard, A. (1985) 'Counting the Cost of Alcohol: Gaps in the Epidemiological Knowledge', *Community Medicine*, 7, 4–17.

Maddux, J.F. and Desmond, D.P. (1992) 'Methadone Maintenance and Alcohol Recovery from Opioid Dependance', *American Journal of Drug Alcohol Abuse*, 18, 63–74.

Manski, C.F., Pepper, J.V. and Thomas, Y.F. (eds) (1999) *Assessments of Two Cost-Effectiveness Studies in Cocaine Control Policy*, Washington, DC: National Academy Press.

Marcus, M. (1994) 'Synthèse du colloque d'Antony', in M. Schiray (ed.) *L'économie souterraine de la drogue*, Paris: CNV.

Marpsat, M. and Laurent, R. (1997) 'Le chômage des jeunes est-il aggravé par l'appartenance à un quartier en difficulté?', in *En marge de la ville, au cœur de la société: ces quartiers dont on parle*, Paris: Editions de l'aube.

Marvell, T. and Moody, C. (1994) 'Prison Population Growth and Crime Reduction', *Journal of Quantitative Criminology*, 10–4, 109–140.

Mauer, M. (1990) *Young Black Men and the Criminal Justice System: a Growing National Problem*, Washington, DC: The Sentencing Project.

Maynard, A., Hardman, G. and Whelan, A. (1987) 'Measuring the Social Costs of Addictive Substances', *British Journal of Addiction*, 82, 701–706.

Miceli, T. (1977) *Economics of the Law*, Oxford: Oxford University Press.

Miron, J. and Zwiebel, J. (1991) 'Alcohol Consumption During Prohibition', *American Economic Review, Papers and Proceedings*, May, 81, 2, 242–247.

Miron, J. and Zwiebel, J. (1995) 'The Economic Case Against Drug Prohibition', *Journal of Economic Perspective*, 4, 9, 175–192.

Mirrlees, J. (1975) '*The Theory of Moral Hazard and Unobservable Behavior – part 1*, Oxford, Nuffield College.

Monterosso, J. and Ainslie, G. (1999) 'Beyond Discounting: Possible Experimental Models of Impulse Control', *Psychopharmacology*, 146, 339–347.

Moore, M.H. (1973) 'Policies to Achieve Discrimination on the Effective Price of Heroin', *American Economic Review*, 63, 2, May, 270–277.

Moore, M.H. (1977) *Buy and Bust: The Effective Regulation of an Illicit Market in Heroin*, Lexington, MA: D.C. Heath, Lexington Books.

Moore, M.H. (1990) 'Supply Reduction and Drug Law Enforcement', in M. Tonry and J. Wilson (eds) *Drugs and Crime*, Chicago: University of Chicago Press, pp. 109–157.

Morel, B. and Rychen, F. (1994) *Le marché des drogues*, Paris: Editions de l'aube.

Musgrave, R.A. (1954) *The Theory of Public Finance*, New York, NY: McGraw-Hill.

Myers, S. (1983) 'Estimating the Economic Model of Crime: Employment Versus Punishment Effect', *Quarterly Journal of Economics*, 98, 157–166.

Nadelman, E. (1994) 'Pour un droit d'usage contrôlé', *Futuribles*, 185, 105–110.

NCIS (1994) *International Narcotic Control Strategy Report*, April, Washington, DC: NCIS.

NIDA (1990) *NHSDA: National Household Survey on Drug Abuses: Main Findings*, Rockville, MD: US Government Printing Office, NIDA.

NIDA (1991) *Epidemiologic Trends in Drug Abuse*, proceedings of the Community Epidemiologic Work Group (CEWG), December, Rockville, MD: NIDA.

Niskanen, W. (1962) *The Demand for Alcoholic Beverages: An Experiment in Econometric Method*, Santa Monica, CA: The Rand Corporation.

NNICC (1990) *Report 1989*, Rockville, MD: US Government Printing Office.

North, D. (1990) *Institutions, Institutional Change and Economic Performance*, Cambridge: Cambridge University Press.

Observatoire Français des Drogues et des Toxicomanie (1995) *Drogues et toxicomanies: Indicateurs et tendances*, Paris: MILDT.

Observatoire Geopolitique des Drogues *La dépêche internationale des drogues*, monthly letter edited by Alain Labrousse, Paris.

O'Higgins, M. (1981) 'Measuring the Hidden Economy', *British Tax Review*, 5–6, 286–302 and 367–378.

ONDCCP (2001) *Global Illicit Drug Trends*, Reproduced from P. Reuter and V. Greenfield (2001) 'Measuring Global Drug Markets', *World Economics*, October–December, 2, 4.

Ornstein, S.I. and Hanssen, D.M. (1985) 'Alcohol Control Law and the Consumption of Distilled Spirits and Beer', *Journal of Consumer Research*, 12, 200–213.

Orphanides, A. and Zervos, D. (1995) 'Rational Addiction with Learning and Regret', *Journal of Political Economy*, 103, 4, 739–758.

Ostrowski, J. (1990) 'The Moral and Practical Case for Drug Legalization', *Hofstra Law Review*, 18, 3, Spring, 607–647.

Padieu, R. (1990) *L'Information statistique sur les drogues et les toxicomanies*, Paris: DGLTD.

Phares, D. (1975) 'Heroin and Society: an Economist's Perspective on Public Policy', in R. Rachin and E. Czajkoski (eds), *Drug Abuse Control: Administration and Politics*, Lexington, MA: Lexington Books, pp. 129–143.

Pigou, A.C. (1920) *The Economics of Welfare*, London: Macmillan.

Polich, J.M, Ellickson, P., Reuter, P. and Kahan, J. (1984) *Strategies for Controlling Adolescent Drug Use*, Santa Monica, CA: The Rand Corporation.

Polinsky, A.M. and Shavell, S. (2000) 'The Economic Theory of Public Enforcement of Law', *Journal of Economic Literature*, 38, 1, 45–77.

Polinsky, M. and Shavell, S. (1984) 'The Optimal Use of Fine and Imprisonment', *Journal of Public Economics*, 24, 89–99.

Pollak, R.A. (1970) 'Habit Formation and Dynamic Demand Function', *Journal of Political Economy*, 78, 745–763.

Pommerehne, W. and Hall, A. (1993) 'Drogue: le point de vue de l'économiste', *Futuribles*, 174, 49–66.

Pyle, D. (1983) *The Economics of Crime and Law Enforcement*, London: Macmillan.

Quirk, P.J. (1996) Macroeconomic *Implications of Money Laundering*, Washington, DC: IMF draft paper.

Rachin, R.I. and Czajkoski, E.H. (eds) (1975) *Drugs Abuse Control: Administration and Politics*, London.

Rawls, J. (1971) *A Theory of Justice*, Cambridge, MA: Harvard University Press.

Reuband, K.H. (1995) 'Drug Use and Drug Policy in Western Europe. Epidemiological Findings in a Comparative Perspective', *European Addiction Research*, 1, S32–S41.

Reuter, P. (1983) *Disorganized Crime*, Cambridge, MA: MIT Press.

Reuter, P. (1984) 'The (Continued) Vitality of Myticals Numbers', *The Public Interest*, Spring, 78, 135–147.

Reuter, P. (1992a) 'The Limits and Consequences of U.S. Foreign Drug Control Effort', *Annals of the American Academy*, 521, 151–162.

Reuter, P. (1992b) *Hawk Ascendant: The Punitive Trend of Drug Policy*, draft paper, Santa Monica, CA: Center for Drug Policy, The Rand Corporation.

Reuter, P. (1993) *Rand Corporation: Cross-National Comparison*, Santa Monica, CA: The Rand Corporation.

Reuter, P. (1994) 'Setting Priorities: Budget and Programme Choices for Drug Control', in *Toward a Rational Drug Policy*, Chicago, IL: The University of Chicago Legal Forum, 99, 145–173.

Reuter, P. (1996) 'The Mismeasurement of Illegal Drug Markets: The Implication of its Irrelevance', in S. Pozo (ed.) *Exploring the Underground Economy*, Kalamazoo, MI: Upjohn Institute.

Reuter, P. (2001) 'Why Does Research Have so Little Impact on American Drug Policy?', *Addiction*, 96, 373–376.

Reuter, P. and Caulkins, J. (1993) 'Public Health Policy Forum: Redefining the Goals of National Drug Policy: Recommendations from a Working Group', *American Journal of Public Health*, August, 85, 8, 1059–1062.

Reuter, P., Caulkins, J. and Feinleib, J. (2002) *Illegal Lemons: Price Dispersion in Cocaine and Heroin Markets*, Mimeo. Santa Monica, CA: Center for Drug Policy.

Reuter, P. and Greenfield, V. (2001) 'Measuring global drug markets: how good are the numbers and why should we care about them?', *World Economics*, 2, 4, 155–173.

Reuter, P. and John, H. (1989) 'The Organization of High Level Drug Markets: An Exploration Study', Santa Monica, CA: The Rand Corporation.

Reuter, P. and Kleiman, M. (1986) 'Risks and Prices: An Economic Analysis of Drug Enforcement', in M. Norval and M. Tonry (eds) *Crime and Justice: A Review of Research*, Chicago, IL: University of Chicago Press.

Reuter, P. and MacCoun, R. (1995a) 'Assessing the Legalization Debate', in G. Estivenart (ed.) *Policies and Strategies to Combat Drugs in Europe*, Amsterdam: Kluwer.

Reuter, P. and MacCoun, R. (1995b) 'Drawing Lessons from the Absence of Harm Reduction in American Drug Policy', *Tobacco Control*, Autumn 4, S28–S32.

Reuter, P., MacCoun, R. and Murphy, P. (1991) *Money from Crime– A Study of the Economics of Drug Dealing in Washington, D.C.*, Santa Monica, CA: The Rand Corporation.

Rey, G. (1992) 'Analisi economica e evidenza empirica dell'attivita illegale in Italia', *Quaderni di Ricerca*, ISTAT, Milano, 67 pp.

Rey, H. (1996) *La peur des banlieues*, Paris: Presses de la FNSP.

Rhodes, W., Hyatt, R. and Scheiman, P. (1994) 'The Price of Cocaine, Heroin and Marijuana, 1981–1993', *Journal of Drug Issues*, 24, 3, 383–402.

Rhodes, W., Langenbahn, S., Kling, R. and Scheiman, P. (1995) *What American's Users Spend on Illegal Drugs, 1988–1993*, Washington, DC: Office of National Drug Control Policy.

Rice, D.P., Kelman, S., Miller, L.S. and Dunmeyer, S. (1990) *The Economic Costs of Alcohol and Drug Abuse and Mental Illness: 1985*, DHHS Publication No. (ADM) 90, 1694, San Francisco, Institute for Health and Aging, University of California.

Riley, J. (1997) *Crack, Powder Cocaine and Heroin: Drug Purchase and Use Patterns in Six Cities*, Washington, DC: National Institute of Justice.

Robert, P., Aubusson de Cavarlay, B., Pottier, M.L. and Tournier, P. (1994)

Les comptes du crime: Les délinquances en France et leurs mesures, Paris: L'Harmattan.

Robert, P., Pottier, M.L. and Lagrange, H. (1999) 'Mesurer le crime – Entre statistiques de police et enquêtes de victimisation (1985–1995)', *Revue française de sociologie*, XL-2, April–June pp. 255–294.

Rosa, J. (1996) 'Le coût social de la consommation de tabac et l'équilibre des finances publiques: le cas de la France (actualisation)', *Cahiers de Recherche en Economie de l'Entreprise*, Paris: Institut d'Etudes Politiques de Paris.

Rottenburg, S. (1968) 'The Clandestine Distribution of Heroin, its Discovery and Suppression', *Journal of Political Economy*, 76, 1, 78–90.

Rydell, C.P., Caulkins, P. and Everingham, S.S. (1996) 'Enforcement or Treatment? Modeling the Relative Efficacy of Alternatives for Controlling Cocaine', *Operations Research*, September–October, 44, 5, 687–695.

Salama, P. (1994) 'Macro-économie de la drogue dans les pays andins', *Futuribles*, 185, 43–57.

Schefrin, H.M. and Thaler, R.H. (1981) 'An Economic Theory of Self Control', *Journal of Political Economy*, 89, 2, 392–406.

Schelling, T. (1971) 'What is the Business of Organized Crime?', *Journal of Public Law*, 20, 61–78.

Schelling, T. (1976) 'Economics and the Criminal Enterprise', *The Public Interest*, 7, 61–78.

Schiray, M. (1989) 'Essai sur l'illégalité en économie: l'économie de la drogue', *Sciences Sociales et Santé*, 7, 3, 5–25.

Schiray, M. (1994) 'Les filières stupéfiants: trois niveaux, cinq logiques. Les stratégies de survie et le monde des criminalités', Futuribles, 185, 23–43.

Schiray, M., Coppel, A., Duprez, D., Joubert, M. and Weinberger, M. (1994) *Economie souterraine de la drogue*, Paris: Synthèse des Recherches, Conseil national des Villes.

Seagrave, J. (1973) 'Economics of Heroin: a Discussion', *American Economic Review*, 63, 2, 278–279.

Shavell, S. (1992) 'A Note on Marginal Deterrence', *International Review of Law and Economics*, 12, 345–355.

Shavell, S. and Polinsky, M. (2000) 'The Economic Theory of Public Enforcement of Law', *Journal of Economic Literature*, 38, 1, 45–77.

Sickles, R. and Taubman, P. (1991) 'Who Uses Illegal Drugs?', *American Economic Review*, May, 81, 2, 246–251.

Silverman, L. and Spruill, N. (1977) 'Urban Crime and the Price of Heroin', *Journal of Urban Economics*, January, 4, 1, 80–103.

Single, E., Robson, L., Xie, X. and Rehm, J. (1998), 'The Cost of Substance Abuse in Canada, 1992', *Addiction*, 93, 993–998.

Slemrod, J. and Yithzaki, S. (1987) 'The Optimal Size of Tax Collection Agency', *Scandinavian Journal of Economics*, 89, 183–192.

Spelman, W. (1994) *Criminal Incapacitation*, New York: Plenum Press.

Stigler, G. (1976) 'The Optimal Enforcement of the Law', *Journal of Political Economy*, 78, 526–536.

Stigler, G. and Becker, G. (1977) 'De gustibus non est disputandum', *American Economic Review*, 67, 76–90.

Tanzi, V. (1983) 'The Underground Economy in the United States: Annual Estimates', *IMF Staff Papers*, 30, 2, 283–305.

Tillman, R. (1987) 'The Size of the "Criminal Population": The Prevalence and Incidence of Adult Arrests', *Criminology*, 25, 3, August, 561–580.

Tirole, J. (1988) *Theory of Industrial Organization*, Cambridge, MA: MIT Press.

Tribalat, M. (1997) "Chronique de l'immigration. Les populations d'origine étrangère en France métropolitaine", *Population*, 1, 52, January–February, 163–219.

Turvani, M. (1994) *Illegal Markets and New Institutional Economics*, Paris: ATOM Paris 1.

UNCDP (1997) *World Drug Report*, Vienna: UNCDP.

UNDCP (2000) '*Global Illicit Drug Trends*', Vienna: UNDCP.

Usher, D. (1986) 'Tax Evasion and the Marginal Cost of Public Funds', *Economic Enquiry* 24, 563–586.

Van de Werf, R. and Van der Ven, P. (1996) *The Illegal Economy in the Netherlands*, StatisticsNetherlands, unpublished paper.

Van Duyne, P. (1992) *Estimates in the Fog*, Paris: La Haye.

Van Ours, J. (1995) 'The Price Elasticity of Hard Drugs: The Case of Opium in the Dutch Indies, 1923–1938', *Journal of Political Economy*, 103, 2, 261–279.

Varese, F. (1994) 'Is Sicily the Future of Russia? Private Protection and the Rise of the Russian Mafia', *Archives Européennes de Sociologie*, 35, 224–258.

Viscusi, K. (1994) *Cigarette Taxes and the Social Consequences of Smoking*, Working Paper No. 4891, Cambridge, MA: NBER.

Wagstaff, A. and Maynard, A. (1988) *Economic Aspects of the Illicit Drug Market and Drug Enforcement Policies in the United Kingdom*, London: HMSO.

Warburton, C. (1932) *The Economic Results of Prohibition*, New York, NY: Columbia University Press.

White, M. and Luskesitch, W. (1983) 'Heroin Price Elasticity and Enforcement Strategies', *Economic Enquiry*, 21, 557–564.

Williams, T. (1990) *Cocaine Kids*, Paris: Gallimard.

Williamson, O. (1985) *The Economic Institutions of Capitalism: Firm, Markets, and Relational Contracting*, New York: The Free Press.

Winston, G.C. (1980) 'Addiction and Backsliding', *Journal of Economic Behavior and Organization*, 1, 295–324.

Witte, A. (1980) 'Estimating the Economic Model for Crime with Individual Data', *Quarterly Journal of Economics*, February, 57–84.

Witte, A. and Tauchen, H. (1994) *Work and Crime: an Exploration Using Panel Data*, Working Paper No. 4794, Cambridge, MA: NBER.

Yaniv, G. (1999) 'Tax Evasion, Risky Laundering, and Optimal Deterrence Policy', *International Tax and Public Finance*, 6, 27–38.

Zaitch, D. (1998) 'The Dutch Cocaine Market in European Perspective', Amsterdam, unpublished.

Zaitch, D. (2002) *Trafficking Cocaine: Colombian Drug Entrepreneurs in the Netherlands*, The Hague: Kluwer Law International.

Zedlwski, E. (1987) *Making the Confinement Decision*, Washington, DC: US Department of Justice.

Index

addiction: consumption and 7, 44–5; hypothesis of changes in taste 50–1; hypothesis of non-convexity of preferences 48–50; model of rational 51–4, 65; modelling 48–51; normal 55; psychoanalytic approach 4–5; term 52
Afghanistan 14 (Table 1.1), 15 (Figure 1.1), 16, 17
Ainslie, G. 63
Akerlof, G. 109, 144
alcohol: attitudes to 5; elasticity of demand, 47, 75; modification of tastes 50; social cost 126, 128; status 195, 196; studies 46, 47, 93; US prohibition 74–5
Allingham, M.G. 170
Andreano, R. 26
Arlen, J. 10, 175, 178, 179

Ball, J.C. 151
banking system: collective action 181–2; conditions for generalization of standard of good conduct 182 (Figure 7.3); laundering 9–10, 175–8; regulation (Anglo-Saxon model) 9–10; regulation (Continental system) 10, 180–5; regulation (US model) 174–80, 183, 184
Becker, G.: influence 133, 198; works: (1968) 8, 90, 100, 105, 109, 110, 172, 189; and Mulligan (1997) 53; and Murphy (1988) 1, 46–7, 50, 57–8, 60, 62–5; et al. (1990) 47; et al. (1991) 50, 54; Stigler and (1977) 50–1
benefits of drugs 126–8
Bentham, J. 119, 120, 122
betrayal 32, 36–7, 166
black market 125–6
Blair, R. 45, 147, 148, 149

Blum, J. 160
Blumenstein, A. 25
Bolivia: coca leaf 15 (Table 1.2), 16 (Figure 1.2), 22 (Table 1.6); cocaine 15
Bourgois, P. 71
Boyum, D. 96
Bretteville-Jensen, A.L. 47
Britain, repressive public policy 134
Brown, G. 46
Buchanan, J. 9, 26, 185, 187, 191
buprenorphine 148
Burma *see* Myanmar

Calabresi, G. 86, 87–8
Camdessus, M. 156
Cameron, S. 100
Camorra 164
cannabis: attitudes to 5; compared to other substances 4; culture of 14; origin 14; production 16; sales 158 (Table 7.1); seizure 16; status 87, 196
capital, allocation of 40–1
Capone, A. 168
cartels 20, 23, 29, 32, 164
Caulkins, J.: (1990) 20, 21, 46; (1994) 46; (1995a) 46, 133, 135; (1995b) 46; and Feinleib (1995) 146; and Reuter (1998) 173; et al. (1997) 151
Chaloupka, F. 47, 76, 133
Chicago School 185, 187, 192
Chinese triads 28, 164
choice(s): ethical 119 (Figure 5.2); social 118–20; temporal consistency 58–64
Choiseul-Praslin, C.H. de 136–7
Chou, S.Y. 47
cigarettes, price and consumption 47